Gardening for People

(who think they don't know how)

by DOUGLAS MOON

illustrated by JUDY DANIEL

JOHN MUIR PUBLICATIONS SANTA FE

Library of Congress Card Number 74-84449
ISBN 0-912528-10-9

Published by
John Muir Publications
P.O. Box 613
Santa Fe, New Mexico 87501

Distributed by
W. W. NORTON & COMPANY, INC.
500 Fifth Ave.
New York, New York 10036

Printed in the United States of America

CONTENTS

I wish to thank Barbara Luboff for setting this book, Ken Luboff for living with her while she had to deal with me, Martha, my wife, for bearing with me through all phases of its production, and Judy Daniel for illustrating it far above and far beyond the call of duty.

I also wish to thank Clifford Burke, John and Eve Muir, Mary Forrest and Tony Vigo for any number of things, not the least of which is managing to be very nice people in times when son-of-a-bitchery is the practical norm.

This book is for **Karen De Lapp**,
who convinced me to write it

PART ONE

GENERALITIES *

1 ABOUT THIS BOOK

This Book

This book was written, I'd like to think, by popular demand. I have among my friends and acquaintances the reputation of being a successful amateur gardener. Because of that reputation, I get asked a lot of questions about gardening, all of which I love to answer, if I can, because who among us can, if given the chance, resist playing the expert? Certainly not me.

This book is intended to spoil some of my fun. I've noticed over the years that, whatever the particular question, the questioner often could have answered it himself if he knew just a little bit more about what the whole of gardening is all about, if he had just a little better sense of what a garden is.

(I'm going to be using *man* and *he* and *himself* and not *woman* and *she* and *herself* in this book for absolutely asexual, purely stylistic reasons. I don't want to get bogged down in a swamp of *men or women*, *hes or shes*, and *himselves or herselves* any more than I want to put anyone off because it may look like I don't think much of women as gardeners. A talent for and an enjoyment in gardening seems to me to be distributed between the sexes with remarkable randomness. For every woman who feels that gardening is man's work, you can find a man who considers gardening effeminate. To avoid this stylistic problem altogether, I might have used the imminently practical *one-oneself*, but that, unfortunately, has come to suggest to readers that the writer thinks he's a cut or two above them, and I personally happen to find *person-itself*, despite its current popularity, unstomachable. "The person who wants to acquaint itself with some of the basics of gardening," however hilarious, just isn't English.)

It's my hope that when the reader has finished this book, he will have gleaned from it a sense of the garden and of what a garden *means*, and it's toward that goal that the first section of this book is aimed. If he finds out, and a lot of people may, that he really hates what it means and decides to give up his garden and move into an apartment far off the ground, this book will have been well worth the reading. A non-gardener who doesn't garden is, after all, a success.

If, on the other hand, he finds out that he can turn his gardening chores into a hobby or even a sport, then mine will be the incomparable pleasure that comes from making a convert and he, I'm sure, will find his life considerably less painful in the future.

Most readers, I suspect, won't attain either of these two extremes but will fall somewhere in between. It's for these, the middle gardeners let's call them, that this book is really intended. I hope to be able to help the middle gardener find out for himself just how much of him is gardener and how much isn't, and I hope to be able to help him achieve a garden that meets all of his gardening needs as well as a garden whose needs he himself can comfortably meet.

Most people fail at gardening, or think they do, because the results they achieve don't meet their expectations. It doesn't matter that their expectations were unrealistic to begin with, both in terms of what nature can deliver and, perhaps more important, in terms of what they themselves are willing and able to contribute. Kidding yourself about what you can or will do in the garden may well do more damage to your garden—and to your soul—than a plague of locusts, a killer frost, or a flood.

Who Is This Middle Gardener?

Most likely this middle gardener is someone who's acquired a garden indirectly, probably along with a house he's moved into. He hasn't acquired a garden because he specifically wanted one, and he hasn't had much previous gardening experience. As a kid, he may have mowed his parents' lawn reluctantly and done some weeding and planting under even greater duress. He may be sorry now that he didn't pick up some general information back then along with his blistered hands and sweaty brow, but he didn't and he certainly can't be blamed for it.

Why Is He Gardening?

He's gardening because he has to, because there isn't anybody else around to do it, and because he feels guilty if it isn't done, if only because his neighbors are casting wary glances over the fence at his uncut lawn and weedy flower beds. His own son may now be doing the mowing and the weeding, but our man's still the one who has to decide, from his lounge chair in the patio, just what has to be mowed, weeded, and even what's a weed and what isn't.

What's His Garden Like?

That's pretty hard to say, but there's a chapter later on in this book, Chapter Two to be precise, which is concerned with what to look for in a garden when what you're really looking for is a house.

If there's a common factor in the middle gardener's garden, it's probably its size. It occupies a largish part of a city lot which is approximately fifty by a hundred feet in area, that part of the lot which isn't occupied by the house, garage and driveway. If the middle gardener's acquired much more land than this, a small ranch, let's say, and he doesn't know what to do with it, he doesn't need a gardening book, he needs a head doctor and a hired man.

If he's got considerably less than five thousand square feet, he can't very well concoct a major horticultural disaster for himself, but he might be able to get some useful information from this book, particularly from Part Two, which talks about how to make a small garden look bigger than it is.

Where Does He Live?

Just about anywhere. I live in California and my years of gardening experience have been about equally divided between the southern part of the state and the northern. Naturally, where I've done my gardening is going to affect what I know and what I think about gardening, but this book is, wherever I could make it, of general interest.

The knowledge that I happen to prune my fuchsias in February isn't going to be of much use to you if you have frosts well into March or snow into May or think of fuchsias as temperamental greenhouse plants that can be stuck into shady places in the garden only after summer has arrived with conviction.

Even if you live in Texas, Florida, or Maine, a lot of what I have to say in this book should be of use to you if you're a middle gardener, because the problems of the middle gardener are not problems of climate. They're essentially conflicts between nature, man, and art. If what I have to say applies specifically to California and other mild, coastal, Mediterranean climates, I've tried to remember to make that clear.

This mild, coastal, Mediterranean climate, by the way, entertained temperatures of 14° and below last winter, and I had the distinct displeasure of seeing my lawn and bird bath frozen solid twenty-four hours a day for ten days, so my gardening experience, in terms of climate, has recently been greatly expanded much to the detriment of my garden and my peace of mind.

What This Book Isn't

This book isn't the unwritable *Complete Guide to Gardening*, although some of my friends have expressed the hope that it might be. I call such a book unwritable because there are just too many different kinds of plants, too many different climates, variations in soils and rainfall, kinds and numbers of garden pests and weeds and, finally, roads to Rome and ways to skin the cat. If such a book were written, and it won't be, you'd have to cover your entire lot with buildings in order to house it and then, of course, your garden would be gone and you wouldn't have any use for the book.

Gardening for People isn't precisely a manual either, although I've tried to compensate for that fact with a comprehensive index at the back. It's one man's reasonably complete theory of gardening with illustrative examples wherever possible, and it's a talky book, I grant, because the author is not only prone to run off at the mouth but thoroughly enjoys it.

This book is intended to be read by a fire in the winter but read with a pencil in hand so that you can make notes of just where my gardening experience, my theories are relevant to you. You might even read this book every winter until it's clear to you that my gardening experience and theories are no longer relevant to you at all. That'll mean that you've graduated.

What's the Aim of This Book?

If this book has a single aim, it's simply this: to help you create your garden whole in your head so that you can create it with confidence, ease, and maybe even joy on, in, and above your ground.

And now down to business.

2 WHAT TO LOOK FOR IN A GARDEN

Garden Hunting

Because it was probably the house that carried the majority of the weight in your decision to rent or buy a house and because it may well be the garden that will give you the majority of your future headaches, it would have been ideal if you'd been able to read this chapter before acquiring your one-sixth of an acre.

Still, it may not be too late to reappraise your garden as it now stands in terms of what it was like when you got it. In doing so, you may be able to diagnose some of your past failures with it and send it off in another, better direction. Gardens, being organisms, are always going somewhere, if it's only to hell.

There are, I think, roughly four kinds of suburban gardens. One is the non-garden or what you usually get with a brand new house. Another is the wildly overgrown garden, the veritable jungle long ago abandoned by its owners when they became too old to take care of it. The third is that perfect jewel of an Eden, the garden that makes your eyes water with appreciation and that anyone's natural avarice would make them ache to own. The fourth and last is what, for lack of a better term, I'll call the ordinary garden, the garden that's been created with a certain amount of imagination and tended with interest if not devotion. This garden looks pretty much like the rest of the gardens on the block and excites neither admiration nor contempt.

The Non-garden Garden

Here we have the lot that up until a few months before was a part of a field, orchard, pasture or woodland. It's usually totally barren except for the house, some hardy weeds, and perhaps a few trees which the builder spared in order to increase the saleability of the house or which the trucks and bulldozers simply happened to miss.

If there are trees on the lot, it's a good sign even if you intend to remove them as soon as you move in. The presence of trees or any other permanent kind of greenery means that the builder hasn't done much to disturb the original soil. If the lot is totally barren, it can mean that the builder has either scraped away all the top soil and moved it some place else or that he's filled over the top soil with, if he's typical, whatever's nearest and cheapest.

With a new lot, if you have any doubts at all about the condition of the soil, you'd be wise to have it analyzed by a soil expert before you plunk down your down payment. If the soil is poor, it will mean that you're going to have to rebuild it before you can even think about landscaping or a lawn, and that means hours of back-breaking labor and a financial investment that will amaze you.

If you go ahead and plant in sub-soil or in inferior fill without adding the necessary amendments, you'll be wasting the price of the plants as well as the effort it takes to put them in the ground. The plants will either wither and die or perform so poorly and so slowly that your confidence as a gardener will be forever shaken.

Even if the soil is first-rate, there are still disadvantages to a new lot. I've never met anyone who, having once put in a new lawn, ever wanted to put in another one, and the initial investment in plants, since you'll be starting completely from scratch, can be staggering.

A new lot also has a few advantages, the main one being that you can lay out just exactly the kind of garden you want without continually stumbling over the garden that the previous owner left behind. You won't be faced, as I was, with an unbelievably messy *datura* dropping its plethora of leaves and flowers everywhere and with the knowledge that removing it will open your patio to the neighbor's window. Thank God, I guess, that the recent killer frost wiped the damn thing out at ground level.

If you are faced with some of the disadvantages a new lot has to offer, we'll discuss how to handle them later on in this book.

The Jungle

This is the lot that the previous owners neglected completely and allowed to go its own way over a number of years. It may be that you almost decided not to buy this house because the garden looked too formidable, but this garden can, if it's handled correctly, be a blessing in disguise.

The first thing to do with the jungle is absolutely nothing, and do that for at least a year. If you're itching to get to work somewhere, work on the house. It's probably not much better off than the garden and can use all the immediate attention you can afford to give it. The garden, left to itself for another year, isn't going to change—or deteriorate—perceptibly.

During the year that you're not gardening, keep your eye on the garden and make notes about any plants which are doing things you like. Any plant that bursts into brilliant bloom in the spring, turns a brilliant red in the fall, bears fruit in the summer, or is simply pleasant to look at all year round deserves to be earmarked for salvation, and you might do your earmarking literally, perhaps with pieces of colored plastic, so that you'll remember, when you start to work in earnest, that you liked a certain plant at one time even if it doesn't happen to look like much at the moment.

In a year's time, you'll have become acquainted with the performance spectrum of each plant as well as that of the whole garden, and you'll have a much better idea of what you want to keep and what you want to get rid of. You won't make the mistake of ripping out in December a bunch of sticks which are going to become a brilliant mass of flowering quince in the early spring, and you won't chop down a ratty looking eyesore of a tree which may produce for you some of the tastiest apricots you've ever eaten, a tree that, with a little imaginative pruning, might even turn into a landscape asset.

With a jungle garden, you can also be sure that every plant in it is a hardy specimen. Otherwise, they wouldn't have survived. The weak and the frail have long since perished, and what remains is obviously what needs the least care, the least artificial watering and fertilizing and, except for pruning, the least future attention from you.

If you can possibly restrain yourself, don't go after your jungle with a machete. Older, taller, bigger plants are worth more than smaller ones, both in terms of landscape value and in terms of cold, hard cash. If you doubt that, pay a visit to your local nursery and price something in a one gallon can and compare that to the cost of the same thing in a five.

Eden

This is the garden that has been painstakingly created over the years by one and maybe two garden enthusiasts and plant hobbyists. It may have been one of the chief selling features of the house, but unless you're the same caliber of enthusiast with an equal amount of time on your hands, this little paradise can soon become a first class headache.

This garden was created—and I stress this—to consume time, not to save it. Plants which perform well with little care have probably been replaced by or overlooked at the nursery in favor of rarer, more difficult specimens. Attractive but invasive or troublesome plants may abound because the people who tended them had the time and the patience to see that they didn't get out of hand.

If you don't have the time and the skill this kind of garden demands, you'll be treated to the agony of watching it deteriorate before your very eyes, and you may be left in the end with little more than a desert or a bamboo forest and the problem of having to start your landscaping all over again from scratch, and all this after you've shelled out plenty for a garden that isn't there anymore.

If you don't have the skills or the time to maintain Eden, watching it deteriorate is really about all you can do, that and convincing yourself, or trying to, that the garden isn't so much deteriorating as it is adjusting itself to you. It's best, unless you're a second Adam, to avoid acquiring Eden in the first place, and here are a few hints about how to identify one if you stumble across it.

A dead giveaway, of course, is a greenhouse or lathhouse full of lush foliage, seedlings in flats and cuttings sprouting out of pots. Another clue is a quantity of plants, healthy ones, hanging in containers. This means that a rigorous watering schedule is maintained, a schedule so rigorous that summer vacations are unfeasible without the aid of a trusted plant sitter.

The lawns of Eden will look like carpets, and there will be an abundance of different kinds of plants around. The whole garden may look very natural, very casual, and very much ungardened to the unpractised eye, but don't let this deceive you. It's often much more difficult to create and maintain a natural looking, woodland kind of garden than it is to create and maintain a more formal one.

If you're already stuck with such a garden, the best thing to do with it is to remove those plants which are failing and let the less demanding and more vigorous take over where they can. Simplify, in other words. If you wish to replace plants that have died, do so with less demanding specimens. Your nurseryman can be of great help here. Most important, don't lose heart. What's happening to your garden, however depressing, really isn't your fault. You have, in a sense, been sold a bill of goods.

The Ordinary Garden

There's not too much to be said here about this kind of garden, except that it's the kind of garden we'll be talking about most in the rest of this book. If you've just acquired one, it's not a good idea, I think, to contemplate any major changes in it until you've seen exactly what it will do over a year's time.

For the first year with any established garden, your efforts should be directed almost solely toward maintenance. Keep the weeds pulled, the lawn mowed, and try to maintain a watering schedule that doesn't differ appreciably from the one the garden's been used to. Too much more or too much less water is going to upset the garden's balance and may cost you the lives of some of your new flora.

If it's possible, ask the departing gardener how he went about his gardening and if there's anything special that you ought to know. He'll probably be more than glad to tell you, especially if he took any interest at all in the garden himself.

3

WHAT A GARDEN'S FOR

Garden Uses

We live in a house that was built some sixty years ago. We chose an old house when we bought because of all the little luxuries it affords us which aren't available in newer houses, luxuries such as big rooms, big closets, high ceilings, and solid construction. Aside from its prehistoric wiring, which with the energy crisis may become the wiring of the future, the house has only one major defect, a defect that's common to most houses of its age: the house is virtually cut off from its own back yard.

The only windows which open to the back are those of the downstairs bathroom, service porch, the upstairs windows of the smaller bedrooms—those intended for the children—and a series of tiny windows over a built-in breakfront in the dining room, windows which are intended only to let light in, not to let sight out.

It's not difficult to come up with the reasons for this flaw. Sometime in the last sixty years we simply stopped seeing the area behind our houses as a back yard, a service area, and started looking at it as a garden, an outdoor living area. The chickens have long since gone, either by choice or city ordinance; the clothes lines have for the most part been brought inside by the clothes dryer; and, unfortunately, the vegetable garden and the fruit trees have been replaced by the supermarket, although both seem to be making their way back into the garden again.

It used to be, back in the days when our house was built, that the only actual living done in the back yard was done by the children who played there and who may have been allowed a Saturday picnic, if only to get them out from underfoot. Their parents wouldn't have dreamed of joining them.

Now, with the advent of the American patio, the parents are actually entertaining their friends in the back yard while the children are probably somewhere inside watching television. The back yard has, in cases like this, assumed some of the old-fashioned sanctity of the parlor, an idea that our great grandparents would have found as improbable and possibly as foolish as moon rockets.

Today, if I were building the house we live in, I'd completely reverse the floor plan so that the living areas would be in the back and the service area in front. It would, of course, be necessary to put a slightly different face on the service side to make it more presentable for public viewing, but that wouldn't present much of a problem, and it would be well worth it to me to be able to sit in the living room and look out on the garden instead of the street and to sleep on the quiet side of the house, leaving the street bedrooms to children and guests who, I'm certain, are better able than I to take the noise.

The urban-residential Spanish and North Africans solved their outdoor living problems years ago. They placed their gardens completely within the walls of their houses. This afforded them easy access to the outside from every room, gave them complete seclusion from their neighbors, and protected them as much as possible from the noise of the streets.

We American city-dwellers, however, borrowed our ideas from Northern Europe, and the houses we inhabit are essentially Northern European farmhouses. The surrounding farm land, the land which once, because of its area, offered us privacy, recreation, and peace and quite, has shrunk around us to almost nothing and left us more exposed to each other than perhaps is good for us.

If not actually borrowing the idea from the urbanites of the Mediterranean but rather responding to similarly crowded environments, some of us are now beginning to enclose our front yards and incorporate them into our houses as living areas. This is usually done by placing a fence or wall, one high enough to screen out the street entirely, a few feet in from the sidewalk as well as along the driveway and opposite property line. The area between the fence and sidewalk, the public area, is then landscaped to satisfy the esthetic demands of the neighborhood, and the area behind the fence is given over to some kind of patio paving, outdoor furniture, and a different kind of landscaping.

With such an arrangement as I've described, you can relax or entertain in your front yard out of the view of passers-by just as you do in the back. You have also, in case you didn't notice it, completely eliminated the front lawn, and the lawn, of all gardening chores, is the most time-consuming, tedious, back-breaking, and finally unrewarding.

Lawns, to digress a bit, were invented by people who could afford to rely on gardeners to do their dirty work for them, and phasing one out can easily cut your gardening time—and your gardening headaches—in half, but we'll get deeper into lawns in a later chapter on that specific subject.

The point I've been leading up to, however slowly, is that the novice gardener should, before he starts to get involved with the specifics of gardening, sit down and have a little talk with himself about what he wants from his garden, and having decided on that, how best to get it.

He may want nothing more from his little bit of land than that it leave him pretty much alone. If this is the case—and there's no reason to feel guilty if it is—it's best to face that fact from the start and to plan accordingly. A later chapter will show how to create an attractive garden that requires almost no attention except for the time it takes to put it in.

Many people, I assume, will want something more from their land, a patio, perhaps, or a play area for the children, one where they can run loose without wreaking accidental havoc on the decorative part of the garden, an area to hang out clothes in, a small vegetable garden, or even a lawn. The more ambitious may be entertaining ideas of a swimming pool, a lath-house or greenhouse, or even a gazebo or a Japanese tea house.

Whatever your plans and however distant they may be, it's best to put them down on paper right from the start. This will help you to remember next year what you had in mind last. A plan on paper also makes any project more interesting, in some cases helps you to realize it sooner, and keeps you in touch with your garden on cold winter days.

For drawing such plans, I use big brown paper bags from the grocery store. When disassembled, they provide a much larger drawing surface than any other kind of paper commonly found around the house, and they have the additional advantages of being durable, of withstanding frequent erasures and of standing up to any number of foldings and refoldings without splitting along the seams.

If you like drawing plans—and I must confess that I'm somewhat of a frustrated draftsman myself—you might make up three different sets. The first should depict exactly what you have now, leaving out the weeds, of course; the second, what you think you can realistically achieve in, say, five years; and the third, a dream plan, what you'd like to achieve given all the time and money you'd need to achieve it. In such plans, you should include all trees, sizable shrubs, paved areas, structures, lawns, and the like. You'll go quietly crazy if you attempt to include every single marigold and daisy. Clumps of such lesser growth should be depicted as "annual bed" or "perennial bed." Single plants, unless they're of particular importance to you, should be forgotten.

You'll also endanger your sanity a bit if you don't set your mind to doing some fairly accurate surveying at the start. If you're using a scale of one-quarter inch equals one foot and a certain tree of yours is an inch off its mark on your plan, it'll be four feet off its mark in the garden and perhaps, just as it's reaching maturity, in the middle of the deep end of your swimming pool.

To start your surveying, arm yourself with a long tape measure (a twelve-footer at least), some string, a few stakes, a hammer, and the knowledge that George Washington, having failed to be born in a log cabin, made it to the Presidency by doing just exactly what you're marching out into the garden to do yourself.

You won't, of course, have to measure the distance between every single shrub or tree, but you should accurately determine the location of enough landmarks so that a few of your educated estimates are proven, via the tape measure, to be accurate within a foot or so.

Once your plans are limned out, you can begin to think about planting and planting priorities. If your gardening time is limited, and whose but mine isn't, don't waste it this year on a lot of little things. Instead, plant the tree that you're going to want to shade your patio.

Even if you don't get around to putting in the patio for five years, by the time you do, the tree will be ready to do some shading. Put in the big things—or the things you want to get big—first, the trees, shrubs, the slow growers or, in other words, the future landmarks of your landscape.

4 WHAT A GARDEN IS AND WHERE IT CAME FROM

History

This chapter might as well have been called "The History of the Garden." I rejected that title because I was afraid that you, in your panic-stricken quest for practical information, might pass this chapter over. How important, after all, is the history of the garden when your roses are being eaten alive by aphids and brown spots are appearing all over your carefully tended lawn? Important enough, I hope, to merit a very few pages in this book.

Whether or not you realize it, the history of the garden, the way in which gardens were born and developed, has determined to a large extent how all gardens look and how we think about them. Since the appearance of your garden and your attitude toward it are concerns of this book, I don't think I can, in good conscience, pass over the historical aspects of gardening without doing you something of a disservice.

If you're still not convinced to go on reading, let me tempt you further with two promises: first, that

Egyptian Garden

this will be one of the shortest, most concise, and more interesting histories you've ever read and second, that once you've read it, I'll relate your reading to some of your more practical gardening concerns.

The first gardens to appear on earth or, at any rate, the first to leave historical records behind them, appeared in Egypt about two-thousand years before the birth of Christ. As you might expect, they were an outgrowth and development of agriculture. Man planted food before he planted flowers.

Contributing more immediately than hunger to the creation of the first gardens were the vagaries of the Nile. The Nile, during the rainy season, produced vast flooding, but during the hot, dry summer months, when water for any purpose was at a premium, the Nile was reduced to little more than a muddy trickle.

To compensate for the ups and downs of the river, the Egyptian farmer, at some point in history or prehistory, arrived at the idea of saving water from the floods and using it during the dry months to irrigate his crops, his livestock and, no doubt, himself. The reservoir was born.

For reasons of convenience and ease of maintenance, these early reservoirs were located near the farmhouses, and they were constructed—or dug—in either square or rectangular shapes, a fact which may seem of historical interest only but nonetheless a fact which may have had more effect on the world than any other apsect of Egyptian culture.

Either by design or simply because there was year around moisture available to them, trees, shrubs, and flowers began to appear along the banks of these reserviors. With the addition of this greenery, a sort of artificial oasis was created, and it surely wouldn't have taken long for the Egyptian farmer and his family to realize that the best place to be on a hot summer's day was in the shade of the trees beside the water, which would help to cool any breeze that might happen to cross it.

At that moment in history when an Egyptian farmer—or perhaps more likely, his wife—decided to add a tree or flower himself or to beautify and enhance the area around the reservior in any way, the first garden and the first gardener were born.

Moses, who probably wrote *Genesis*, almost surely got his idea for the Garden of Eden from the gardens he must have seen while living in Egypt, a thought that may anger the fundamentally fundamental. Still, one can't help but wonder why Adam and Eve, having been forced out of a garden they loved, would have left the idea of a garden behind them as well, unless of course Adam, like so many middle-aged men, had simply grown tired of mowing the lawn, and the apple of his eye had her eye on a condominium east of Eden.

From Egypt, the garden made its way eastward into Persia and India and ultimately into all of Europe and finally to the Americas and Australia. The Persians, Indians, and the Europeans borrowed more than just the idea of a garden. They borrowed the shape as well, the geometrical shape which had been predetermined for the Egyptian gardens by the squares and rectangles of the early reservoirs.

French Garden

The rectangular reflecting pools of the Taj Mahal and your neighbor's rectangular swimming pool owe their shapes directly to the ancient Egyptian reservoirs just as the formal gardens of Versailles and your own clipped hedge owe theirs to the gardens that surrounded those reservoirs.

The formal, geometrical garden, established completely by accident, set a precedent which endured unbroken and remarkably little modified in that part of the world we can conveniently call the West until, and for reasons still in doubt, the English in the eighteenth century, four thousand years later, came up with an entirely different garden, an informal, more natural-looking one based on the configurations of nature instead of on the square. No garden like it had ever before been seen in Europe, the Middle East, or India. The Western garden had up until that time always been a strictly formal affair.

The history of the Eastern garden couldn't be more different, nor could the garden which the East produced. The Western garden, as we've seen, was a direct outgrowth of agriculture, a product of the lowly farmer. The Oriental garden was a reaction against agriculture and a product of the aristocracy.

Pre-agricultural China was not, like Egypt, a desert wasteland subject to alternating droughts and floods. It was a horticultural paradise abounding in lush greenery and brilliant color, a veritable Eden where the ancestors of many of the plants we now consider strictly garden items grew wild. As the population of China increased, however, the natural landscape gradually became field and farm, and the original natural beauty of the land was left intact only in the mountains and in other uncultivatable nooks and crannies.

Chinese warlords stormed over these fields and farms in quest of land, people, and glory for themselves. When a particular warlord felt he'd conquered enough and that his conquests were secure, he would set aside a certain amount of the newly conquered farmland for his personal use to accommodate his victory palaces and to serve as a park to satisfy his hunting needs.

The grandest of these hunting parks, one called the Western Park, was begun by the Emperor Sui Yang Ti in 607 A.D. The Western Park occupied no less than seventy-five square miles and required no less than a million workers to construct. It contained five lakes and four seas, the largest sea measuring thirteen miles in circumference. All the lakes and seas were dug out of the farmland by hand and the excavated earth used to build hills and mountains. The park was landscaped and stocked by imperial command with every available bit of flora and fauna within the Emperor Sui Yang Ti's jurisdiction, including full grown trees which, naturally, had to be dug up, carried in, and planted by hand.

The Western Park was an undertaking of such magnitude that it could hardly be called a garden as we understand the term. It was also not a garden in the strictest sense because its primary purpose was to serve the Emperor and his court as a private game preserve. No one else was allowed to have anything like it on any scale, however small, or for any purpose. One merchant prince who tried to copy the Emperor found his lands and goods confiscated and himself in the hands of an executioner.

Still, the first imperial hunting parks could probably be considered prototypes of the Eastern garden. At some point in their development—and there are no records to tell exactly when—they came to contain the essential elements of what we think of as a Chinese garden, the lakes and seas dug out of flat or rolling farmland and the hills and mountains created from the excavated earth in imitation of the virgin landscape of the nearby mountains, arrangements always dictated in part by myth and religion.

It was Buddhism, however, that accounted for the first appearance of true gardens in China. In the fifth century, it became fashionable for court officials to make religious retreats to Buddhist monasteries located in the mountains.

Chinese Garden

The court officials were so impressed by the natural beauty of the mountain landscape that they began to recreate it on their own estates when they returned to court. These early imitations of nature were, to be sure, on a much smaller scale than the imperial parks, and they were not used for hunting, making them gardens in the truest sense.

It was at this same time that the Japanese first made their way into China. The visiting Japanese were so taken with the gardens they saw there that they borrowed the format behind them in its entirety and took it back with them to Japan. For that reason, the first Japanese gardens were no more than imitations of the Chinese originals, but in time a uniquely Japanese style evolved, and by the seventeenth century, the Japanese had developed a garden which, to my mind, can only be approached, if not actually touched, by the very best English gardens of the eighteenth century.

Japanese Garden

The Japanese contribution to the Eastern garden is twofold. They gradually eliminated the flowering annuals and perennials of the Chinese gardens and came to rely almost entirely on shrubs, trees, and ground covers to achieve the effects they wanted, color effects included.

For spring color, the Japanese used and still use flowering trees such as the cherry, which is now famous the world over. For fall color, they came to rely heavily on the Japanese maple, the leaves of which, in its many varieties, cover the entire autumn color spectrum. At no time of year does a Japanese garden look drab, forlorn, or out of season. Even in winter it's an artistic success, the snow becoming as integral and intentional a part of its beauty as the spring cherry blossoms.

The second Japanese contribution to the Eastern garden is the use of perspective, the placement of larger trees and shrubs in the foreground and smaller ones toward the back to create an illusion of depth and distance. If there happens to be mountains in the background, a well-executed Japanese garden appears to extend without interruption from the feet of the viewer to the peaks of the mountains miles away.

How or why the Japanese stumbled on perspective isn't known, but it's interesting to observe that the great Japanese gardens of the seventeenth century, although created, like the gardens of China, by the aristocracy, were created by an aristocracy which had been deprived of its power and its ability to conquer and rule, an aristocracy which was under permanent house arrest and which, deprived of its normal functions, turned its attentions to gardening. The Western Park of the mighty Sui Yang Ti was truly grand. The gardens of these later Japanese aristocrats only appeared to be grand, suggesting by means of art a grandeur that had been lost to them.

The two great traditions of gardening, Western and Eastern, took, as we've seen, a long time in developing and changed very little in the process. The Western garden grew out of agriculture as a reaction against nature and its cruelties. The Eastern garden developed as a reaction against the monotony of agriculture and in imitation of natural landscapes that weren't

English Garden

cruel but beautiful. All the changes that took place in either tradition were slow and gradual, evolutionary rather than revolutionary.

Because of this, I find it hard to believe, as some people do, that the English of the eighteenth century staged the first and only revolution in the history of gardening. It cannot be denied that, for some reason, some of the English abandoned their four-thousand year old tradition of formal gardens and began creating out of whole cloth informal, natural-looking essentially Eastern gardens. The proof is incontrovertably there in books and growing to this day in the English countryside.

Why the English did this is another matter. Did someone walk out one morning and announce that he had just invented an entirely new kind of garden or did someone pay a visit to the Orient and return with a description or a sketch of the gardens he'd seen there? The latter possibility seems to me far and away the more probable of the two, the one more in line with the history of gardening everywhere. That the English did it, however they did it, is still a remarkable feat, and one that's made a permanent mark on all the gardens of the West.

It's probably all too apparent by now that of the two styles of gardening, I have a definite preference for the less formal, for the kind of garden created by the Chinese, the Japanese, and the English, which, for lack of a better term, I'll call the Anglo-Oriental garden. I prefer this style of garden to the more formal Egyptian influenced garden for two reasons. The first is purely esthetic, a reaction not against the monotony of agriculture but against the monotony of cities, against buildings and blocks, the endless urban parade of squares and rectangles that meet the eye at every turn. I like having something, if only my own back yard, to remind me, however artificially, that there's more to the world than man and his creations.

My second reason is purely practical, one which, even if you don't agree with my esthetics, may still be of interest and use to you. An Anglo-Oriental garden, in any of its infinite possible forms, is far less demanding and much easier to care for than a formal Western garden in any of its more finite forms.

To prove this to you, let's imagine that you've purchased a dozen marigolds from the nursery. Following the Western tradition, you plant them in a straight line, equally spaced as a border along your lawn. If some garden monster or dog or child gets to one of the marigolds and it dies, you'll have a glaring hole in your planting, a hole that will catch your eye and hurt your heart every time you stroll through the garden. Instead of noticing eleven healthy plants, you and everyone else will notice one missing one.

If, however, you plant your twelve marigolds in a randomly spaced grouping along a *curve* of your lawn and the same thing happens to one of them, the only way you'll notice it is to actually see the dead plant. After you've removed it, I grant that the strength of the planting will be reduced one-twelfth, but the total design of the planting will be virtually unchanged and your joy in it unhampered.

Or take the garden hedge. If you have a formal hedge, it will require weekly trimming during the summer to keep it from looking shabby, and it will never look as good as it did the minute you finished trimming it. With a formal hedge as with a new car, there is one perfect shape only and an infinite number of imperfect and undesirable ones, of possible dents and unwanted outcroppings.

Unless you're Louis XIV or his modern equivalent and have a bevy of master hedge-trainers at your beck and call, you're much better off in terms of garden maintenance with an informal hedge, one that you can occasionally prune—not clip—in order to give it body and keep it from straying into places where it doesn't belong, a hedge that can be left alone indefinitely without its suggesting that it's been abandoned.

Many of the English, refusing to abandon the Western tradition entirely, incorporated a few formally clipped shapes into their otherwise informal gardens. These formally maintained plants serve much the same function as garden sculpture or statuary. They act as focal points for less formal arrangements and give the garden greater visual interest and character.

At no time in history has the amateur gardener had more and more varied material to draw from than he does today, especially now that the influence of the Japanese garden is really starting to be felt in the United States. In a later chapter on garden design, we'll employ some of the features of each gardening tradition to help you create for yourself a garden that's a pleasure to see, easy to care for, and one that looks bigger than it is, a garden that makes it look like you're doing more work than you actually are.

5 WHAT PLANTS DO FOR YOU

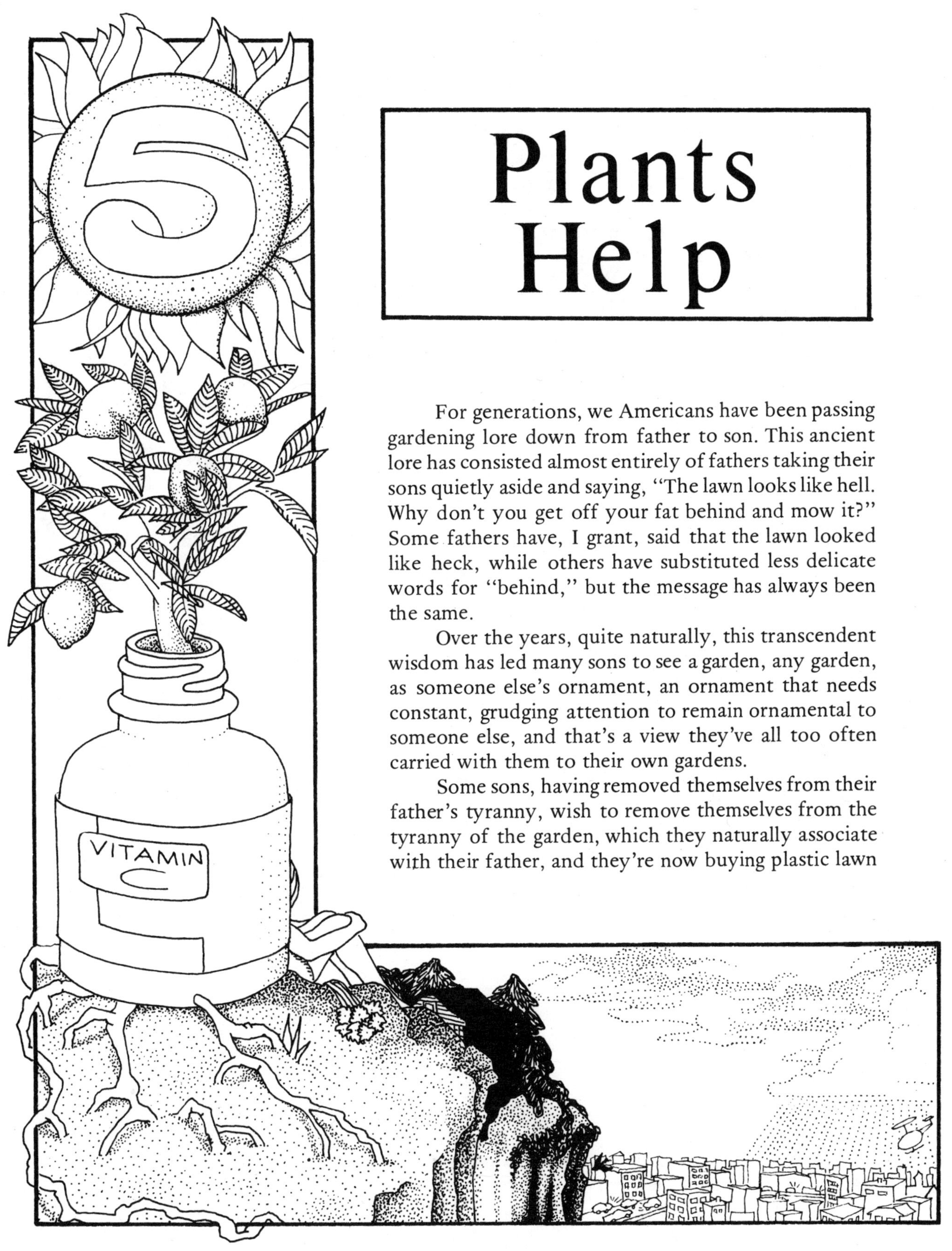

Plants Help

For generations, we Americans have been passing gardening lore down from father to son. This ancient lore has consisted almost entirely of fathers taking their sons quietly aside and saying, "The lawn looks like hell. Why don't you get off your fat behind and mow it?" Some fathers have, I grant, said that the lawn looked like heck, while others have substituted less delicate words for "behind," but the message has always been the same.

Over the years, quite naturally, this transcendent wisdom has led many sons to see a garden, any garden, as someone else's ornament, an ornament that needs constant, grudging attention to remain ornamental to someone else, and that's a view they've all too often carried with them to their own gardens.

Some sons, having removed themselves from their father's tyranny, wish to remove themselves from the tyranny of the garden, which they naturally associate with their father, and they're now buying plastic lawn substitutes and plastic flowers, trees, and shrubs to stick around the borders of their plastic lawns.

According to those who sell plastic natureware, all your gardening headaches will forever be over once you've purchased and installed their space age, heaven-sent product. Anyone who's ever owned a plastic garbage can will tell you that that's not strictly true. Plastic anything has a nasty habit of cracking, splitting, tearing, and fading. It also melts, and a plastic tree, no matter how beautiful on the day you buy it, will never look that good again. It will deteriorate. A real tree, on the other hand, can grow, become greener, and can even become more beautiful.

This isn't, I suppose, the place for a full-scale tirade against plastic greenery, although I'd love to give one. I'd love to rant and rave and scream and holler for at least six pages. But I'm not going to do that. Instead, I'm going to soothe myself by assuming that you wouldn't be reading this book if you'd given up trying to grow things and that, between turning these pages, you're not looking over at a relative and saying, "The lawn substitute looks like hell. Why don't you get off your fat behind and vacuum it?"

I'm also not going to try to convince you that one of the main functions of a city garden, especially the front yard, isn't ornamental and decorative, because I'm convinced that it is and I hope it will remain so. The only alternatives to a basically ornamental front yard seem to be food production or parking lots, depending on whether it's the human or the automotive population which eventually carries the day. I hope things don't come to that.

What I am going to do here is talk about some of the things, other than merely looking nice, which plants do and do for you, things which should be taken into consideration before you put in a new plant or take out an old one. By the time you've finished reading this chapter, the plant world will, I hope, hold a few new dimensions for you.

Plants As Insulation

This subtitle, I expect, jarred you just a little. Like most people, you probably think of insulation in terms of the hardware store or building supplier's rather than the nursery, but the nursery can, if used properly, insulate you against an impressive number of elements, both natural and man-made.

Against Rain

Trees don't make acceptable roof substitutes, and I'm not going to suggest that they do. Their roots, however, and the roots of all plants are valuable when it comes to holding down the soil. Anyone who lives on a hillside is probably already aware of this use of plants or they've found a significant part of their hill in the valley below after a good hard rain.

You don't, however, have to live on a hillside to benefit from the soil-retentive properties of roots. A planting of shrubs around the base of your house will help to keep the soil, if there's any movement of water at all, from washing out from under your foundations, which can, if it happens to you, become a very costly experience.

A similar planting will also keep soil from washing up against the foundations and raising the soil line around them. If this happens, and it usually happens too gradually to be noticed, it leaves you more open to dry rot and termite damage since it makes it easier for moisture and termites to get from the soil into the wood superstructure above the concrete.

This same planting of shrubs will also keep the rain from splashing mud up against the outer walls of the house, a phenomenon that's particularly noticeable with new houses which haven't yet been landscaped. Besides being unsightly, mud may stain and damage paint jobs and, because of its moisture holding tendencies, can actually do more permanent damage to wood and stucco surfaces.

Against Wind

You've probably sat in a forest on a windy day and listened to the wind howling through the tree tops above and marveled how you yourself were barely caressed by the smallest of breezes. In case you missed the point of what was going on—and the Oklahoma dust bowl suggests that it's a point not obvious to everyone, it was the trees themselves, not some mysterious force or unseen geographical feature, which kept the wind off the ground and above your head.

The point I'm making is, simply, that the larger the planting around your house, the less susceptible it will be to the wind, the blasts of chill or heat it can bring, and the damage it can do.

A very low planting, a lawn for example, keeps the wind from picking up the soil and carrying it away. A planting of medium height will slow the wind considerably as well as trap dust particles in the air and ease the burdens of that housewife whom we've all heard complain that she doesn't know how so much dust finds its way into the house unless it's through the very walls themselves. A planting that's taller than the house will, if it's large enough in area, keep the wind above the house and off it entirely, and that can make a significant reduction in winter heating costs.

Using plants to break the wind isn't reserved for careful farmers alone, nor is a windbreak necessarily a mile long column of hundred-foot tall eucalyptuses. Twenty feet of six-foot hedge properly placed can do wonders.

In planting against the wind, some judgement will have to be used. You won't want a highly flexible tree between you and the wind because the wind may whip it around and put one of its branches through a window or even a wall. You also won't want a shallow rooted giant hovering over your house because a windy rainstorm might uproot it and land it firmly in your attic.

Conifers, because of their rigid central structure and deep roots, make the best large windbreaks.

Against Sun

Planting as insulation against the sun is a time-honored practice, one we're all familiar with to some extent and have benefitted from at one time or another just by sitting in the shade of a tree on a hot summer's day.

Plants outside the house can also make life more pleasant inside it. Say, for example, you're cursed with a hot south wall that turns the rooms along it into ovens during the summer. A heavy planting along that wall will prevent the sun from beating against it, keeping the temperature inside a good deal lower than it otherwise would be. Keeping the sun off that wall will also prevent much of the damage the sun does to wood and paint.

During the winter, it may be that the sun and its warming properties are welcome along that very same wall. In that case, nature has supplied us with a large number of deciduous plants whose summer verdure will fall away in winter and let the desirable rays of the winter sun through their branches and onto the wall. If a planting of shrubs is for some reason impossible or impractical, there are deciduous vines like Boston ivy which will serve the same purpose.

A large deciduous tree can do the same thing for a roof, keeping the sun off it in summer and letting it through in winter, although such a tree may cause more problems than it solves, since there's the danger of falling branches damaging the roof and the nuisance of leaves clogging up the rain gutters. Nothing, unfortunately, seems to be simple.

Against Climate

Every garden is, in a sense, its own ecological unit with its own mini-climate, a climate slightly different even from that of your nearest neighbor's garden, the differences determined to some extent by the amount of artificial moisture you pour or don't pour on your garden and by the size and varieties of plants you're fostering.

A heavily planted garden will, in general, maintain a more uniform temperature around your house than will barren ground. You'll be warmer in winter because of the protection such a garden will give you from the wind, and you'll be cooler in summer because of the shade and the large amount of cooling moisture which plants pour into the air.

To be sure, a substantial planting of large trees may make your mini-climate undesirably dark and damp in winter, but such a situation can be avoided by careful arrangement and corrected by judicious pruning and thinning.

Against People

This section could just as well have been called "Insulation for Privacy." Privacy is afforded you to a certain extent by fences, but most city ordinances do not allow you to build a fence over six feet tall without a permit and rarely, if ever, over eight feet with one, and some city ordinances are, I've learned from personal experience, hopelessly vague when it comes to the question of privacy screens.

In some cases, especially in neighborhoods where most of the houses are two stories high, even an eight foot fence may not provide you with the privacy you need. It won't for example, cut off the inevitable nosey neighbor's view of your patio from said neighbor's second story window.

Happily, there are no city ordinances, or none that I know of, which limit the height of trees and shrubs, so in the case of a nosey neighbor or a badly placed window, you might pay a visit to your local nursery and acquire a tree that's guaranteed to allow you to sunbathe in your own back yard in whatever state of dress or undress your mind and body may dictate. Exhibitionists will, on the other hand, want to make a survey of their yards to see what trees must be removed in order to give them maximum exposure.

City ordinances are also, I understand from the newspapers, vague when it comes to just how naked the law entitles you to be in your own back yard. "Officer, I just happened to be up on my roof dusting my television aerial when I saw this naked..."

Or your privacy problem may be of an entirely different nature. Perhaps the unfathomable priorities of your city planner have allowed the house across the street to be torn down and now, instead of looking out of your front windows and into the neighbor's front yard, you have an unobstructed view of a cracker box apartment house or even of that great beauty of all great beauties, the gas station.

In a situation such as this, a large planting in your front yard, a sizeable hedge or some fast-growing, low-branching trees, can completely obstruct that view and in some ways provide you with a better one, since you'll no longer have to feast your eyes on passing automobile traffic.

Large plantings at the front of the house have by no means been the standard practice in the residential sections of most American cities, although the cottages in quiet English villages and along quiet country lanes have for centuries been shielded from better views and far less traffic by thick, tall hedges in order to give their tenants greater privacy and peace of mind. It seems to me that this type of planting is one truly effective method of combatting a lot of urban unpleasantness and of making life in the city more bearable for those of us who have to live there. Perhaps more of it will be done in the future.

Against Noise

Using plants as insulation against noise is apparently such a novel idea that I hadn't heard of it until I thought of it myself. The reason for the novelty of the idea may be that until recently most of the noises that reached the human ear from outside were pleasant noises: birds singing, children at play, even the slamming car door of an expected guest.

Now, however, the city dweller's aural privacy is increasingly being invaded by ever more unpleasant and louder sounds: speeding cars, diesel trucks, horns of all kinds, screeching sirens, tires, and brakes, private burglar alarms, airplanes, mufflers which magnify, the moans of stabbing victims, airplanes, more airplanes, and that newest and most damnable noise of all, the helicopter. Imaginative planting can't cut these noises out entirely, but it can do a lot to weaken their force and to muffle them in the older sense of the word.

Bare walls, for example, especially if two of them abut on a concrete driveway, become a perfect echo chamber. Unpleasant noises seem to bounce down them indefinitely, adding many times over to the strength and duration of the original noise. A planting along either or both walls will absorb and diffuse much of the reverberating racket in just the same way that adding furniture, drapes, and rugs to an empty room will soften and dilute the sounds within it.

A shrub or series of shrubs with many small branches and small leaves will, of course, provide a great deal more noise insulation than a tree which has most of its foliage above the line of the roof, and a dense, compact plant will come much closer to approximating the acoustical properties of a velvet curtain than will a loose, open one.

Protection for Nasties

Nasties are people that we're afraid of: robbers, muggers, purse-snatchers, Commies, bandidos, highwaymen, and the Gestapo. They're the only reason I can think of for minimizing the size of the planting around a house, since large shrubs and trees give nasties a place to hide and lay in wait for us. Correct lighting, intelligent planting, a little pruning, and some proper paranoia can help you solve this problem without forcing you to denude your garden of its foliage.

I've noticed, too, that most people who give the existence of nasties as the reason for removing a big and beautiful shrub are also convinced that a one-foot high boxwood hedge should be removed for the same reason. These same people, for reasons known only to them, seem confident, however, about their ability to detect a hidden nasty through six feet of their own automobile parked in a driveway.

This peculiar phenomenon has led me to suspect that what we're really afraid of is, oddly enough, Indians. Indians were always hiding behind trees, while we hid behind our cars, or covered wagons, as we used to call them. Relax, friends, the final tally is in. The score is we and our cars 100, Indians and trees 0.

Greenery

I see, without surprising myself in the least, that I've opted at virtually every turn in this discussion for big plantings, and I will confess, now that I've been caught, that big plantings are very definitely my preference and that I very definitely would like to make them yours. If I haven't converted you on practical grounds, I'm now going to have a go at it on esthetic and spiritual ones.

Some day when you've got a few hours to spare, find an old established neighborhood, preferably one that hasn't been allowed to deteriorate, if that's possible. Park your car, force yourself out of it, and spend an hour or two walking under the big old trees and absorbing the atmosphere around you. When you've finished, hop back in your car and take off for the nearest and newest housing tract. You will be able to identify it from a sign reading Wonderful View Gardens. It's called that because it isn't wonderful, there's no view, and nothing is growing there.

When I've found myself in either of these two neighborhoods, strange things happen to me and my soul. In the old neighborhoods, I perceive that I am, in some truly significant way, related to my surroundings. The big trees and the large shrubs seem to act as a buffer between me and the sky, softening my presence in the scene and making me less conspicuous to myself.

In the new, treeless neighborhoods, I feel like nothing more than a lone cornstalk standing on an empty Kansas plain, waiting, hoping for a wind to blow me over and integrate me into the landscape, a feeling which, oddly enough, I've never had standing alone on an empty plain in Kansas. Kansas and its plains have their own beauty, however surrealistic you may find it.

If that's altogether too metaphysical for you—or if you read it as a symptom of impending mental illness on my part, we'll pass over any further discussion along spiritual and esthetic lines, for the time being at least. I've still got a few more reasons, practical ones, for big plantings, and I'd like to toss them out.

The first has to do with something you probably already know, that plants are great producers of oxygen, an increasingly rare but nonetheless pleasant commodity, particularly when it comes to breathing. It seems to me that the bigger the plants and the greater their number, the more oxygen they'll be able to produce. I approve of that.

The second reason for promoting trees and such involves recent studies, which, I'll be the first to own, can and do prove almost anything that anyone feels the need of proving, but the recent studies I'm talking about I happen to believe for the simple reason that they seem to me to be true.

These studies show that plants absorb, digest, and dissipate air pollution by ingesting it through their leaves. Naturally, plants do this to their own detriment, just as humans and other animals absorb, digest, and dissipate air pollution to theirs.

Although I am by no means in favor of increasing air pollution, I am most certainly in favor of increasing the plant world's share of it, and it seems to me that there's no better way to do this than by increasing the number and size of the plants around us. Anyone who wishes to establish a Begonia for Better Breathing Society may count me as a charter member.

I see where my soap box is beginning to creak and wobble which must mean that it's time for me to return to the ground.

Planting for Color

Planting for color is, strictly speaking, using plants for ornamental purposes, and that's a subject which I hadn't intended to broach in this chapter. I mention this kind of planting here not as ornament for the garden, however, but as ornament for the house, which is a secondary use of plants and therefore in line with the professed goals of this chapter and in keeping with the order I'm having a hard time maintaining in this book.

If you like having cut flowers or cut greenery in the house, you can, with a little advance planning, satisfy your needs in this regard on a year round basis and, if you're inclined to use the florist, save yourself a good deal of money at the same time.

One way to go about this is to reserve a small, out of the way area in your garden for growing cut flowers and nothing else, an area which isn't part of the garden's overall landscape, a vegetable garden for flowers, to put it succinctly.

In this area, you might plant florist-type carnations, which are poor landscape plants at best but which make, as you might expect, excellent cut flowers—if you take the time to stake the blooms, which you have to do to keep them from falling over into the dirt. For summer color, add a row of snapdragons, zinnias, and large marigolds, and for autumn color, a row of long-stemmed florist-type asters and a couple of clumps of your favorite kind of chrysanthemums, which, like carnations, make poor landscape plants but excellent cut flowers, perhaps the most durable cut flowers of all.

Any number of other kinds of flowers might be added to this area. The only requirements that they'd have to meet to merit a place are that you like them, they're cuttable, and they're durable in a vase. The one important requirement that they wouldn't have to meet is that they be attractive as plants.

Besides being out of the way, your small flower farm should be located in a sunny area, since very few flowering annuals and perennials will tolerate shade. The farm should also be out of the way of overhead sprinklers. Overhead sprinkling increases the chances of diseases in some plants, such as zinnias, and in most cases, the weight of the water on the flowers will cause them to droop, dangle in the mud, and even break off well down into the plant, which can seriously hamper flower production.

Cuttable greenery can more easily be incorporated into the overall landscape of the garden. In the winter, you can combine some of your winter pruning chores with your Christmas decorating if you've had the foresight to plant a pyracantha or an English holly. (If you like your holly complete with red berries, you'll have to plant two, one of either sex, or trust to luck that there's another holly close by in the neighborhood.)

In the spring, if you have flowering fruit trees in the garden, you can bring in sprigs of plum, cherry, and apple and enjoy some of the benefits of the season long after the sun has set. A branch of magnolia soulangiana in a vase is an instant—and durable—Japanese flower arrangement and gives almost as much pleasure as the tree itself in all its spectacular bloom. You may already know this tree as the tulip tree, which it's sometimes erroneously called.

For late autumn color, after the flowers have gone, you might supply a basket of homegrown decorative gourds or a vase full of autumn leaves. If you live in an area where there's no frost or where it frosts too late to turn the leaves, add a liquidamber to your landscape. The oak-like leaves of this particular tree turn brilliant reds and oranges even in the mildest of climates.

Using your garden to grow flowers for the house can sometimes get you into trouble outside. As a case in point, I'll cite the almighty rose, probably the most popular, best-loved, and most beautifully scented of all flowers. As a garden plant, however, the rose is quite another matter.

I don't believe, for example, that I've ever seen a rosebush which, without its flowers, could by any stretch of the imagination be considered beautiful. The best that could be said for it is that it looks healthy, and even that can't be said very often since, by early summer, at least one of the myriad of pests which afflict roses has done something to make the leaves look miserable. In January, a correctly handled rosebush looks like nothing so much as a bunch of sticks stuck into the ground by a blind man using his toes. If it weren't for the flowers they produce, roses would have disappeared from the garden a long time ago.

The first drafts of this book contained a long discussion on the pitfalls of growing roses as well as on the unattractiveness of rosebushes. It was a very negative piece of writing but one which, strangely enough, got me interested in the roses I'd inherited with my garden and caused me, for the very first time, to add new roses to my inherited collection.

Because of this weird turn of events, I'm forced to conclude that my diatribe no longer has a place in this book, and I've taken it out and replaced it with a chapter on rose growing which is somewhat more positive in approach and which you'll find toward the end of the book.

Before dropping the subject entirely, however, I'd like to say, in deference to my deleted tirade, that rose-growing is probably best ignored by anyone starting to garden for the first time, by anyone who's easily discouraged, and by everyone whose gardening time is fairly limited. Roses are demanding but worth it, I now find, for those who are willing, able, and have the time to meet their demands.

Edible Ornamentals & Ornamental Edibles

Some plants, besides being nice to look at and performing some or all of the functions we've been talking about in this chapter, do even more: they produce something we can eat. If I were awarding a first prize in this category, it would go to the lemon.

A healthy lemon tree or lemon bush or even lemon hedge, with its thick masses of emerald green leaves and bright yellow fruit, is a joy to behold, and the powerful fragrance of its blossoms ranks with the aroma of star jasmine, roses, and lilacs. As if this weren't enough to expect from any one plant, the lemon also produces a valuable crop, especially for the French cook, a crop that keeps remarkably well on the tree and which can pretty much be picked as needed. In Mexico, where lemons abound, a delicious tea is made from the leaves by crushing several of them, adding a stick of cinnamon to the pot, and pouring boiling water into it.

Many areas of the United States are too cold to grow lemons outside the year round, but it's possible to grow the dwarf varieties in tubs and bring them in during the winter if you have some place, a glassed-in sun porch, for example, to put them. Lemons, like all other citrus fruits, make ideal container plants, and a tubbed lemon on the patio during the summer will, of course, make its owner the envy of his neighborhood if he lives in an area where lemons don't normally grow.

During last winter's cold spell, I learned a lot about just how much cold citrus fruit would take. As I mentioned in the first chapter, the temperature here dropped to at least 14° and stayed well below freezing for ten days.

A lime tree of mine, one that had just started to come into its own, and a Meyer lemon, the easiest of lemons to grow, were burned almost to the ground. The Meyer, nearly a year later, has recovered its leaves and most of its previous size, but there's still no sign of fruit. The lime I removed.

A Eureka lemon, the variety most often sold in the market, lost very few leaves. One of my Washington navel oranges, a very young one, was killed to the ground but managed, finally, to put forth a shoot, probably and unfortunately from the root stock rather than the graft. My other Washington navel sustained damage only at the tips of its branches, while my neighbor's orange trees, the names of which I don't know, were not damaged at all.

Citrus fruit are somewhat tricky even in the most favorable climates. Young ones will sometimes sit for years and do nothing until suddenly and for no obvious reason they'll take hold and begin to flourish, but because of their beautiful foliage, attractive shape, wonderful aroma, and the valuable crops they produce, they're worth experimenting with even at the risk of total failure in the end.

Other fruit trees, deciduous ones like apples, nectarines, plums, peaches, and apricots, are less tricky than citrus and can be grown in a much wider variety of climates. If you have a penchant for any of these fruits, you might consider adding a tree or two to your landscape. Dwarf varieties of most fruit trees are available for people who don't have a great deal of space or who don't want to be burdened with a mountain of the same kind of fruit all in the space of a week or so.

Dwarf trees, because they grow only to about the size of a large shrub, are much easier to service and harvest than the full scale varieties. When it comes to picking and pruning them, you won't find yourself at the top of a tall ladder or, as sometimes happens, too quickly at the bottom.

Deciduous trees are more demanding than citrus when it comes to pruning, but they're not by any means impossible to handle, even for the amateur, and shouldn't be rejected for that reason by the dubious pruner, who will find fairly thorough instructions on the art of pruning in the third part of this book.

A fruit tree in full bloom in the garden is one of the surest and most delightful signs of spring, so delightful, in fact, that a number of flowering, non-fruiting varieties have been developed for people who love this spectacle but don't want to be bothered with the fruit it usually produces.

During the winter, deciduous fruit trees of all kinds and varieties are available at the nursery in bare root stock and at considerable savings, but once you've decided on a certain kind of tree, an apple or a plum, don't rush out and buy the first variety you lay eyes on. Do a little research first.

If you've definitely decided you want an apple tree, check into the different varieties. Do you want a red apple or a green one? An apple primarily for eating or mainly for cooking or one that's good for both? Do you like your apples especially firm and crisp, tart or sweet? Is it important to you that the apples store well?

After you've selected the four or five apples that best suit your needs, pay a visit to the nursery and ask the nurseryman which of those on your list are best suited for your climate, and plant one of those.

If I were recommending an apple, it would be the Golden Delicious, a great eating and as good a cooking apple as I've run across. The Golden Delicious is especially firm and crisp. It's also sweet and juicy, and it has an underlying tart taste which I'm particularly fond of. The tree is an asset in almost any landscape, and it does well almost anywhere, hot, low desert regions excepted.

Of the smaller plants that can be used for landscaping as well as food, the strawberry is one of the more versatile. It makes an attractive ground cover and can be used in rock gardens or as lawn substitute in areas where it won't get walked on and from which you don't demand lush greenery during the winter. For a prolonged strawberry harvest, plant one of the ever-bearing varieties.

The prostrate, low-growing, varieties of rosemary, a tasty and useful herb, make an excellent and durable ground cover for small areas and will cascade handsomely down a wall. The upright varieties can easily be pruned into small, bonzai type trees to show off their picturesquely gnarled trunks and branches. In winter and spring and again in the fall, the dark green foliage of my rosemaries is covered with tiny, electric blue flowers which, when they turn to seed, attract goldfinches to the garden.

Purple or variegated sage makes an attractive addition to any part of the garden that's kept dry enough. My own watering habits, unfortunately, have killed more sage plants than I care to think about. There is also a variety of deep purple basil which can be planted in borders or groups to set off flowers and provide contrast for green and gray foliage. Basil is an annual and will have to be replanted every year.

The main thing to consider if you're thinking about adding a food-producing plant, particularly a fruit tree, to your garden is whether or not you're really going to make use of what it produces. One spring day you may fall in love, and with very good reason, with someone else's flowering crab apple and decide then and there that you have to have one of your own, not realizing that, come some fine summer, you're going to have crates of crab apples to dispose of.

The first year the tree reaches maturity, you'll probably make crab apple jelly, quarts of it. The second year, you'll start giving the apples away along with your recipe for jelly. The third year, you'll begin dumping the apples in the trash, and the fourth year, you'll start to think about cutting the damn tree down because destroying all those apples is making you feel guilty, making you hate yourself.

Another problem with fruit trees is that the entire crop may come ripe while you're off on your summer vacation. You'll leave home anticipating a golden harvest on your return, but when you actually do get back, you'll find your golden harvest rotting on the ground, a stinking mess occupied by an army of ants and air forces of flies, bees, hornets, yellow jackets, and the like.

With fruit trees as with any other plants, *plant your needs and abilities, not your dreams.*

We'll call that Gardening Rule of Thumb, green thumb, Number One. If you can bear a bit more home-grown gardening philosophy, keep in mind that all the plants you're in charge of are your servants, not your masters. When you march into the garden to do your chores, assume the attitude of a benevolent despot. You're kind, firm, and very definitely in charge, a strict and loving disciplinarian.

Now that you know some of the things that plants can do for you, besides looking nice, we'll go on to the next order of business, which is what you have to do for plants to insure that they'll do what you want them to, and what you want them to do is grow.

6 MEETING THE PLANT AND ITS NEEDS

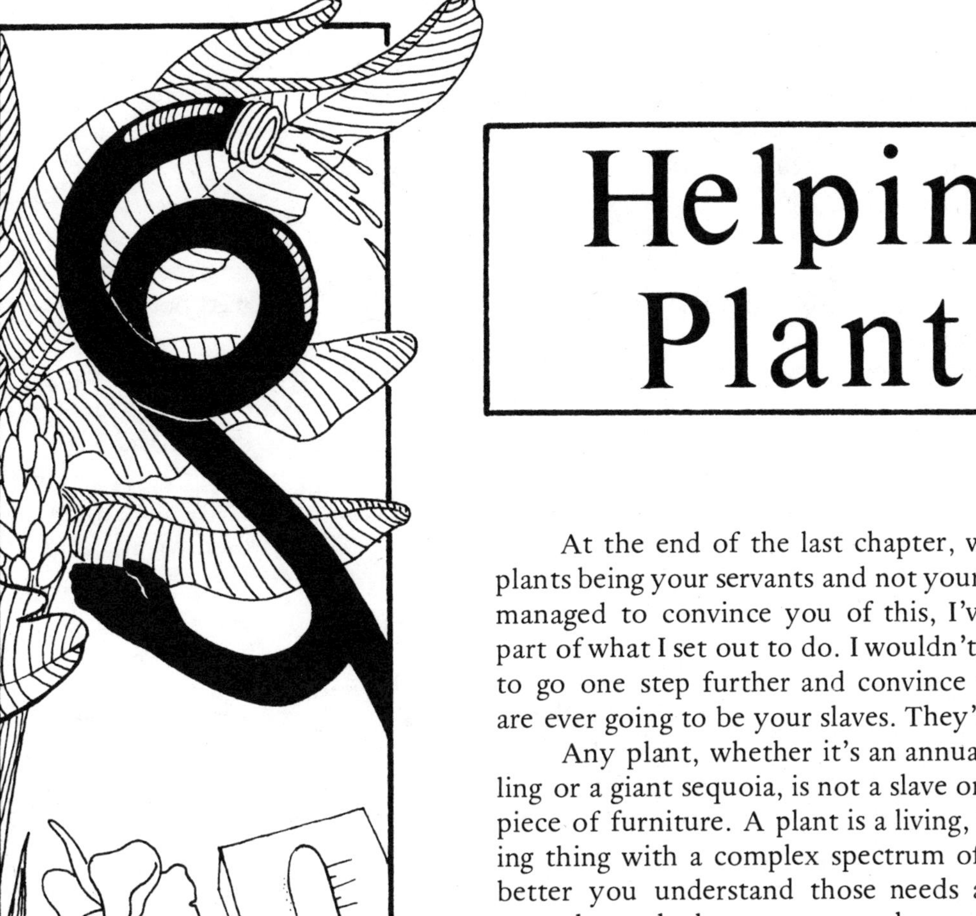

Helping Plants

At the end of the last chapter, we talked about plants being your servants and not your masters. If I've managed to convince you of this, I've accomplished part of what I set out to do. I wouldn't, however, want to go one step further and convince you that plants are ever going to be your slaves. They're not.

Any plant, whether it's an annual rye grass seedling or a giant sequoia, is not a slave or a machine or a piece of furniture. A plant is a living, breathing, feeding thing with a complex spectrum of needs, and the better you understand those needs and are able to meet them, the better are your chances of success with any plant.

To me, and perhaps to you, this seems grossly obvious, so obvious in fact that it almost embarrasses me to mention it, but I do mention it because it's become apparent to me that it isn't obvious to everyone. It certainly isn't obvious to a neighbor of mine.

My neighbor entertains a passion for Colorado

blue spruces, which on the whole isn't a bad passion to entertain. Blue spruces are lovely trees, and every year my neighbor purchases a new one and pays a professional gardener to plant it for her. However, if you're picturing a city lot covered with a small forest of blue spruce, you're making a mistake.

You see, this professional gardener—a man of questionable ethics or small courage—plants the new spruce, according to my neighbor's instructions, in exactly the same spot where he planted the one the year before, the one that died and has had to be removed before the new one could be planted in its place.

Next spring, this year's tree will be dead, and my neighbor, as is her habit, will have it replaced with yet another. I assume this cycle of death will continue until my neighbor herself goes the way of her spruces or at least until she passes into bankruptcy, for it costs her, she tells me, some fifty dollars a year to maintain this lone spruce habit of hers.

The two of us haven't discussed spruces beyond their replacement cost. My neighbor isn't the sort of person who solicits—or even condones—advice. If she were, a dam within me would burst and a well of information gush forth. I'd let her know in no uncertain terms that, as far as I can see, she's never going to get a spruce to survive, much less grow, in the particular spot she's chosen for that end.

For one thing, the spot she's chosen is a swampy bog for much of the year, and swampy bogs are about as conducive to growing Colorado blue spruce as the Arctic Circle is to the cultivation of bananas. One pictures—or at least I do—Colorado blue spruces growing in the rocky, fast-draining soil of the Colorado mountains, and my neighbor provides instead something more akin to a Louisiana backwater bayou.

For another thing, as if things weren't bad enough already, she's also chosen a spot where the winter sun shines not at all but where the spring sun starts banging away full force sometime during those two weeks when the day time highs around here jump from the fifties into the high sixties and seventies—and even eighties, nineties and hundreds, California weather being, as it is, eternally unusual.

Consequently, if the already belabored spruce has somehow managed to struggle through the wetness of winter and has by chance forced out any new growth, this new growth is soon fried alive on the tree by a sun the tree hasn't seen for three months. Imagine, for example, what would happen to a human being just out of three months of solitary confinement if some ghoul were to place him naked and exposed on an equatorial beach.

It's also about this time of year that spring gardening fever hits my neighbor, and she totters out of her house, takes stock of those few plants that have survived her attentions, and notices for the first time that her spruce is ailing. It has, in fact, turned from a sickly blue-green to a morbid brown in a matter of two weeks, and the needles are dropping like proverbial flies.

To remedy this problem, which we can call death, my neighbor puts the garden hose under the dying tree and leaves it running there for several hours each day. This act of charity quickly quenches any small sparks of life that the tree may have been harboring, and it dies. In a month or so, there will be a new one in its place.

If trees wonder, hers must have quite a few questions to ask when they get to that great Colorado in the sky. I've done some wondering, too. For a time, I considered that my neighbor saw the Colorado blue spruce as a kind of huge evergreen annual, a fifty-dollar-a-throw giant petunia. Her last ditch efforts to save her drowning, sun-burnt trees by watering them convinced me otherwise. She wouldn't be watering them, I'm forced to conclude, if she didn't want them to live.

I finally reached the conclusion, and I think it's the correct one, that she sees the blue spruce and every other form of plant life as pieces of furniture. She likes a particular plant, she has a spot in the garden she wants filled, and she fills it with the plants she likes. She decorates her garden with plants just as she decorates her walls with pictures. A picture, of course, doesn't care where it's hung, but a plant cares very much where it grows, and if it doesn't like where it's growing, it lets you know about it by dying.

Decoration is an important consideration when you're creating a garden, but it's a secondary consideration. What nature has in mind must come first. After you've figured out what choices nature gives you, you can make your choice from among nature's selection which, however limited, is still bound to be a large one. If you reverse this order, make your choice first, and then let nature pass on it, you're running an unnecessary and really rather foolish risk.

An Analysis

Let's return to my neighbor for the moment and take a closer look at her problem to see what would happen if it were handled with more thought. The problem, first of all, is two-fold. My neighbor wants a Colorado blue spruce, *and* she wants a tree to grow in a particular spot in her garden. We've already seen that, as things stand, she can't satisfy either of her wishes by combining them.

If her desire for a spruce is pre-eminent, she should, simply, look around her lot to see if there are any places on it that are better suited to growing spruces. As it turns out, there are many such places, places which get more uniform sunlight all year around and places which are considerably drier, places which don't, as the one she's chosen, bear the responsibility of draining a large portion of the clay hillside we live on.

If her desire to have a tree in the particular spot we've been talking about is pre-eminent, she should find a tree that will endure or even thrive under the conditions the spot provides. In this case, a birch, an alder, a willow, or an ash, all of which appreciate a lot of water, would be infinitely preferable to a spruce. If my neighbor insists on an evergreen, a redwood would be her best alternative.

There is, however, a third possibility, that something could be done to the spot in question to make it more suitable for spruces, suitable enough to expect one to grow in it. In the case of my neighbor, however, such a solution isn't practical. It would involve demolishing her living room so that the tree could have winter sun, and it would mean that she would have to replace enough of her heavy, slow draining soil with a looser, faster draining medium to support the root system of a tree that can reach as high as a hundred feet.

All this brings us to one simple fact which should by now be clear to everyone: no matter how overriding anyone's need is for a particular plant in a particular place, that need is going to be overriden in the end by the needs of the plant itself.

The Needs of Plants

The needs of plants can be nicely distributed among the four classical Greek elements of Earth, Air, Fire, and Water, which should give you some idea of just how scientific plain dirt gardening is, if for Air we understand temperature and for Fire, sunlight.

For every plant, there is probably a perfect point on each of these four spectra, but it won't be one of your gardening chores to determine exactly what that point is and provide it. God and Luther Burbank forbid. If, however, you can get a general idea of what's involved in each of these elements and what they mean in terms of what you grow, you'll be that much closer to some kind of horticultural success.

You'll also find that if circumstances force you to cheat a little with one of these elements, you can often convince a plant to perform by working on and perfecting one of the others, one which is in your power to control. I have, as a case in point, gotten my too shady (Fire), too cool (Air) vegetable garden to produce vegetables by making the Earth as nearly perfect for vegetables as possible and by keeping a close eye on the Water it gets.

Earth

As far as plants are concerned, there are two important aspects of soil, its *chemical* and its *physical* make-up.

Chemically speaking, any soil has to be acidic, alkaline, or neutral. Acidity-alkalinity is measured on a scale of 0 to 14. Soil with a *pH* factor, as the chemists call it, of 7 is neutral. Soil with a *pH* factor of 0 is highly acidic, while soil with a *pH* factor of 14 is highly alkaline.

This information, expressed thus technically, isn't of great import for the amateur gardener. Grandma got along just fine without ever having heard of *pH* factors, although she probably gave her lilacs a shot of lime now and then and saved her coffee grounds for her azaleas, which was her way of dealing with the same problems. I mention *pH* factors here mainly because they crop up again and again in books and articles on gardening and often without any explanation as to what they refer to.

In general, soils which are subject to heavy rainfall are acidic, while soils which get little rain are alkaline. This information is of direct importance for the amateur gardener, because it tells him that if he lives in a low rainfall area and wants to grow plants native to high rainfall areas, he's going to have to do more than supply his plants with the extra water they'll need. He's also going to have to *amend* his soil, to make it acidic rather than alkaline.

This type of amendment can be done, in part, by leeching out the excess lime through repeated and heavy applications of water and by making sure that the lime-bearing water is able to drain away. Adding organic matter to the soil in the form of compost, leaf mold, peat moss, steer manure, ground bark, and sawdust will also increase its acidity as will the addition of gypsum, calcium sulphate.

To reverse this procedure, to make an acid soil more alkaline, you simply add agricultural lime to it and make sure that the lime isn't carried off by the rain and normal garden watering. Lime is available from most garden supply outlets.

Many plants aren't terribly fussy about the acidity or alkalinity of the soil they grow in. They'll do well in whatever soil the gardener can provide unless, of course, his soil is extremely acidic or extremely alkaline. If you live in an area where the soil has a very high or very low *pH* factor, you'll know it or can quickly find out about it by talking to a few of your neighbors. If you don't already know it or your neighbors don't have any idea what you're talking about when you ask them, your soil, like most soils, is probably fairly close to neutral.

Plants which have their origins in areas where the rainfall is extreme in either direction and the soil strongly acidic or strongly alkaline are, of course, going to be more demanding in this regard than most plants. If, for example, you want to grow cacti in any place but a desert, you're almost certainly going to have to add lime to your soil to achieve any kind of success.

Conversely, if you're planning to grow such rain forest natives as ferns, azaleas, rhododendrons, and camellias anywhere but in a rain forest, you'll have to increase the acidity of your soil by adding organic matter to it. We'll explore this subject at greater length further on.

The last generalization I have to make about soil chemistry is that heavy clay soils tend to be alkaline just as light, loose soils tend to be acidic, the determining factors being the amount of rain they receive and the speed and thoroughness of the run-off.

By and large, you'll never have to learn to think about your soil chemically. If you learn to think about it and handle it physically, the proper chemistry will follow. In my own garden, for example, I become a soil chemist only when I spread a little lime around the lilacs or add a little to the soil when I'm planting peas. I dig in organic matter whenever I'm adding a new plant to the garden, and I increase the amount if the new plant happens to be a rain forest native.

Physically speaking, soil is composed of three main ingredients: clay, sand, and organic matter. Clay and sand, I'm sure, are familiar to everyone. Organic matter, to approach the subject in a slightly different way than I did above, is any decayed or decaying vegetable material and sometimes, as in the case of blood meal and bone meal, decaying animal material.

(A decaying corpse is, as you might suspect, in the process of returning to the soil all the things that it still owes it, a debt which the users of air-tight, water-proof coffins are, for reasons that I don't understand, declining to repay. Personally, I'd prefer to think that part of my rotten old self might end up as part of a tree rather than to know for certain that all of my rotten old self was going to remain forever locked inside a padded, pink satin box, but since that's the undertaker's "forever," not Nature's, I suppose in the long run it doesn't make very much difference.)

Unlike organic matter, vegetable or animal, clay and sand by themselves contain no plant nutrients. Their contributions to the soil are of a purely physical nature, while organic matter contributes both chemically and physically. Clay holds the soil together, gives it stability, slows down drainage, and holds in water. Sand breaks up the soil, facilitates drainage, and helps to furnish those small pockets of air that the soil must contain if plant roots are to breathe, something that all roots must do.

Too much clay or too much sand in the soil makes for poor soil. Too much clay retards root growth, keeps air out of the soil, and holds in water that may rot the roots that do grow.

Too much sand drains water away too quickly, which may cause plants to dry out and die.

An excess of either clay or sand can, to a certain extent, be corrected by adding balancing proportions of the other to the soil. The addition of organic matter will improve the quality of both sandy and clayey soils and provide necessary and desirable plant nutrients as well.

This is how it works. Organic matter mixed with clay prevents the small particles of clay from forming larger ones, from forming dirt clods in other words. The air pockets necessary to root growth can thus be maintained between the particles of clay, and excess, undesirable water can more easily pass between them and drain away. The looser structure which organic matter gives to clay soils will also allow roots to work their way more readily through the soil, which provides for more vigorous root growth and more vigorous plant growth above it.

The addition of organic matter to sandy soil helps to hold the sand particles together and keeps them from shifting around, a condition which is almost as unconducive to sustained root growth as tightly packed clay. Organic matter also permits sandy soil to retain moisture, something which sand by itself doesn't do for long.

I should point out here that pure sand is an ideal medium for rooting cuttings because it provides almost no resistance to root growth. It must be remembered, however, that the sand in this situation is tightly contained, usually by the walls of a flower pot or the sides of a nursery flat, and that any water applied to it must of necessity be applied very gently.

People frequently complain that their soil is either too sandy or too clayey, but I've never heard anyone despairing because his soil contained too much organic matter. If I did, I'd be tempted to treat him like the man who complained about having too much money. I'd offer to relieve him of his problem by relieving him of its cause. If there really is anyone who thinks he's suffering from this problem, he can easily solve it and without my help. If he just digs down a foot or so, he'll find plenty of inferior soil which he can work up into his overabundance of organic wealth to help dilute it.

The back yard soil test. To determine the quality of your soil, take a handful of it when it's damp and squeeze it. If you end up with a loose, crumbly ball, your soil's in good shape. If the ball is solid and hard, you've got too much clay. If there's no ball visible at all, you've got too much sand, and by now you should know how to set about remedying either defect.

For the serious gardener, maintaining and improving the quality of the soil isn't a one-shot affair. It's not something that can be done once and forgotten about. It's an on-going process, something that the gardener always has at the back of his mind no matter what other gardening chore he's performing. Top quality soil is something few people have to start with. It's something that you work towards, slowly, patiently, and relentlessly, because the rewards are great.

A point of importance. If you've decided to buy or borrow sand for your garden, make sure that it's river sand. Beach sand, with its high salt content, will make your garden look like what Rome did to Carthage, to name a remoter horror than the one which leaps more readily to mind. If you're in doubt about whether you're getting beach or river sand, swallow your scruples and taste it. Beach sand, to no one's great surprise, will have a decidedly salty taste.

Plant nutrients, the various elements and compounds which are found in the soil and are necessary for plant growth, will be discussed in the chapter on fertilizers which follows.

Water

Next to lawn-mowing, watering is probably the gardening activity most familiar to everyone. Everyone knows that plants need water. That's simple enough. What's complicated is when, how, how much, and where to water.

In part, of course, the amount of water poured onto your garden in a year's time is going to be determined by the annual precipitation in your area. The kind of soil indigenous to your area will have been to a large extent determined by the amount of precipitation you receive, and together the rainfall and the soil will have achieved just the perfect balance necessary for growing the kinds of plants which are native to your area.

If you're only growing natives, you'll never have to think about using a garden hose. The modern garden, however, is usually a highly non-native and unnatural place, far more so than its counterpart of a hundred or even fifty years ago. Your garden, even if it's a small one, probably contains plants which had their origins on all seven continents. Some of these plants will, of course, have come from areas as distant but as similar as California, the Mediterranean, and certain parts of South Africa. Others will have come from dissimilar areas where conditions, rainfall patterns among them, are very different from yours.

If you live in an area where summer rains are scarce or non-existent, you can make up the slack for those plants that need the water with the selective use of the garden hose as is the custom of almost every Californian who maintains a garden. It's more difficult, of course, to keep rain off a plant that doesn't want it, short of putting a roof over it, and that isn't terribly practical.

Luckily, however, it isn't so much the amount of water a plant gets that counts. It's how much water the soil around the plant keeps which really matters. Consequently, by making sure that plants which like it dry are planted in loose, fast-draining soil, you can often convince them to put up with more water than they would normally stand.

This brings us to the difference, which I've hinted at above, between *water retention* and *moisture retention,* two names which on the surface sound very much the same but which, underneath the ground, are very different indeed.

Water retention is just what the name implies, the containment of water in much the same way a bowl or a cup contains water. It's the condition one finds in swamps, bogs, and aquariums and is conducive only to the growth of swamp, bog, and aquarium plants, plants which can, like fish, take the air they need directly from the water or, like cetaceans, appear on the surface to get it when they need it, and these are not plants which grow, for obvious reasons, in most gardens, water lilies being the commonest exception.

Water retentive soils retain water at the expense of air. Moisture retentive soils, on the other hand, retain water and air together in much the same way as a damp sponge, and they do not retain moisture at the expense of air. The roots of plants grown in moisture retentive soil have access to both moisture and air as they need it.

Clay soils and soils with a high clay content are water retentive. If these soils aren't watered judiciously, the roots of plants grown in them will suffer the consequences of too much water and not enough air. They'll drown and rot. For this reason and because water moves very slowly through clay, clay soils should be watered infrequently but deeply, to insure penetration.

Sandy soils and soils with a high sand content are neither water retentive nor moisture retentive. If sandy soils aren't watered judiciously, the roots of plants grown in them will suffer the consequences of too much air and not enough water. They'll dry out and die. For this reason and because water moves very quickly through sand, sandy soils should be watered frequently but lightly.

And now we come to soils rich in organic matter or *humus* as it's sometimes called. These soils are moisture retentive but not water retentive. Excess water passes quickly through them, leaving air pockets as well as desirable moisture behind it.

This fact is of particular significance to the gardener because it means that he can indulge in overwatering or underwatering without endangering the lives of his plants. In either case, humus will help to compensate for his watering errors and minimize their potentially dangerous consequences. Humus rich soil, in other words, does some of the gardener's work for him, and this is just another reason why the constant improvement and enrichment of his soil should be one of the gardener's most important concerns.

So far we've talked only about water in terms of what it does and what happens to it below the level of the soil, where water does its most important work and where too much or too little of it can do the most damage to plants. There are a few things of somewhat lesser importance to be said about water and watering above ground level.

It's a rule, one almost without exceptions, that any plant in the garden is going to be grateful for having its leaves washed clean either by the rain or by you and your garden hose. If you run out to wash everything off just as the thermometer is about to drop below 32°, you are, of course, going to create unnecessary problems for yourself, but if you're crazy enough to start watering at that temperature, you may deserve them.

Some of the exceptions to the overhead watering rule involve roses, zinnias, and marigolds. Overhead water applied late in the day, especially when the weather is cool, can cause mildew in roses. Roses shouldn't be sprinkled unless you're sure that they'll have time to dry off before the sun sets.

Overhead watering also causes rust in zinnias, and it's probably best not to water them in this way if you can avoid it. Irrigate your zinnias. Overhead watering doesn't promote diseases in marigolds, but the weight of it on the flowers often causes them to fall over and break off.

All three of these conditions are easily diagnosed and shouldn't cause the gardener undue concern. Mildew is a light, white, powdery substance which usually covers the leaves and to which red roses, for some reason, are particularly susceptible. Rust appears as brown spots on the leaves of zinnias, and a broken down marigold is just that and nothing more.

There has in the past been a great deal of discussion among gardeners about overhead watering when it's hot. One side says that it should be avoided at all costs because the standing water drops act as tiny magnifying glasses through which the sun can and does burn tiny holes into the leaves of plants. The other side suggests that it's a good idea because it lowers the temperature of the entire garden, preventing or reducing the danger of heat damage to sensitive plants, and because it allows plants to quickly replenish the vital moisture they're rapidly losing because of the heat.

I belong to the second school of thought, the one that believes more damage is done by excess heat and moisture loss than by the thousands of tiny magnifying glasses, but with one small exception: if you do water in the heat, don't just sprinkle, pour it on. If you sprinkle, you'll only succeed in creating the magnifying glasses without producing any significant drop in temperature or any significant increase in moisture level.

In general terms, as we've seen, watering above the ground is useful for freshening and cleansing plants, for lowering garden temperatures, and for raising the level of humidity in the garden. The more specific and practical aspects of watering will be covered in a later chapter on the subject, but before I go on to Air, there's something I'd like to say about lawn watering.

For years, the people at *Sunset* magazine, people for whom I have great respect, have disagreed with me when it came to how and when a lawn should be watered. They've always recommended watering deeply and infrequently. I've always contended that a lawn should be kept moist at all times and never be allowed to dry out.

Recently and somewhat timidly, the people at *Sunset* came around to my way of thinking. I can't, however, take any credit for this minor victory, even though I found it satisfying. For one thing, I never let them know that I disagreed with them and, for another, my way of thinking isn't really mine. It was my grandfather's.

My grandfather, I don't believe, ever laid eyes on a copy of *Sunset*, but he maintained a rigorously green lawn throughout the often horrendous summers of Southern California, and he did it by pouring on the water. His lawn was always wet, I well remember, because my valuable shoes and I were continually being kicked off it by some authoritarian voice or another.

Just how my grandfather arrived at his then unorthodox views on the watering of lawns, I don't know for sure, but it may have had something to do with a belief that the summer rains of Iowa were what God had really intended for the earth but had forgotten about when he created the Los Angeles basin. My grandfather was just doing what God had forgotten to do.

Air

By Air, as I've said, I mean temperature, although I'm mightily tempted to throw in a few more comments about smog, something the ancients didn't have to bother about when they came up with the Earth, Water, Air and Fire scheme, a scheme, by the way, that's broad enough to include smog if smog is designated as an admixture of Air and Earth catalyzed by Fire, and that isn't all that far from the truth of the matter.

Air, or air temperature, is the one element over which the gardener has least control short of building a greenhouse, and I'm not going to take up greenhouses in this book because I've never been fortunate enough to own one, which shows remarkable restraint and perhaps even dubious thrift on my part.

Outside in the garden, however, and away from greenhouses real or imaginary, we're pretty much stuck with the temperature variations that the climate we live in affords us, and since virtually nothing can be done to alter temperature range artificially, the gardener must learn to live within the range by not planting outside of it, although of course the temptation is always there.

I myself didn't learn until last winter that the San Francisco Bay Area isn't suitable for citrus fruit, fuchsias, and the Brazilian princess flower, and I'm afraid it's going to take a couple more winters of equal severity to teach me that particular lesson because it's a lesson that I'm not much interested in learning.

Generally speaking, however, people do tend to think of warmer climates as infinitely preferable to colder ones when it comes to growing things. If asked to name the best place of all for plants, most people, if they thought about it for very long, would, I suspect, come up with that greenhouse we've been talking about.

The inhabitants of temperate and less than temperate climates seem to hanker after subtropical and tropical zones and the flora they produce, the orchids and bananas, mangoes and papayas, and for many, the oranges, limes, gardenias, hibiscus, and tangerines, the fruits and flowers of paradise.

What's often forgotten in these spiritual migrations to the southern climes is that many trees, shrubs, bulbs, and perennials require low temperatures in order to perform well and that many of the flowers and fruits we like best simply couldn't be grown in the tropics.

Plants which suffer the effects of winter temperatures that are too warm don't as a rule suffer as dramatically as subtropicals which have been devastated by a hard frost. Instead, they languish, and since any number of other factors can cause a plant to languish, an absence of cold weather is rarely pinned down as the real culprit.

I wasn't aware of just how true this is until the advent of the Great Frost I've mentioned before. I was, of course, very much aware of the damage that frost did, and if anybody had told me at the time that any good was going to come from that frost, I would have laughed in his face. But as that winter passed into spring and spring became summer, the positive results of the frost became visibly apparent. Almost all of those plants which are native to climates colder than this one, deciduous shrubs and trees, spring bulbs, and those perennials which disappear into their root systems in winter, leafed out and grew with a vigor none of them had previously shown.

With the evidence of my eyes before me, I did a little research into the subject and learned that I could expect two or three more years of truly vigorous growth from my cold climate natives because of that one hard frost. They had, in effect, been made to feel more at home and showed it by making themselves visibly comfortable.

Prior to the Great Frost, I had known that cherries, for example, require a number of hours at temperatures below 40° in order to prosper and that, because of this requirement, cherries are marginal trees in the Bay Area. They grow, but they don't grow well, and they don't produce a great deal of fruit.

Lilacs and peonies, both great cold climate favorites, are also marginal here, but I've managed to produce better than average blooms from both by growing them in the colder sections of my garden, places which don't get too much winter sun and which get no reflected or trapped heat from walls and fences, those places, in other words, where citrus fruit and other subtropicals would be least happy.

By locating or creating warm, protected spots in your garden as well as colder, more open ones, you can to a certain degree extend the range of the plants you grow, just as I have, as I mentioned, been able to grow citrus on the one hand and lilacs on the other in the same garden, although all three are fairly marginal here, the first happier further south and the latter two more at home up north or back east.

The gardener can, in part, compensate for his inability to control temperature range by making himself aware of the temperature requirements of the plants he's considering growing, by not planting much beyond those requirements, and by learning to think of his garden in terms of micro-climates: warm spots, cold spots, windy spots, protected spots, and so forth.

The gardener is also helped in this regard by nature and by horticulturalists, both of whom have developed different varieties of certain plants which do better in different climates. If you live in the Bay Area, for example, and are thinking about planting a cherry, don't plant the cherry you like best at the market. Plant the cherry that's least fussy about chilling, and plant it on the assumption that a few cherries of any kind are better than no cherries of the best kind.

This is, I suppose, the proper place to discuss what to do when the thermometer starts to drop below freezing if you live in an area where frosts are considered unusual and are known to be undesirable.

The first thing to do, of course, is to stop all watering if you haven't already. More water means more ice both on the plants and in them, and more ice means more death. If you've got anything growing outside in a pot that you suspect might be fragile, bring it inside. Permanently placed plants of a delicate nature should be covered with tarps, blankets, or even sheets. Ground covers and low-growing plants can be mulched with straw, if it's available.

When the temperature begins to drop five to ten degrees below the normal low point, the sheets, blankets, and tarps will start to prove less effective than prayers, and you might as well not bother with them. All you can do at these temperatures is adjust yourself to your losses and hope for a better tomorrow.

If tomorrow does happen to be better, don't—and I stress this—run outside and start pruning off frostbitten branches and digging up frozen plants. *Leave everything alone.* What looks frozen to you now may, when the weather warms up permanently, start putting out new growth further down a branch, or new growth may suddenly appear from the roots.

Although the dead material at the tops of frozen plants may be ugly and unsightly, it's still serving a purpose. It's helping to protect what's alive below it from further frost damage, and by cutting it off before all danger of frost has passed, you may make a dead plant out of one that was only badly wounded.

Come spring, what's really dead and what isn't will become readily apparent, and the plants themselves will tell you what needs to be pruned off and what should be dug up. By June at the latest, anything that hasn't shown some sign of life isn't going to show any, and you can safely get rid of it then.

Fire

Ah, the sun! How I'd like to see a little more of it this fogged over August afternoon, and how I hated it last June when it forced the temperatures up toward 110° and burned the living bejesus out of a couple of my hydrangeas that were just starting to come into bloom.

Sunlight is almost, but not quite, as hard for the gardener to regulate as temperature. In the case of the sun, however, the paraphernalia of civilization, the walls and the fences, are often a blessing and allow a gardener to grow things that wouldn't normally survive if they were more exposed.

North and east facing walls provide shelters for plants which like light or partial sun but which can't stand the full force of the hot afternoon sun. South and west facing walls can actually raise temperatures high enough to grow plants which, if grown in the open, would find the climate decidedly too cool.

In hot, sunny climates, shade-loving plants can also be grown under lath or in the filtered shade of a tree, two other ways the gardener can get around some of the problems the sun presents. Because of the addition of a birch tree on the south side of the house, I can now, for example, grow a couple of azaleas and a rhododendron in a place where I very much wanted them but where they otherwise, because of the southern exposure, wouldn't have stood a chance.

The main problem with the sun, if the sun can be said to present problems, is that it moves north and then south in the sky as the seasons change, and one of the main problems for the gardener, and gardeners can be said to have many, is that he tends to forget this little fact of life.

The gardener may, as I myself have done, place a shade-loving plant in a spot that's shady from September to April only to find to his horror in June that this very same spot gets a good strong dose of direct sun during the hottest part of the day just when the days are the hottest and longest. Good-bye, shade-loving plant.

In my particular case, the trickiest spot in the garden is along the northwest front of the house. This area gets no direct sun for most of the year, but it gets full sun during the summer months from two o'clock in the afternoon until the sun sets around eight. This solar phenomenon makes it a particularly difficult area to garden, and it certainly is no place for the shade-loving hydrangea my predecessor planted there, the hydrangea that I keep promising myself I'll move but which I always forget about until the June sun turns it into something resembling a shredded gunny sack.

It would take constant, accurate observation, an elephant's memory, and a full year's acquaintance with any garden to get a true and complete picture of just where the sun was and wasn't going to be at any particular time. That's too much to ask anyone to do, it seems, but I'll confess that if I'd started thinking in those terms a little earlier, I could have spared myself a number of stupid and costly mistakes. I think in those terms now. At any rate, I keep reminding myself that I ought to.

If too much sun can be corrected by planting trees, erecting a lath house, and utilizing north and east walls, too little sun can sometimes be corrected by the judicious pruning and thinning of trees and shrubs or by getting rid of them entirely. That, however, is something I'd give a lot of thought to before doing. The removal of a tree from a small garden can do a lot more than give you more sun. It can change the overall climate of the garden drastically and bring about the destruction of smaller plants which you had no intention of getting rid of.

If the offending tree happens to belong to a neighbor, you can have a heart-to-heart talk with him or, better still, learn to live in the shade he's providing just as my vegetable garden has learned to live with the three large redwoods which abut it. I would, you can be sure, take my redwood-owning neighbors to task if it looked for a moment like they were thinking about removing those trees, which, because of their great age and beauty, take precedence over my vegetables, although you might not realize I thought that to hear me talk.

You can also, to a certain extent, compensate for too much shade or too much sun by using water wisely and well. A sun-loving plant that gets more shade than it wants will have a better chance of survival if you keep it on the dry side, just as a shade-loving plant can put up with more sun than it wants if the ground around it is kept moist and if you can remember to focus a light mist on it on those days when the sun is most vicious.

That, in perhaps too rough and general a way, describes the world the plant lives in. If you can keep the framework of that world and the interrelationships between its elements at the back of your mind when you're dealing with plants, you'll have begun to think like a gardener; and, in case you haven't noticed it yet, that involves thinking like a plant. One day you're a cabbage, the next an orchid. Gardening's a mind broadening experience, and avid gardeners are, they tell me, sometimes a little strange. Now you know why.

7 GARDENING WITH AND GARDENING AGAINST NATURE

Nature

Gardening is, strictly speaking, an unnatural activity, an activity which, like all other forms of agriculture, is conducted to a certain extent against nature. Mother Nature gets along perfectly well—and all too often a lot better—without man. She needs us not at all, we need her absolutely.

The American Indian understood man's relationship with nature perfectly, and because he did, if it hadn't been for us, he could have survived indefinitely on this planet. Our tenure here is limited. We are killing the goose that laid the golden egg, the only goose of any kind we'll ever know.

The first symptoms of this shortsightedness of ours appeared about eight thousand years ago when we first cut into the earth with a plow to make it give us more than it was willing to provide on its own. And this was a major step indeed, going from accepting the gifts of nature to taking them unasked, but it's a step the earth might have survived. It's also a step that led directly to everything we think of as civilization, and it's a hard step to imagine not having made.

Eight thousand years after the Agricultural Revolution, man made another big step forward, the Industrial Revolution. At this point in history, we advanced from taking the gifts of nature unasked to destroying the capacity of the earth to give them at all. We have advanced, if that's the proper word, from grace to rudeness and from rudeness to suicide.

A case in point, and such cases are legion, is strip-mining where, for the sake of stealing one of earth's many products, we kill its capacity to yield up all the multitudes of other things we need from it, things we may need more than coal or gold. We are cutting down the entire apple tree just to get the one apple which remains at the top out of our reach.

This message, and message it is indeed, may not have a place in a book such as this one. It will only depress those who already know it, and it will convince those who don't that I'm some kind of fanatic. I've given the message in part because I can't help myself and in part because I often read a gardening column in one of the local newspapers, a column which always brings the message to the front of my mind no matter how hard I try to hide it in the back.

Reading this column, which is written by a man whom I have no doubt knows a great deal more about gardening than I do, is a very strange experience, at least for me. I don't, as I suppose I should, get a picture of the columnist as a gardener at all. Instead, he comes across as some kind of horticultural warrior who daily marches forth into his garden armed to the teeth with weed killers, deadly insecticides and laden down with chemical fertilizers.

Gardening for this gentleman is, it seems, nothing short of war, which he wages relentlessly against treasonable insects, invading weeds, and finally even against his own recalcitrant charges, his plants, which stubbornly, in spite of all he's done for them, refuse to grow fast and lush enough to meet what must be an absolutely meglomaniacal need for success.

However great his final success might be, to me this man's a failure as a gardener. He's missed about every point there is to miss, this green thumb general of the Industrial Revolution. If gardening is turned into an all-out war against nature, as this man has done, there can never be any fun or pleasure in it at all, unless you're some kind of sadist, and I admit I had my doubts about this expert until I learned that he has for years been in the employ of one of the major oil companies, a company which manufactures and sells carloads of chemical garden products. It's not madness apparently. It's money.

My personal feeling is that if you're too lazy to pull up an unwanted weed by hand, you'd better leave it where it is. If you can't bring yourself to murder garden pests red-handed or learn to put up with a few of them, you're sadly out of tune with nature, and if you're too lazy to prepare your soil naturally and wait patiently for nature to do its work, you might be better off staying out of the garden entirely.

We'll go into the problems of pests, weeds, and fertilizers at greater length in later chapters, chapters in which I'll be forced to confess, much against my will, that I don't always have the moral character to follow my own lofty edicts to the letter, no one being perfect and certainly never perfectly consistent, certainly not me.

By and large, however, gardening is most rewarding in all respects as a cooperative effort with nature. If nature wants something very badly that you don't want at all, cooperate by giving in. You may be able to stay the judgement of nature temporarily with chemicals, and you may even be able to use them to alter the course of nature slightly, but you'll almost surely pay for it in the long run. You'll pay in terms of ruined, sterile soil and giant insects which are immune to the harshest chemicals, chemicals to which you and yours will have developed no immunity at all.

Sometimes it's only possible to win by submitting, something that Westerners, male Westerners in particular, find hard to understand, since we're taught almost from birth to stand up against even the most outrageous odds and to die before giving in. For some this is bravery, for others it's foolishness. It's always foolishness if nature is the enemy.

Native Plants

In the garden, the easiest way to be wise, the most comfortable way to submit to nature is to grow only those plants which are native to your area, those which come from similar areas, and those which will easily adapt to yours. With this kind of garden, your duties as a gardener will be minimal. You'll only have to involve yourself with locating the plant, putting it into the ground, and shaping it occasionally with pruning tools.

You won't have to worry about soil alteration, watering, fertilizing, mulching, or even acute variations in the weather, since native plants will have survived every extreme your climate has to offer, extremes which you yourself may never have experienced and probably never will.

You also won't have to consider expense much beyond the price of the plant, and you won't have to worry too much about pests, since natives will long ago have established a balance of their own and since the advent of civilization may even have tipped that balance in their favor by driving some of their natural predators into abeyance and by completely eliminating others, the suburban gopher, for example.

There are some gardeners who specialize in nothing but native plants, and in some places, the Bay Area for example, these gardeners have established native plant societies. If you're interested in creating a similar garden of your own, you might give a thought to looking up such a society and asking it for a list of native plants and for information about how and where to acquire them.

If no such society exists in your area, you can try your county agricultural office or the department of agriculture at the nearest university. Some universities and even some cities maintain botanical gardens devoted entirely to native plants. A visit to one of these will give you a first-hand look at prospective candidates for your garden, and a talk with one of the gardeners might even end up by getting you a start on one or two plants.

Armed with this kind of information and cursed with more ground than you feel you can handle comfortably, it might be possible for you to create for yourself a garden which would require almost no attention and survive almost any amount of neglect, a garden that you could thoroughly enjoy and be deservedly proud of. Who knows, you might even become a fanatic of sorts, looking down your nose at impurists like me who still insist on catering to the whims of Chinese, South African, Australian, and European imports.

More probably, you may find a few natives that you didn't know existed before and which will prove to be useful, beautiful, and remarkably undemanding. I myself stumbled more or less by accident on the Pacific wax myrtle (*Myrica californica*), and a fortunate accident it was. This large, elegant shrub has shiny green leaves which look fresh and new all year long. The wax myrtle, cousin of the Eastern bayberry, is also a very versatile plant. It can be shaped into a grand, informal hedge, pruned into a small tree, or left alone to stand in the background as a full-time complement to anything you choose to set in front of it. The fact that it isn't, to my knowledge, used at all by local public landscape architects is a sad comment on the extent of their knowledge and the depth of their vision.

Most of us, myself included, tend to be more adventuresome on the one hand and lazier on the other than the native specialists. It's simply easier to buy what the nurseries stock than it is to hunt around for something that may be difficult if not impossible to find. We've also grown accustomed to many imports and tend to think of them as belonging to us. If their nurture presents difficulties for us, we tend to think that the fault lies with us rather than with the plant, and so it will no doubt continue.

Still, if your gardening time is severely limited or your spirit of adventure small, the time it takes you to locate those plants which fit comfortably within the natural range of your climate, soil, and rainfall is going to be time well spent in the long run.

Naturalized Citizens

If the research route of societies, universities, and public agencies doesn't appeal to you or happens to be impractical, there is another way to locate plants which will do well in your area. Take a survey of your neighborhood, and look for those gardens which have been neglected and for those plants in them that you like and which are doing well in spite of the neglect.

Beg, borrow, or steal a sample of each of the plants you like, and take it to your nurseryman. He'll be happy to tell you what it is and duplicate it for you if he can. While you're there, you might also ask him if any of your candidates have any severe drawbacks.

Some hardy individuals, even when neglected, do too well. Vines like honeysuckle and Virginia creeper can easily run rampant and will, if left unchecked, cover and destroy everything in sight. Some kinds of bamboo, if provided with adequate moisture, will spread like wildfire and choke out less hardy competition. Papyrus (*Cyperus diffusus*) is an attractive plant, but it sows itself extravagantly and can create a weed problem for you the likes of which you've never seen.

The black acacia (*Acacia melanoxylon*) also self-sows, and its powerful, invasive roots can uproot sidewalks and foundations. The plant world has its Mafia, too, and your nurseryman can help to steer you away from introducing any of its members into your garden.

Tricking Mother Nature

I've spoken out rather strongly in this chapter against gardening as a war against nature. There are times, however, when small conflicts arise and when it doesn't hurt to subvert nature just a little. To do this, you have to have a picture, a pretty clear one, of just what nature has in mind.

What nature has in mind, or rather what every plant is harboring, is one driving ambition and one ambition alone: reproduction.

If the foliage of a certain plant is beautiful to you and an end in itself, to the plant it's merely the means to an end, and that end is reproduction. If the flowers are gorgeous in your eyes, the perfume a joy to your nose, the plant couldn't care less. It's the eyes and the noses of the insects who will pollinate it that the plant is trying to attract.

Once pollination is accomplished and seed production underway, the plant will concentrate most of its energies—and if it's an annual, all of its energies—in that direction, and it will do so to the detriment of its beautiful foliage and at the expense of further flower production.

So, unless you're specifically after seeds, *remove all flowers from all plants as soon as the flowers have begun to fade.* And this, simple as it is, may be the single most important statement this book makes.

In the case of annuals, roses, fuchsias, and other plants which flower over an extended period of time, removing the faded flowers will mean more flowers for an even longer time. In the case of plants which, like lilacs, bloom for shorter, more specific periods of time, removing the faded flowers will allow the plants to concentrate their energies on the production of lusher foliage, stronger stems, and hardier roots, which will mean a bigger and better flower display for next year's fling with the bees.

That's one way that Mother Nature's goals can be subverted to bring them more in line with man's, and it's harmless unless you can bring yourself to believe that no plant can ever be truly happy if it doesn't attain mother or fatherhood, and I imagine that there may be one or two souls wandering the globe who feel that way. I picture them somewhere throwing a baby shower for a pregnant banana tree.

Sometimes Mother Nature manages to trick herself, and sometimes she gets tricked inadvertently. An example of each of these situations along with its diagnosis and cure may be of some help to you if you've got other plants with similar problems. Plants may differ a great deal in shape, size, color, outward behavior, and use, but the natural principles which underlie their total performance are remarkably similar and, if you can come up with some of the underlying generalities, the seemingly endless and confusing parade of particularities may come suddenly clear.

The Non-flowering Flowering Dogwood

You have planted a dogwood tree in your garden because you've fallen in love with the dogwood's beautiful spring bloom. The tree is doing beautifully except in one very important respect: It absolutely refuses to bloom. To correct this condition, to bring the tree into bloom, you're going to have to, horror of horrors, score the trunk of the tree. You're going to have to wound the tree but not, of course, enough to kill it.

No, this isn't punishment for the tree's having failed to live up to your expectations. What's happened is that you've planted the tree in such an ideal spot and given it so much of everything it wants that it's convinced it's going to live forever and, consequently, it's forgotten all about reproducing itself. Damaging the bark simply convinces the tree that there really is a tomorrow and sets the tree on its way to preparing for it. By scoring the trunk you get your flowers and at the same time convince the tree of a very important truth.

The Fruitless Tomato

Like millions of others, you've discovered the vast difference between store-bought and vine-ripened tomatoes, so this year you've planted a few tomatoes of your own in some very rich soil of your own concoction. The vines are doing very well, too well in fact. They're lush, deep green, and growing vigorously in all directions. The only problem is that they're not producing any little yellow flowers and of course no tomatoes.

The chances are that the problem lies with you. You're almost certainly giving your tomatoes too much water. Too much water in conjunction with very rich soil tells the vines that it's still spring, the time when tomatoes concentrate almost wholly on vine growth.

If you keep up the water, you may succeed in convincing the tomatoes that it's spring right up until the first frost convinces them otherwise by killing them, and that's a very successful argument. If you ease up on the water, however, you'll let them know that summer has come, and they'll turn their energies, as nature intended, to reproduction, to cranking out those succulent red seed cases that you've been waiting for.

I mention this problem in connection with very rich soil. If your soil is too poor, the tomato will realize from the start, no matter how much water you give it, that it's in trouble, and it will probably begin producing tomatoes before the vines have fully matured. If this happens, the tomatoes will be small and few and far between, so don't plant tomatoes in poor soil even if you're afraid of overwatering them. That's not a proper approach to this particular problem.

When almost any plant, not just the tomato, finds itself growing in a hostile environment, it will focus its energies on speed of reproduction and sacrifice both quantity and quality of reproduction to achieve it. This is only natural. If a plant took its sweet time reproducing itself when conditions were unfavorable, it would, in a purely natural environment, become quickly extinct.

Mother Nature seems to make human beings behave in a remarkably similar way when they're faced with the human equivalent of bad growing conditions. During a war, the birth rate always jumps sky high, and the percentage of male over female births increases dramatically to compensate, it would seem, for those adult males who are out in the field busily killing each other off. For me, that's a very convincing argument for Fate and against Free Will. It's odd, I suppose, to think of Mother Nature as a Moslem—unless, of course, you happen to be one yourself.

Juggling & Pruning

The failure of many would-be gardeners stems, it seems to me, from a two-fold misunderstanding of gardening and their role in the garden. They tend, first, to think of gardening as a series of small chores, which makes gardening unnecessarily complex because it obscures the relationships between the chores, making them seem both endless and arbitrary.

If you view gardening in this way, learn the list of chores, and perform them well, it's possible, I suppose, to garden with some success, be it the success of a well-programmed robot. If you, however, can learn to see gardening as a process, one that closely reflects the processes of nature, the arbitrariness of gardening disappears and the chores become finite if frequent.

An understanding of the larger concepts, an awareness of how nature works, which is something within anyone's grasp who cares to think about it and who'll read this sometimes awkward book with loving care, automatically answers most of the endless numbers of small questions that can be asked about gardening. Such questions simply disappear into the larger picture.

The second mistake that many would-be gardeners make is to see themselves as somehow in charge of taking care of Nature. Nature, in the strictest sense, doesn't need to be taken care of by man. Nature takes care of herself, although gardens do not.

Gardens don't take care of themselves or, put another way, nature doesn't take care of gardens because a garden is a purely human expression, a painting, if you like, done by man with paints, brushes, canvas, and easel supplied by nature. To paint the picture, the artist must understand the medium, the proper use of the tools, and learn to live within the limitations of both, but the final product is all his own. In other words, the only real chores a gardener has are those directed at achieving his ends, not nature's, providing that his ends aren't in conflict with hers, of course.

A garden is, essentially, an enhancement of nature, a complication of it, dictated by the gardener's own needs, tastes, and abilities. He effects this enhancement by acquiring and arranging exotic plants—and an exotic plant is any plant which nature herself couldn't or wouldn't have placed in the garden—by enriching the soil and changing its chemical and physical make-up to accommodate the exotics, by creating shade and admitting sunlight, and by taking advantage of warm and cool spots within the garden to extend the garden's range and give it character.

All gardens are, I suppose, in a sense striving to be paradise, a word that comes from Old Persian and means, interestingly enough, "walled garden," and the gardener, pushing his garden always in that direction, becomes a kind of juggler. He juggles what he wants from a garden against what nature can provide as well as against what nature demands. The juggler's hands are soil, water, temperature, and sun and, unlike any other juggler, the gardener is asked to throw his hands into the act and to juggle them as well. The creation of paradise is a hard act to follow—or would be, if paradise were attainable. The fact that it isn't is why the gardener can, when he gets tired, throw everything on the ground and hide in the house. If he couldn't, he'd go bananas. No earthly garden, thank God, can ever be perfect.

While performing his act, however, the gardener always has one relatively free hand, the hand he uses to do his pruning. Pruning, in the largest sense of the word, involves everything from mowing a lawn up to and including removing a hundred foot high tree. Both of these acts are, in terms of their concepts at least, simple things in themselves, but pruning is still one of the least understood aspects of gardening. Very few people feel comfortable doing it or even thinking about doing it.

People tend to think of pruning in terms of doing something to a plant that the plant absolutely has to have done to it. They view pruning as an operation equivalent to the removal of a rupturing appendix or a malignant brain tumor from a human being. They see it as a life-saving operation, and that's simply the wrong way to view it.

Ninety percent of the time, pruning is nothing more than a haircut. It's something that Dad, the gardener, wants the kid to have, although, the kid, the plant in this case, may not think he needs it at all.

Pruning is the gardener's way of keeping plants to a desirable size, of discouraging the fast and hardy so that the weaker and slower will have a chance, and of changing and improving the shapes of plants. Pruning is the gardener's way of imposing discipline on his garden, and by discipline I mean structure and order, not punishment.

Mother Nature prunes her charges, too, in case you hadn't stopped to think about it, and it may help you to understand pruning better if we take a quick look at some of the ways she does it. Sometimes she does it rather dramatically. A bolt of lightning strikes a tree and knocks the top out of it. Perhaps the bolt of lightning sets fire to the whole forest, and the fire clears away all the undergrowth, leaving only the tallest and toughest trees standing. This, too, is pruning.

The rampage of a flooded stream through a narrow gorge prunes the surrounding vegetation, and so does a rabbit nibbling at some tender shoots. A weighted branch breaking and falling to the ground is another example of natural pruning as is a landslide which pours rocks down a mountain into the vegetation below. The wind prunes continually, and anyone who's seen the cypresses on the Monterrey peninsula would have to agree that it shapes rather well, too.

In the garden, however, nature's way of pruning is impractical. It's usually far too dramatic and, from the gardener's point of view, very likely to be messy. A garden, because of its size, won't tolerate the grand artistry of nature. It needs instead the controlled and delicate artistry of man. And pruning is, lest you're still entertaining any doubts, very often nothing but art, not *an* art, but Art with a capital A.

If you're not just a little bit artistic, if you don't have an eye of sorts for shape and design, there is, I'm sorry to say, no very good way to communicate this facet of pruning to you, just as there is no vocabulary to explain the differences between red and green to someone who is colorblind or for the colorblind to explain what they see to the color-visioned.

The remaining aspects of pruning, the myriad of details, will be covered in the third section of this book, and with that I'll conclude what I have to say about the generalities of gardening, the interrelationships between man and nature, gardener and garden. If you still find that you're as much in the dark as you ever were, the specifics which follow may help to lead you out into the sunlight.

PART TWO

LANDSCAPING *

8 SOME BASIC PLANS AND CONCEPTS

8 Ideas

The garden plans I'm going to discuss in this section are intentionally very simple ones because they are intended primarily for people who want a garden which is both pleasant to look at and, above all, easy to care for. As we go along, I hope it will become clear to you the ways in which these plans might be varied, made more complex and, with additional complexity, more interesting. What follows really aren't plans so much as they are ideas.

I've chosen the back yard as a subject because its almost inevitable rectangularity makes it more difficult to landscape than the front and because the landscape of the front is often and to a large extent predetermined by the architecture of the house, the layout of driveways and sidewalks, and the general tenor of the landscaping of the street or neighborhood.

Ideas for landscaping a front yard are also readily available to anyone who's interested if he or she is willing to take the time to stroll down a well-landscaped

Fig.1 The Croquet Court

street and make notes of the things that please the eye. Back yards are less accessible.

The Croquet Court

This part of the book, unlike the rest, has a villain. I'll call this villain the Croquet Court. Figure One shows a generalized plan of such a back yard, and one glance at the plan should call to mind the scores of back yards just like it that you've surely seen.

The horizons of this yard are dominated by fences, roofs, television aerials and, if you're lucky, the tops of other people's trees. It's area is dominated almost wholly by lawn or a reasonable facsimile thereof, and the lawn is surrounded by a foot or two of flower beds which separate the lawn from the fences.

Simple as the Croquet Court is, it's not particularly easy to take care of. The large lawn, which dominates it, has to be mowed and watered frequently—and fertilized if it's to be kept to anything approaching uniform greenness, and it's the uniform greenness of the lawn and that alone which makes this yard bearable to look at. The blotchier the lawn, the more the yard begins to look like a fenced-in vacant lot.

Besides the hours spent in keeping the lawn in shape, some time is also going to have to be given over to keeping it out of the flower beds, a chore that often seems to take up so much gardening time that not much ever gets planted in the beds, which are usually sparsely occupied by a few hardy perennials and some scattered shrubs.

These plants, spread out randomly as they are along the fences and walls, contribute nothing towards suggesting a unified whole, a garden in other words. Standing independently as they do, these plants are on display as individuals and consequently are forced to justify their existence in terms of their own health and beauty, something that few plants, however hardy, can do all year long. If they're not healthy or if they're simply out of season, these randomly scattered plants will only suggest that the fenced-in vacant lot has begun to sprout weeds.

The Croquet Court is a liability as a garden. It's uninteresting and often ugly to look at. It demands a lot of work and insures that very little profit or reward can be derived from the work put into it. It's only an asset if you happen to play a lot of croquet.

In Figure Two, the same area has been totally relandscaped. The boring walkway has been removed and replaced with a patio living area (1). The lawn has been done away with entirely, and part of the lawn area (2) has been planted with a variety of low-growing juniper, from which there are many to choose. Behind the juniper in Area Five, I've planted three to five *Acacia verticillata*, a fast-growing evergreen tree which is dark green in color and which looks very much like a conifer except in the spring when it's covered with masses of bright yellow flowers.

Area Four is occupied by a single liquidamber, a deciduous tree, the leaves of which resemble those of an oak and which turn brilliant fall colors in even the mildest climates. Area Three is reserved for bedding plants, summer annuals such as marigolds.

Figure Two

After it was installed, the maintenance of this garden would be minimal. The acacias might have to be shaped occasionally to keep their lower branches close to the ground so that weeds wouldn't pop up under them. After the junipers established themselves, you'd have to trim them once a year to keep them from growing into the patio and bedding plant area. The leaves of the liquidamber would have to be picked up in the fall and the marigolds you planted in the spring removed.

This garden would, except for the marigolds, require almost no artificial water, and the marigolds could conveniently be watered while you were hosing off the patio to help cool down the house. It would be my estimate that such a garden as this one could be maintained with less than four hours of work a month, less time than you would have spent mowing the lawn which it replaced.

Simple and easy to take care of as this garden is, it still offers a lot of seasonal variety. In the spring, you would have a blaze of golden yellow from the acacias and the fun of watching the liquidamber leaf out; in the summer, the bright oranges of the marigolds, and in the fall, the brilliant reds of the liquidamber. Even during the winter this garden, anchored as it is in the great green expanses of juniper and acacia, would still be pleasing to the eye.

Using the outlines of Figure Two, an entirely different garden could be planted. Ivy might be substituted for the juniper and the acacias replaced with Monterrey pine. Instead of a liquidamber, you might have a Japanese flowering cherry, and chrysanthemums, for fall color, instead of marigolds in the bedding area. For additional variety, and for the more ambitious gardener, a few choice potted plants in attractive containers might be added to the patio.

This garden, because of the ivy, Monterrey pine, and potted plants, would require more artificial water, especially in its early stages, than the juniper garden, and the ivy would need more frequent trimming than the juniper simply because it grows faster. Still, this garden would be an extremely easy one to maintain.

Any number of other trees and ground covers could be substituted in a plan like Figure Two for the juniper, ivy, pine, and acacia that we've been talking about, and the number of accent plants, the liquidamber, flowering cherry, marigolds, and chrysanthemums, is almost endless.

The basic plan of Figure Two can also be altered in any number of ways. To mention but one, an Area Six might be added between Areas Five and Two and planted with a few shrubs of medium height, such as *Pittosporum tobira*, to catch the eye at medium level and add further interest to the garden.

The number of variations are almost infinite. If you can come up with a plan on paper which you like, take it to a nurseryman and discuss it with him. Tell him that here you'd like something fairly tall and evergreen, there you'd like something that bloomed beautifully in the spring, here something of medium height possibly gray-green in color, there something with dramatic leaves for accent. Then have the nurseryman show you what he has and, if you think you might like it, ask him about its requirements and how you can expect it to behave if you plant it. Take notes. That's one of the reasons they made us all go to school.

All this will take some work, hard work initially, some initiative, and a little thought, but if it's done right, it will give you a garden that you can enjoy all year round without ever being a slave to it or, at least, more of a slave than you're willing to be.

Utility Areas

It's possible that you won't want to give all of your garden over to landscape greenery, that you may want to save part of it for a clothes line area, a vegetable garden, a rose garden for flowers for the house, a place to keep your trash cans, an herb garden and so forth.

If that's the case, the best place for such a utility area would probably be along the back fence and away from the house. To achieve it, you would simply move all the plants in the Figure Two plan forward so that the tall background trees separate the garden from the utility area.

If your back fence borders the northern line of your lot, the background trees will keep the sun out of the utility area for most of the year and make it less than ideal for growing anything but shade loving plants. So before starting on your garden, make sure that you locate your utility areas according to their sun requirements and plan your landscaping with the sun in mind.

Perhaps this is so obvious that it's not worth mentioning, but if you're doing your planning in the summer, when the sun is directly overhead, it's all too easy to forget that in a few months certain areas of the garden will be getting no sun at all.

Fences

For me, fences are necessary evils rather than things of beauty. I dislike looking at them, but I'm willing to grant that they're helpful in keeping dogs, plants, children, and property lines from circulating too freely around the centers of city blocks.

To more liberated spirits, this attitude of mine may sound uptight and intolerant, but I find that I'm better disposed to the people behind us if I don't find their three year old making mud pies in my newly planted vegetable garden and ever so much more charitable to the next door neighbor's dog if she hasn't made her way into our garden and eaten our cat.

City life is much more tolerable if certain aspects of it are clearly defined and the definitions formally observed, but this doesn't make me like the looks of those defining fences any better, and I've done my best to landscape my fences out of visual existence. I think I've succeeded, too.

From the house and from many places in the garden, the center of our city block resembles a large park which seems to be shared by a few sparsely scattered houses. Nothing could be further from the truth. In most instances, it's impossible to tell which trees and shrubs belong to me and which are my neighbors', an effect that I've deliberately worked to achieve and to enhance.

And I must confess, too, that I haven't achieved all of it through strictly horticultural means. I've stooped to using theatrical effects as well. I've painted all my fences a brown that's so dark it appears to be black. The idea of a black fence may appall some people, and I will admit that the idea, so expressed, doesn't appeal very much to me.

With plants thickly distributed in front of them, however, the black fences don't appear to be black. They simply don't appear to be there at all, so much so that no one among my all too frank acquaintances has ever made a comment on them. If asked about my fences, they'd probably say that they didn't know what color they were and weren't even sure that I had any.

(To exonerate myself further from possible accusations of bad or extreme taste, I'll have to add that the trim on our house is painted the same color as the fences and that the trim sets off the naturally darkened shingles of the walls tastefully and conservatively enough to please even the most fastidious of exterior decorators.)

For more timid souls who may still be unable to accept the idea of black fences, a brown fence or a fence left unpainted and allowed to weather naturally might be the answer. Either would blend into the flora better than a white one, which, no matter how well hidden by plants, always manages to make its presence and what it's defining felt somewhere.

Whatever you decide about fences, an informal hedge grown in front of one will give the impression of openness and depth behind it, a feeling in other words of untrammeled expanse. If part of your garden is bordered by the walls of the house or garage, you might consider growing a vine against the wall.

Boston ivy, a very attractive climber that will grow almost anywhere, clings unaided to almost any surface. It's also a deciduous vine, affording the wall protection against the heat of the sun in summer and leaving it exposed to the warming rays of the winter sun. Boston ivy offers the grower a problem only if and when it comes time to paint the surface it's growing on.

The harsh lines of fences can also be softened by training vines along the tops of them and by turning them into trellises for such things as climbing roses. Even the Croquet Court, if its fences were hidden behind vines and hedges, would lose much of its vacant lot look and become a warmer, more friendly place to be in.

Fences, even if they're your own, either seem to be penning you in or keeping you out. They're prisons, things on the other sides of which the grass grows proverbially greener. Erect them, enjoy the privacy they afford, but hide them.

Perspective

The Croquet Court, even with its fences hidden by vines and hedges, still looks like the small garden it is because the whole of it is visible all at once from almost any point in it. A garden of the same size but landscaped in the manner of Figure Two will look larger because it's built on the principle of receding heights. The further the eye travels back in this garden, the higher it's raised, and the further it comes forward, the more it's lowered. The Figure Two garden exercises the eye, and if the eye is exercised, the brain thinks "space."

The Figure Two garden takes advantage of what I'll call *horizontal* perspective. If a garden is made to take advantage of *vertical* perspective as well, it will not only ask the eye to look back and up but back and *in* at the same time and thus exercise the eye even more and

Figure Three

make the garden seem larger still.

In Figure Three, again in a highly simplified drawing, I've tried to show how you might build vertical perspectives into a garden. The taller trees in the center of the background have been removed and replaced with an arrangement of some kind, three dwarf Alberta spruce, for example, or maybe a bird bath or even an arbor. It really doesn't matter what so long as the arrangement is eye-catching, appealing, and perhaps suggestive of even more interesting things beyond it, things of course that aren't really there.

If the landscaping of Area A is miniaturized, landscaped with small plants that suggest larger ones, it will seem to the eye that the distance between the patio and Area A is much greater than it actually is, adding even more to the illusion of size in a small garden.

Adding Area A at the back of the garden gives the garden depth and a focal point. The interest of the garden can be further enhanced by planting Area B with a large shrub, small tree, or an arrangement of some kind, the width and heighth of which is somewhere between that of Area A and the larger trees, Area Five, which border it.

Something planted in Area B will make the eye look back and *around* as well as back and up and back and in. Because of the Area B planting, anyone wishing to see the whole garden will have to move around on the patio to see all of it, and if you've convinced someone that he has to move about to see the whole of something, you've convinced him that the something he wants to see is sizable.

If the plant or plants in Area B are somewhat branching and loosely structured rather than thick and dense, you will have added yet another visual dimension to your garden, back and *through*, and in terms of landscaping for visual effect, you will have taken advantage of much of what art has to offer the gardener.

The plans I've given in this section aren't, of course, meant to be followed to the letter or even copied at all. In every instance, they are, as I've said before, gross oversimplifications, and they're intended only to acquaint you with some of the principles of landscaping, principles which can be used to turn a back yard into a garden and suggest that beyond the garden lies a park. A real garden will make use of these principles over and over again to make a much more complex whole than any of the paper gardens we've been talking about.

The Lawn Area

A lawn or paved area in a garden can either add or detract from the illusion of space in a small garden. A plain, recognizably geometrical area such as a square, rectangle, or circle, no matter how large, will appear smaller than it is because it's easily comprehended by the eye, categorized by the brain, and forgotten about by the viewer.

The brain, however, has no means by which to remember a shape like that of the lawn pictured in Figure Four. Such an area is perceived as a shape but not as a particular shape, and for that reason, it keeps, I think, both the eye and the brain attentive longer and makes the garden more interesting, again suggesting that the garden is larger than it really is.

Figure Four

The eyes of anyone standing on the lawn in Figure Four will be drawn naturally along with the lawn into those parts of the garden into which the lawn reaches furthest, those areas marked A in the diagram. If these A areas are planted with specimens of particular beauty or interest or with interesting and eye-catching arrangements, the viewer will feel that he's been rewarded for the tricks the lawn's played with his eyes, and the irregularity of the shape of the lawn will have been explained and justified. It will be seen to have a purpose other than mere artiness for artiness's sake.

Before you proceed to install an irregularly shaped lawn, I should point out that by doing so you're going to increase the length of the lawn's edging considerably. The coastline of little Norway, because of its phenomenal irregularities, is almost as long as that of continent-sized Australia. If, for whatever reason, you have a hard time keeping your lawn out of your flower beds, a perfectly square lawn, which gives maximum area for minimum edging, might be a better lawn for you in the long run, and artistry be damned.

The Last Trick

I have in this section of the book found myself talking about perspectives, eyes, brains, and minds much more than I'd planned to, and I have perhaps strayed into art and the epistemological aspects of art further than anyone should in a book that purports to be about gardening. To compensate for this, I'll say now that the last landscaping trick I have up my sleeve is a purely practical one. It's a maintenance trick, and it's one I use in order to give my garden the look of being better cared for than it sometimes is.

To explain this trick, I've concocted Figure Five, a symbolic representation of the way in which my garden is laid out. If I have only a few minutes to make my garden look loved, I dash out of the house and hose off the patio. Given a little more time, I run the mower quickly over the lawn. Given another half an hour, I take a pair of lawn clippers and trim the edges of the lawn.

With a few hours to devote to the garden, I advance into Area One and tend to the low-growing plants which comprise it. I pick the dead flowers off the annuals, do a little pruning and shaping here and there, pick up the fallen leaves, and cultivate the soil where it's necessary or desirable to do so.

With half a day to spend, I proceed into Area Two, which contains larger and more permanent plants, and do those things to them and their area that need to be done. Area Three is comprised of large shrubs and trees which don't require serious attention very often. They'll survive, thrive and present a satisfactory appearance even if months pass when I don't have the time to reach their area.

It takes a little thought to arrange your garden in this way but not a lot. Any plant which needs a great deal of attention must be placed in Area One. If it's too large to have so far forward in the garden, it should be avoided and an acceptable substitute found for it. On the other hand, nothing small and nothing which requires constant or even frequent attention should be planted in Area Three.

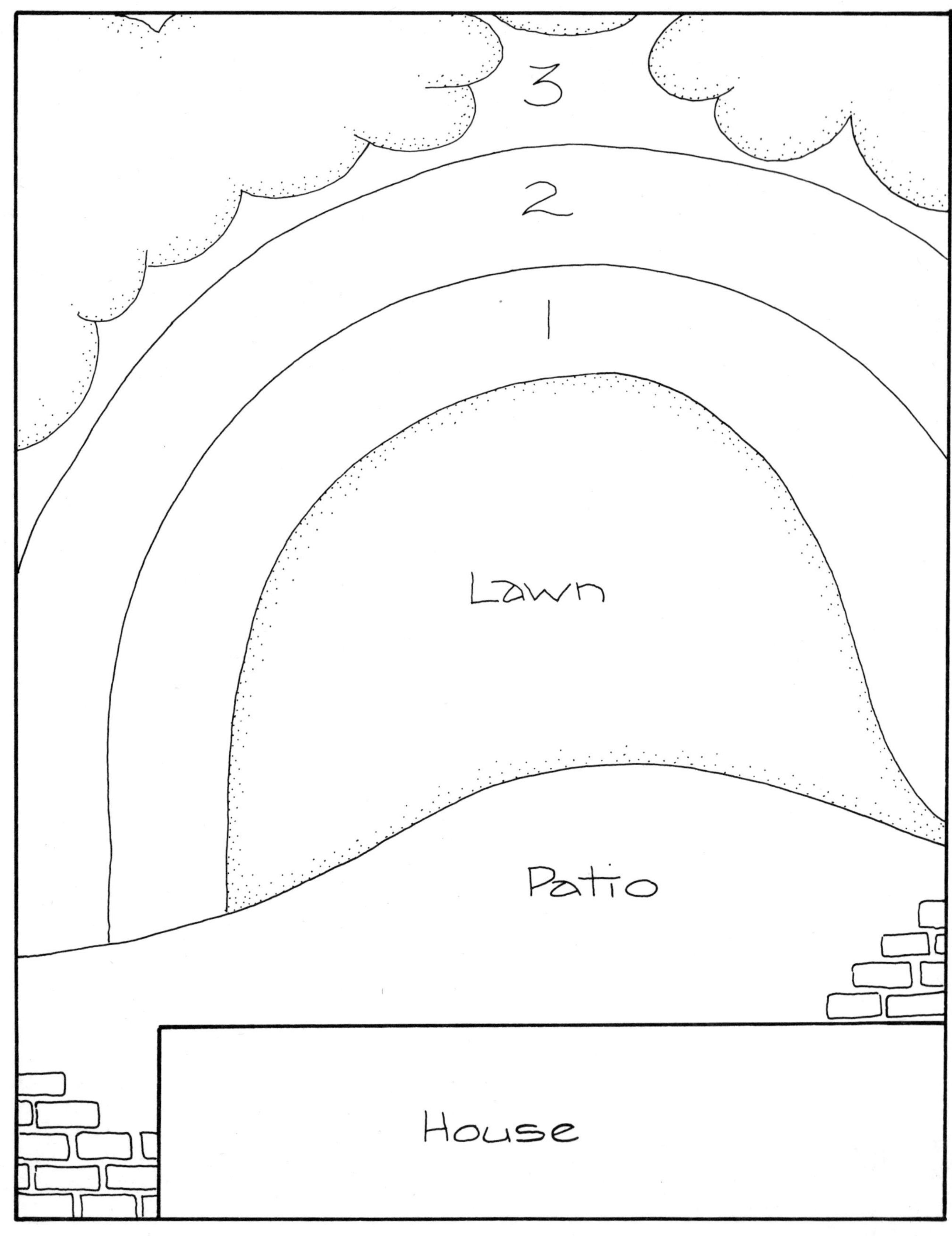

Figure Five

A garden planned and planted in this way is much more apt to get the attention it needs where and when it needs it than one planted more randomly. This kind of garden is also much less apt to get out of hand and give the gardener the feeling that his garden is getting away from him, a feeling that causes a lot of tenuous and tentative gardeners to throw up their hands and say to hell with it, it's too much for me.

My own garden isn't, of course, planned around five concentric circles with their epicenters located in the patio as Figure Five suggests. There are many circles radiating from many different points in the garden. They overlap throughout the garden, and none of them is, I hope, visible to any eye but my own.

The common feature of each set of circles is that it radiates from some point in the garden easily accessible to foot traffic, from those points from which people view the garden and from which I sally forth to tend it. Up to now, these circles have been my secret. Now, I imagine, I'll be asked to delineate them for those of my friends who read this.

If it comes to that, to delineating the circles, I'll probably find myself becoming highly inventive and remarkably fast-talking. Either that or I'll have to explain that my circle theory is best perceived as a theory and that, if it can be perceived as a fact by anyone but the gardener himself, the garden is perhaps organized along overly formal lines.

Unfortunately, this book doesn't allow for a chapter on the Gardener as Liar, and lying is almost as much a part of gardening as it is of fishing or of being President of the United States.

PART THREE

SPECIFICS

*

9 THE LAWN

9 Lawns

Chances are that more of your five-thousand square foot lot will be occupied by lawn than by any other single thing, and that includes your house.

For some reason, one that I don't really understand, most non-gardeners and anti-gardeners feel more comfortable with a lawn than they do with any other kind of planting. In a way, this is madness because a lawn—and by a lawn I don't mean a foot high patch of weeds—demands almost as much time and attention from the gardener as an equivalent spread of hothouses and orchids.

By the time we finish talking about lawns, I think it will be clear to you why this is true, and we'll turn our attention to some possible alternatives, if not for the whole lawn, at least for part of it, alternatives which can make your gardening experience less time-consuming and more enjoyable.

Planting a Lawn

Planting a new lawn is an incredibly involved and often expensive project, more involved and expensive perhaps than putting in a rose garden of equivalent dimensions. I'm not going to go into great detail here about how to install one because the information is readily available elsewhere, in Sunset's *Western Garden Book*, for example, and because I have little or nothing to add to this general fund of knowledge on the subject.

This, very roughly, is what's involved:

1. A soil test to determine the alkalinity or acidity of the area to be planted. A neutral soil is best, an almost neutral soil mandatory. Add enough gypsum to alkaline soil or lime to acid soil to bring it within a *pH* range of 5.5 to 8.3 . (See page 48.)
2. Cultivation to a depth of nine inches of at least three or four inches of organic matter, leaf mold, peat moss, compost, or well-aged steer manure. Finely ground bark or sawdust may also be used and at considerably less expense, but both are iron and nitrogen poor, deficiencies which must be compensated for chemically. If they're not, the bark and sawdust will in the process of decomposing draw valuable nitrogen away from the grass seedlings.
3. Leveling, using a rake, drag, and lawn roller. This is a boring chore but nothing compared to what's involved in trying to level a lawn that's already been planted.
4. Watering in order to locate and correct low spots and force weeds, which are much easier to remove before the lawn has been planted. A plastic tarp placed over the moistened area will aid in forcing weeds and, if the sun's hot enough, will cook them as soon as they sprout.
5. Seeding uniformly either by hand or, preferably, with a lawn seeder. If you choose to do this on a windy day, you may end up with much of your lawn in your flower beds.
6. Covering the seed with a thin mulch (1/4 to 3/8 inches) of peat moss or peat and sand. The addition of sand will help to keep the peat from blowing or washing away. This mulch helps to retard moisture loss and prevents scorching of the sprouts by the sun.
7. A thorough and very gentle watering, preferably with a fine mist or spray. Water applied too heavily or too quickly will wash the seed around and create bare spots in the lawn.
8. Continued, frequent applications of water until the seed has sprouted and established itself. If the lawn area is allowed to dry out, seeds which have just begun to sprout will quickly die, and you'll have to start all over again from Step 5. Because of this danger, it's best to plant your lawn in cool weather and when it can benefit from light rains.
9. A very gentle mowing after the new grass has reached a height of two to four inches. Anything less than gentleness until the seed bed is firmly packed and rooted will endanger the life of the seedlings.
10. Reseeding the inevitable bare and brown spots.

If you've skimped on any of these steps, as I've sketched them out, you'll pay for it later with a stubborn, unresponsive, blotchy, and none too green lawn. If you've carefully followed all the steps and put in the labor of Sisyphus and the money of Croesus, you might well feel that you're entitled to sit back and take the rest of your life off.

I'm sure that you're entitled to nothing less, but as things really stand, you've only just begun. You're now at the stage where you've brought the baby home from the hospital and are faced with all the problems of raising it. And with a baby, you can at least visualize the day when it will become self-sufficient. Not so with a lawn. It'll need your constant attention as long as the two of you live together.

Mowing

If I might carry the baby analogy a little further, let me say that mowing the lawn is a lot like changing diapers. Nobody likes to do it, but it's something that absolutely has to be done, and it has to be done on a regular basis or you run the risk of losing your charge.

With lawns, if not babies, this is particularly true in the summer when you shouldn't try to get by with mowing your lawn less than once a week. If you wait much longer between bouts with the lawnmower, you won't be mowing at all, you'll be harvesting, cutting off the lush top growth, a crop for which you have no use at all, and exposing the weaker undergrowth and surface root system, your future lawn in other words, to the full wrath of a sun it's not used to facing. In a few hours, a hot sun can turn a lawn so exposed into a stubble field, and you'll find yourself back at Step 1.

Ideally, and I say *ideally*, a lawn should be mowed twice a week at the peak of its growing season. Peak growing season will vary according to what kind of grass or grasses you have, but it's easily identified as that time of year when the lawn grows fastest. Besides discouraging sun burn, frequent mowings encourage root and side growth, both of which provide for deeper, richer, fuller, and greener coverage and those, presumably, are your goals.

Frequent mowing will also permit you to leave the clippings on the lawn where they belong without making your lawn an unsightly mess or creating an unwanted mulch on the top of the lawn which can kill the living grass underneath.

If you've always mowed with a grass catcher and never thought anything about it, my comment that the grass clippings belong on the lawn and not in the trash barrel may have come as a surprise to you. If you think about it, however, it makes perfectly good sense.

Removing the clippings week after week, year after year will gradually deplete the richness of the soil under the lawn and, along with it, the capacity of that soil to support the lawn. You can't, as farmers long ago learned, expect to harvest the same crop from the same field forever without eventually ruining the productive capacity of the field.

If you mow your lawn frequently, the clippings will be small enough to dry quickly and soon filter down out of sight through the lawn to the soil where they'll decompose and provide food for the very plants that produced them. You will have established a natural cycle for your lawn, a cycle that will lengthen its life span and strengthen its vigor and its beauty.

Another way to reduce the size of grass clippings and speed them on their way back to the soil is to cut your lawn in more than one direction during the same mowing. I've been called a fanatic for doing this, but I can afford to do it, because I've kept the size of my lawn to a minimum, and in some ways I can't afford not to do it, because my lawn mowed in four directions is a joy to behold. Thus mowed, it resembles a freshly vacuumed and very expensive green carpet, but of course it isn't. It's a highly organic, green and growing thing.

Mowing in more than one direction has some other advantages as well. It helps to prevent lawn build-up, and it aids in keeping the soil underneath the lawn level. Mowing always in the same direction can actually contribute to both of these lawn problems.

Winter can bring partial or, in snow areas, total respite from the lawn. In mild winter areas, the frequency of mowing will be dictated by just how fast the lawn, or parts of the lawn, happens to be growing at the time. Keep an eye on it and don't let it get out of hand even if it isn't taking full summer advantage of your patience and time.

Edging

As Tweedle-dee has Tweedle-dum, so mowing has edging, the curse of keeping or trying to keep the lawn off the walks and out of the flower beds. There's not much to say about keeping the lawn off the walks, except good luck.

As a kid in Southern California, I remember being pitifully grateful when my father finally broke down and bought a power edger. We lived on a corner with its attendant miles of sidewalks and curbings, all of which abutted against lawns comprised almost wholly of Bermuda and St. Augustine grass. Between them, these two grasses quickly built up a two or three inch cushion, and having to push a hand-edger through that overhanging cushion made me a prolific and imaginative swearer at a very tender age.

In the cool summers of the Bay Area, however, a power edger would be about as practical an addition to my tool collection as a helicopter. I have very little edging to do now at all, and what I have to do can easily be done on my knees with a pair of lawn shears. Still, wherever you live, if you're putting in a new lawn, you might consider putting it in slightly below the level of the walks. This will insure, at least for awhile, that all the edging you have to do will be done strictly against horizontal growth and not against both horizontal and vertical growth, as I edged in my youth, and in this regard, my happily lost youth.

Keeping the lawn out of the flower beds is a slightly different matter, mainly because neither a hand nor a power edger can be used to do it—or, at any rate, used with much practical success. I've found that, by keeping the ditch that separates the lawn from the beds as shallow as possible, I can run one wheel of the mower onto the bare dirt and clip off all unwanted vertical growth in that way.

Horizontal growth—the stuff that's creeping laterally into the flowers—can easily and quickly be snipped off with a good pair of grass shears, and the shallower the ditch, the less horizontal growth the lawn will produce.

If you can bring yourself to get down on your hands and knees and perform this little chore once a week during peak growing season and once a month when growth is slowest, it'll hardly amount to any work at all, but if you let it go for too long, it can become a horrendous chore involving spade work, the creation and destruction of dirt clods, the wholesale pulling of weeds and roots, and finally the pain of redefining the margins between the flower beds and the lawn.

It's far better, as my wife tells me from time to time, to put out that small fire today than it is to wait until tomorrow when you might feel more like doing it, and that rule often applies to gardening chores as well.

My wife imparts this sage bit of advice to me because in her college days she lived in an apartment building which caught fire. One night the boys next door threw a drunken party, and one of them, a visiting soldier, set fire to the couch. Since the fire was a small one, they decided to wait until the next morning to put it out, and they all fell asleep.

The visiting soldier woke up when his pants caught fire, and he left the burning building without bothering to tell anyone else what was going on. Twenty-five blocks away, he decided to call the fire department and, even though someone else had already beaten him to it, he was later decorated by the Army for outstanding service to civilians.

I'm not sure that this story has any business in this book except that it might very well have had something to do with Forest Lawn and those underneath it who help to keep it green, one of whom, thanks to the U.S. Army, might have been my wife. Had the Army known the true story, they could have armed this genius of theirs with a six-pack and sent him off to party with the enemy. That's the way to win the war, men.

Watering

I've discussed lawn watering in a previous chapter where I suggested keeping it constantly moist, not soggy, rather than letting it dry out and then watering it deeply. (See page 53.)

Unless you've got the patience of Job and plenty of free time, watering the lawn by hand is an impractical and very often inadequate procedure. The waterer tires too quickly and the lawn soon dries out and turns brown. Some sort of lawn sprinkler is almost mandatory for gardens of the size we're talking about.

What kind of lawn sprinkler to get is another matter, and I'm sorry to say that I've never run across one that I liked well enough to recommend. Ideally, the perfect sprinkler should water all the ground it covers equally. You can test the performance of a sprinkler in this regard by setting empty coffee cans at varying lengths away from it. If the cans fill at approximately the same rate, the sprinkler is performing well.

While you're checking the sprinkling rate, check the connection between the hose and sprinkler, too. If water is pouring out from beneath them, your coverage is going to be poor no matter how evenly the sprinkler itself distributes the water.

Another attribute of a good sprinkler is a clear line of demarcation between what it's watering and what it isn't, since your lawn is almost surely going to need more frequent watering than certain of the flower beds which border it. If you've got a stand of juniper, an apricot or an oak tree, or any other planting near your lawn which demands dryish summer soil, a fine line of demarcation is mandatory. Giving any of these plants the same amount of water necessary to keep a lawn green will, simply, kill them.

If there's one rule that applies when you're buying a lawn sprinkler, it's that you pretty much get what you pay for. A cheap sprinkler almost assuredly will water unevenly and fall apart quickly. I've also found the same to be true of garden hoses. Plastic hoses, although considerably cheaper than their rubber counterparts, don't last, and over a period of two or more years, the more expensive rubber hose becomes much the more economical investment.

While we're discussing garden hoses, I might mention that I've come to prefer hoses with a narrow diameter (up to 1/2 inch) to those with larger ones (5/8 inch and above). Although the wider hoses deliver considerably more water in a shorter period of time, the narrow hoses are much easier to handle and store, less prone to kinking up and the inevitable breaks which follow the kinks, and less apt to do permanent damage to the plants that I, at any rate, invariably find myself dragging the hose over. The longer the hose, too, the more comfortable you'll be with a narrower one. If, however, you only need twenty-five feet to do the job, the diameter is of little consequence.

No doubt the best solution to lawn watering and all garden watering problems is an underground sprinkling system, one carefully planned and engineered to deliver just the appropriate amount of water to each and all parts of the garden. For a long time, this kind of system was pretty much limited to the fairly well-to-do and was considered enough of a real asset to be worth mentioning in the ads which offered such houses for sale.

Now, with the advent of plastic pipe and plastic fittings, sprinkling systems have come within the reach of the less well-off do-it-yourselfer. I don't have such a system myself, but I occasionally dream in that direction, my dreams turning to nightmares when I envision digging deep ditches through the garden in order to lay the pipe. Still, if you're starting a garden from scratch, it might be well worth your while to look into a sprinkling system of some kind and maybe even an automatic timing device to go with it. What a pleasure it would be to be able to leave a garden that would water itself while you were away.

Fertilizing

Fertilizing the lawn is something many people don't do, and that's unfortunate because water alone won't, as some people seem to think, keep a lawn, especially an older one, looking healthy, vigorous, and green.

If you do decide to fertilize, you're faced with a choice between organic and non-organic (chemical) fertilizers. Many people reject chemical fertilizers out of hand for purely ecological reasons, none of which I can argue against successfully. Chemicals speed growth, but they do so at the expense of the organic wealth of the soil, to which they add nothing. Chemicals used improperly can also do more immediate damage to a lawn than they do immediate good, since too heavy an application will burn a lawn and even, if the dose is strong enough, kill it right down to the roots.

Far and away the best, safest, and most ecologically sound method of fertilizing a lawn is to fertilize organically with steer manure, the kind you buy in bags from your local garden supply outlet. Other natural fertilizers, those you may be able to pick up for little or nothing at a dairy, stables, or chicken ranch are possibilities, too, but they present certain dangers and disadvantages.

Commercially prepared steer manure, if the supplier is reputable, will be well-aged, weed-free, somewhat sightly, and, to me at least, pleasant smelling. Unprepared natural manures may be raw enough to burn your lawn, a particular danger with chicken manure. Before you use raw manures, you'll have to age them well yourself, and that can present problems for everyone, especially in a crowded city environment. Unprocessed manures may also contain unsprouted seeds, which will create a weed problem, and they're often unpleasant to handle and apply, especially for the squeamish.

In spite of the relative safety of steer manure, you still have to be careful how and when you apply it. The best time to do this is in the early spring, when the lawn is just beginning to put out its new growth and when you can still count on a fair amount of cool weather and rain. The rain helps to beat the manure into the ground, and the cool weather will insure that the sun doesn't heat up the manure enough to burn the lawn.

I put down a forty pound bag of steer manure for about every one-hundred square feet of lawn, and I do it by hand, although spreaders are made for just this purpose. Whatever method you use, it's a good idea to use a bamboo rake on the lawn afterwards to make sure that the coverage is as even as possible. I'm satisfied that the job has been done correctly when the manure shows everywhere but buries nothing.

If steer manure isn't readily available to you, you might consider using completely aged and finely screened compost applied in exactly the same manner. Compost and steer manure have very nearly identical nutritive and organic value, and with compost you run no risk of burning your lawn.

Weeds

In time, most lawns, even well cared for ones, seem to become little more than an acceptable collection of trained weeds which more or less complement each other. Once you've come to accept this fact, you can start to view your lawn's weed problems as something you can easily handle and, unless you've got more acres than scruples, handle by hand.

I loathe chemical weed-killers, and I hated them long before the ecology movement became fashionable. With weed-killers, it's simply too easy to do too much damage too fast, damage that it may take years to correct if it can be corrected at all.

Selective weed-killers, however discriminating their name may make them sound, are pretty much of a myth, too. They select only between lawn plants with narrow blades and lawn plants with broader leaves. The weed-killer that wipes out the dandelion will take the clover and the dichondra along with it—and, if misapplied, may take along the whole lawn and large parts of the surrounding landscape.

It's my feeling, a somewhat snobbish one I grant, that if you're too lazy or too busy to bend over and dig up a dandelion by hand, you should spend a couple of hours before the fire some winter night and, through contemplation of the dandelion's many beauties, learn to love and live with it.

If you can't bring yourself to do that and find that you're still determined to remove the offending dandelion, by hand of course, make sure that you get all of it, every last and little bit of root. The dandelion has the capacity to regenerate itself from even the smallest piece of root, so if you don't get all of it, you really don't get it at all. It's rather like having your finger cut off, sprouting a new finger, and having the old finger sprout a new you.

If you're postponing the actual disinterment of the dandelion, keep the flowers picked off so there won't be a lot more little dandelions popping up all over the place in the meantime.

Lawn weeding can actually be kind of fun if you wait until a nice warm day, put on a bathing suit, stretch yourself out comfortably on the grass and pull away at your leisure, if you'll pardon the expression. I got rid of twenty-two million crab grass plants in just this fashion.

Pleasant Weeds

There are two plants, very different from each other, which don't normally belong in a lawn but which can give it additional character and beauty as well as hiding some of its flaws.

One of these is the original English daisy (*Bellis perennis*), which produces small white daisy-type flowers, as you might guess, all through the lawn, giving it somewhat the feeling of a floral carpet. The flowers are attractive and visible enough to divert attention from less attractive intruders and from ugly brown and bare spots.

The other pleasant weed is baby's tears (*Soleirolia soleirolii*), a low-growing plant with miniscule round leaves which are suggestive of moss. In moist, shady places where most lawn grasses falter, baby's tears will thrive, producing a dense, richly green and virtually flawless carpet. Baby's tears are, unfortunately, susceptible to heavy frost, which turns them into black mush, but they recover quickly when the weather warms up.

Bermuda Grass & Clover

Bermuda grass is like the proverbial bad back, if you've got it you're stuck with it and, like a bad back, you can spend a fortune trying to get rid of it only to have it show up time and again. Learning to live with Bermuda grass isn't quite as painful as accepting a bad back, however, because it mostly involves learning to tolerate a brown lawn in winter. There are harder things to overcome.

If the brown winter lawn really does get to you, there is at least a partial solution for it. Seed it with clover. I've seen clover thriving above the brown in the dead of a California winter in all its rich green splendor, but then there are those, I understand, who can't stand clover, a prejudice that I myself can't quite fathom.

If you happen to be one of the clover-haters and want to get rid of what you've got, the best way to go about it is to set your mower very low to the ground. Close mowing removes most of the clover leaves and exposes the sensitive root area to the killing rays of the sun. To encourage clover, you do just the opposite.

Selecting the Right Grass

When it comes time for you to choose a grass, don't just run to the nursery and grab the first box you come across off the shelf. There are a number of different kinds of grasses and any number of different mixtures. Some of them will be more suitable to your needs than others.

If you can tell the nurseryman what kind of soil you have, what condition it's in, how much sun the lawn will get and when, how much water you'll probably be giving it, and how much foot traffic you expect it to receive, he can direct you to the perfect mixture for you or help you to create one for yourself out of what he has in stock.

If you're creating a new lawn of any size, it will really pay you to spend some time determining what your lawn needs are and locating a competent nurseryman who can respond to them. If for some reason you're not satisfied with the competence of your nurseryman, try another, and keep on trying until you get two identical answers from two different people.

Dichondra

Hopefully, the great dichondra myth is dead, but in case it isn't, I'll attempt to kill it over again here. The myth, if you don't remember it, went something like this: Dichondra will solve all your lawn problems. It never needs mowing, almost. It chokes out any weed it comes across. And it's eternally a deep, dark, and luxuriant green.

A lot of very conscientious people bought that myth, set to work tearing out their old lawns completely, and started all over again from scratch with dichondra. In the early days of the myth, you planted dichondra from plugs carved out of nursery flats at about five dollars a throw. Later on the seed became available and you could sow it, either by itself or mixed with clover.

Planted from flats, your lawn looked like it had a symmetrical case of the measles. The measles grew a little, but then generally got about as high as they did wide. By the time you realized you'd better mow your measles, they were so high that the mower topped them and killed off the center.

The dichondra did choke off a few weeds here and there, but most of them it didn't even manage to reach, and those flourished like never before in the well-prepared soil between the measles. If the dichondra was planted where Bermuda grass had once flourished, the Bermuda was soon flourishing again.

During the winter, after a little cold spell, the dichondra languished. A little colder, and it disappeared temporarily, and if it really got cold, the dichondra was gone forever, leaving you with the memory of a lot of hard work and a patch of weeds or, if you'd seeded it, perhaps a healthy stand of clover.

The following spring, you started over again with whatever handicap the winter had provided. This year you fertilized frequently and lightly and watered deeply, heavily, and constantly. If you let the lawn dry out in the hot sun, you lost it early. If you were conscientious about fertilizing and watering, it appeared, come fall, that you might have, in another year, a lawn that would look as good as the one the dichondra replaced, and then you and your lawn again had to face the perils of winter.

If you were smart the next year, you started mowing the weeds, the clover, and what was left of the dichondra early and regularly, and finally your lawn began to resemble a real lawn once more. In five years' time, if you really looked closely and if the winters hadn't been too severe, you could still see a little dichondra here and there. It was a pleasant green, as promised, and it made a nice, unobtrusive filler for your real lawn.

Between drafts of this chapter, different friends of mine have approached me on separate occasions with their dreams of a mower-free dichondra lawn of their own. One of them I managed to discourage, but the others, at last word, were still planning to forge ahead into that great green dream where you save half an hour's mowing time by putting in ten hours of digging, planting, fertilizing, watering, and swearing. And no argument of mine seems to have been able to stop them.

If there is an argument that might prevent you from falling victim to the great dichondra myth, it's a simple one. Before you start to put in such a lawn, find one, just one dichondra lawn somewhere that looks like the one you're planning to grow. Surely, if dichondra is anything like its myth cracks it up to be, there should be one such lawn somewhere.

For my part, I've never found it, and I've known people who really tried, who put more work into their dichondra lawn in a year than I put into my ordinary one in ten. Sometimes, in spots, the lawn would be lush and green if somewhat bumpy and rolling, but for every lush, green spot, there would be two brown and bare ones, and the whole effect was always that of a carpet well-worn in spots and badly in need of replacement.

I'm not, as you've now got a perfect right to suspect, totally and passionately opposed to dichondra. I've seeded some into my lawn from time to time but without ever deluding myself that it would someday take over completely. It hasn't and it won't, and with last winter's deep freeze, it all disappeared, so I was forced to seed it again.

I seeded it again because it makes a nice filler, as I've said, because it makes the lawn more versatile, more resistant to the various things that plague a lawn, and when it disappears in winter, as mine invariably does, it departs gracefully without leaving a trace of a bare or brown spot behind it. If it did, I'd consider it a weed.

Why a Lawn at All?

A question well worth the asking, I think, especially following a discussion of what it takes to produce and maintain a halfway decent lawn. The best answers are that no other planting can come near a lawn when it comes to absorbing and withstanding foot traffic. No surface is better or safer for adults and children to play on, with the possible exception of sand, and a well-tended, carefully maintained lawn is a thing of real beauty to behold if not a joy to take care of.

If you've got more lawn than you or your children need, however, and if the only real foot traffic it gets is the plodding of feet behind the lawn mower, it might be well worth your while to consider replacing at least part of it with a less time-consuming and demanding substitute.

Lawn Substitutes

A few years ago at a party, I met a couple who had just purchased a new house and had solved all of their lawn problems in one fell and virtually irretrievable swoop. They had covered their entire lot, except for the house, with a four-inch concrete slab and upholstered the slab with that kind of green plastic which now passes for grass in stadiums around the country and which has created whole new realms in sports-related injuries.

I really felt like strangling this couple then and there on general principles but decided to leave them to the fate they'd so cleverly contrived for themselves, to cook in the middle of a desert of their own creation, a desert which doesn't have to be mowed, mind you, but vacuumed. I wonder, too, how they're handling the liquid and solid deposits of the neighborhood dogs and any number of other natural, biodegradable phenomena.

I wonder if perhaps they haven't created many more problems for themselves than they could possibly have solved, and I wonder, when it comes time to sell the house, if they'll be able to locate another couple with similar tastes in concrete. Perhaps, if worse comes to worst, they can sell to a matched pair of Chevrolets. I've even found myself wondering if they haven't solved their carpeting problems by planting a lawn inside, and this Christmas I'm sending them a hole in the ground just to see if they can tell what it is.

There are, I'm convinced, better substitutes for lawns than concrete and plastic, and two of the most common ones in the Bay Area are ivy and prostrate juniper, both of which can and will grow in a wide variety of climates.

Ivy

Nothing, including a lawn, can touch ivy when it comes to uniformity, density, and regularity of coverage and its ability to hold and knit the soil. Ivy's only serious drawback as a ground cover is that it will stand little or no foot traffic and, of course, there are those who have been known to get bored with it since, once it's established, it manages to look exactly the same all year long.

Ivy is usually planted from nursery flats in soil that ideally has been prepared in much the same way as that for a regular lawn. If part of your reason for choosing ivy is to avoid that kind of preparation, you can circumvent it by plowing the area to be planted and preparing only the holes where the actual plants are to be placed with aged organic matter and sand, if necessary. Unless your soil is of a hopelessly poor quality, this kind of preparation should insure a healthy stand.

The best time of year to plant ivy is in the fall when the young plants can benefit from winter rains and establish their root systems away from the heat of summer. Once established, ivy will endure fairly long periods of drought, but it does require a good deal of moisture in the beginning.

To help the ivy along the first year or two and to fill in the bare spots between the young plants, you might try planting some nasturtium seed. The nasturtiums will create shade and coolness and help retard moisture loss, all of which will speed the ivy on its way to eventually choking out the nasturtiums altogether. Because of its hardiness, vigor, and ability to reseed itself, the bright orange variety of nasturtium seems to be best suited for this purpose.

Once the ivy is established, the only care it will need, beyond occasional watering, is clipping along the edges with lawn shears or hedge clippers three or four times a year to keep it off the walks and out of the flower beds.

In time, the planting may build up to an undesirable height. If and when this happens, cut the ivy down to ground level with hedge clippers and without disturbing the root system. It's best to do this in early spring just before the ivy starts putting out its new growth. If you cut it back in the fall, you'll be faced with a winter of ugly, bare roots, and if you wait too long into spring, the sun will burn the light sensitive undergrowth, and you may lose all or part of your stand. After you've cut the ivy down, give it a mulch of well-aged steer manure an inch thick.

Ivy can become a day-time hide-out for snails and slugs. If you're not willing to bait heavily for these pests, you might want to avoid ivy altogether, and you certainly wouldn't want to grow anything too near the ivy which slugs and snails feed on. These monsters won't, however, do any noticeable damage to the ivy itself.

Nursery flats are expensive, especially if you've got a large area to plant. If you've got the time, some room, and access to some ivy, it isn't difficult to start it yourself from cuttings. Pure sand or a mixture of sand and peat moss are ideal for rooting ivy. The flats or pots or whatever you use to root the cuttings in should be kept constantly moist and placed in filtered or partial sunlight and in a fairly cool place.

Ivy can also be started in water and then transplanted into a light soil mixture, one part each of peat moss, sand, and good garden loam. If you're planting directly from water into the ground—an easy, economical, and somewhat precarious way of doing things—do it at a time when the weather is certain to stay cool and the area will never dry out. Before putting the ivy into the ground, dig a hole about six inches deep and three inches wide, and fill it with a mixture of half sand and half peat moss. Not all the ivy planted this way will survive, so be prepared to do some replanting.

Ivy should be planted from a foot to two feet apart, depending on how much time and money you want to put in and how fast you want it to cover.

Juniper

Junipers have several advantages over ivy. They aren't at all particular about the kind of soil they grow in and require no advance preparation beyond loosening the soil in the immediate area with a shovel or pitchfork.

Junipers also require little or no artificial water. Most juniper failures, in fact, are caused by overzealous gardeners who pour too much water on them, a particularly hazardous practice if your drainage is poor. Watering once a month during the summer is all the artificial water that a juniper will need.

I have a stand of junipers growing on a slope below my little dab of front lawn. Because of the lawn above them, the junipers get more summer water than they should. So far I've been lucky, perhaps because the slope is steep enough to handle the run-off quickly and because I'm reasonably careful about the amount of water I put on the lawn. I water it frequently and very lightly, but if it ever happens that the junipers start to yellow and fade, the lawn, I'm afraid, will have to go.

This arrangement of lawn above, junipers below was cooked up by my predecessor. I wouldn't recommend it to anyone. In fact, I'd strongly recommend against it, and I'm slowly getting rid of the lawn so that I can quit worrying about the junipers altogether.

The kinds of junipers usually planted as ground covers vary in height from about six inches to two or three feet. They vary in color from variegated yellow-white and green through silver, gray-green, deep green, and blue-green. Because of these variations in height and color it's possible to create a much more interesting and eye-catching planting than you can with ivy.

I've often thought that it might be interesting to landscape an entire garden with nothing but junipers, using the taller varieties, some of which reach well over twenty feet, as background plants. There's enough variation in color, size, shape, and growth habits in the juniper family to make a very effective garden, although I grant that such a garden might prove a little too tailored, formal, and somber for some tastes. Still, once you'd put it in, you'd never have to touch it again except for minimal shaping and trimming, and very minimal shaping and trimming at that.

Junipers can be planted any time of year when the soil is dry enough to work and the weather dry enough to work it in. Bigger varieties of juniper can be planted as far as five or six feet apart, smaller ones two to three feet, depending, of course, on how quickly you want coverage and how much time and money you're willing and able to spend.

Some Other Ground Covers

In rich, well-drained soil and in a fairly sunny location, strawberries make an attractive ground cover as well as one that will produce a highly desirable crop, if you can keep it away from the non-human fauna who also love it.

Prostrate rosemary takes well to hot, dry areas and poor soil, provides a green carpet dotted with little blue flowers for part of the year, and can be carted into the house for use in the kitchen. Several varieties of thyme can also be used in the kitchen and to cover small areas in hot, dry places.

In shady, moist spots, nothing can compare to the rich beauty provided by an undulating carpet of baby's tears, which, if they find a place they really like, can prove to be a little too hardy. They're difficult to get rid of if for some reason you decide you don't want them. I've never found one myself, however.

Scotch and Irish moss work well in small areas and, since neither is a true moss, will take a lot of sun. Chamomile is an attractive deep green and highly aromatic ground cover, and its flowers can be dried and used to make the tea which Beatrix Potter and Peter Rabbit made famous.

The numbers and kinds of ground covers aren't endless, of course, but there are many more than this book can comfortably accommodate. If you're lucky enough to have a well-stocked nursery close at hand, you might reserve a Sunday afternoon for a visit there just to see what they carry in the way of ground covers and other low-growing, spreading plants.

I think you'll be in for a pleasant surprise, for a whole new world in miniature really, one that you may have missed on previous visits because your eyes were occupied with the bigger, showier competition. You might even decide to turn over a part of your lawn area to a rock garden, the perfect place to show off some of your new found discoveries to friends who, with just a little prodding, might even be induced to show some interest.

10 WATERING

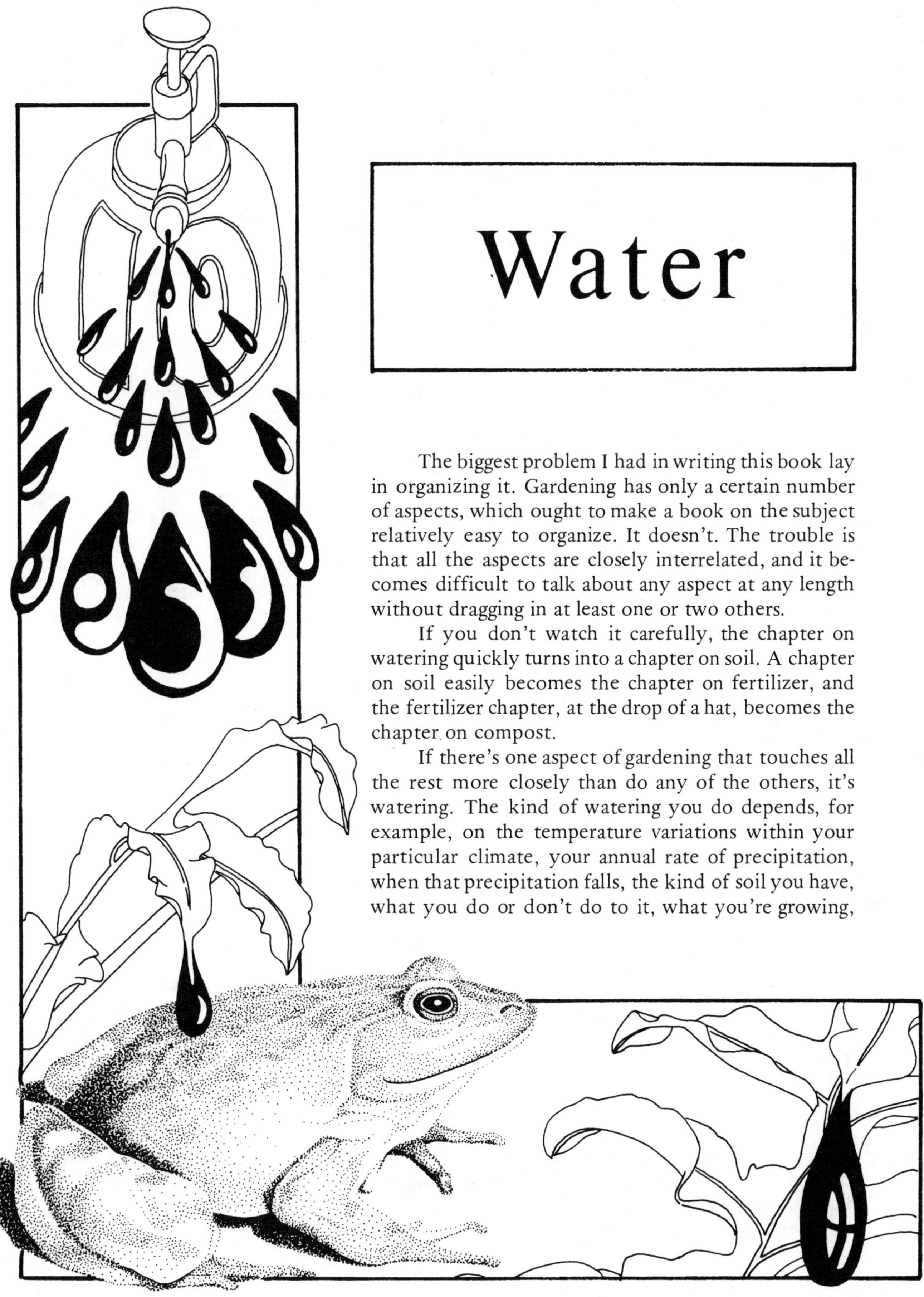

Water

The biggest problem I had in writing this book lay in organizing it. Gardening has only a certain number of aspects, which ought to make a book on the subject relatively easy to organize. It doesn't. The trouble is that all the aspects are closely interrelated, and it becomes difficult to talk about any aspect at any length without dragging in at least one or two others.

If you don't watch it carefully, the chapter on watering quickly turns into a chapter on soil. A chapter on soil easily becomes the chapter on fertilizer, and the fertilizer chapter, at the drop of a hat, becomes the chapter on compost.

If there's one aspect of gardening that touches all the rest more closely than do any of the others, it's watering. The kind of watering you do depends, for example, on the temperature variations within your particular climate, your annual rate of precipitation, when that precipitation falls, the kind of soil you have, what you do or don't do to it, what you're growing, how old that growth is, how much mulching you do or don't do, how much time you're willing to give to watering, and sometimes, at least in California, how much water is available to you.

Because of this lack of delineation and clear definition among the aspects of gardening, particularly when it comes to watering, I'm afraid that you're going to find me repeating myself in this chapter even more than in others. I've decided that repetition, however inelegant it may be, is preferable to omission, particularly if omission means that you're going to have to chase around in other parts of the book for information that by rights belongs in this chapter, information that you might overlook altogether if you took this book off the shelf to see what I had to say about watering and nothing else.

As a reward for your patience and kind indulgence, I will forthwith and without further ado divulge the Great Watering Secret before going on to more complex and mundane matters. The Great Watering Secret is simply this: *Every bit as much and sometimes more damage can be done to plants by overwatering as it can by underwatering.*

Water is something that all plants need in varying degrees, but it is not a medicine, something tonic to be poured on automatically if a plant begins to show signs of failing. That failure may very well be caused by too much water, and if that's the case, more water is just exactly what the plant doesn't need.

You say that you've already figured this out for yourself? Good. I congratulate you. You're fast becoming an accredited amateur practitioner—in theory at least, and now on to business.

When to Water, Time of Year

I hope it doesn't need to be said that when the rains really start, the watering stops. In most parts of California, this means that you won't need your garden hose from November through March or April. A few years ago, we experienced a mid-winter dry spell here, however, that lasted, if I remember correctly, some forty-two days, during which I was forced to do more than a little watering, and in the middle of January, too.

In a case such as the one cited above, I would check the soil after about a week or ten days, depending on how warm the weather has been. If the soil is dry down to a depth of an inch or two, it's time to start watering again. The same advice holds true for October and early November when the rains may be heavy but distantly spaced. Since plants are accustomed to more water at this time of year, it's much easier to sin in the direction of omission, so if you're in doubt, water.

If you live in an area where the rainfall patterns differ from California's, simply ignore the names of the months mentioned above and follow the same directions when the same conditions apply. If, however, you depend wholly or partially on summer rains to water your garden, don't wait ten days for more rain before you water. You may have to start watering a day or two after the last rain if the weather turns hot and/or dry. You'll be able to tell if and when you need to start watering by making the soil test described above.

When to Water, Temperature

All watering should stop when the temperature falls below forty degrees. Watering when the temperature approaches freezing will only serve to compound frost damage when it comes. Most plants become dormant in this temperature range, and being dry will, for once, work in their favor, since there will be less moisture on them and in them that can turn to ice.

If you're mystified by why some plants are killed by freezing temperatures, perhaps I'd better explain. The principle behind this phenomenon is a simple one. The water within the plant solidifies into ice and in solidifying, expands. The expansion explodes the cellular structure of the plant in exactly the same way that too much air causes a balloon to pop, and popped balloons are pretty much what frozen plants are and appear to be when they thaw out.

The higher the temperature rises, on the other hand, the more water you should pour on. This helps to compensate for evaporation and moisture loss, both of which increase proportionately with a rise in the temperature, and it helps to keep plants cool as well. Keeping a delicate plant cool during an unduly hot spell can save its life.

At high temperatures, as I've mentioned before, you should avoid merely sprinkling. Sprinkling lightly won't cool the plants significantly, but it will create water drops on the leaves which act as tiny magnifying glasses through which the sun will burn little holes into the leaves. If you water when it's hot, water heavily.

When to Water, Time of Day

Water early in the morning and late in the afternoon or evening to save water, at noon and early in the afternoon during hot weather to save the plants. In cool climates and during cool weather, watering in the evening will encourage rust and mildew. If circumstances, such as having a nine-to-five job, force you to do your watering at this time of day, you can avoid rust and mildew related problems by irrigating instead of spraying or sprinkling.

If you're not terribly concerned about saving water and your time is pretty much your own, the best time of day to water is between ten and three o'clock when moisture loss—yours as well as your plants—is at its peak, and the plants, particularly the moisture loving ones, will benefit most.

How Much Water

How much water depends partially on temperature, as we've discussed above. It also depends on what kind of soil you happen to have.

Clay soil. Clay soils absorb, evaporate, and drain away water at a very slow rate. To make sure that water will penetrate clay, it should be applied slowly over a long period of time. To insure that excess water has had time to drain and evaporate away, you should water clay soils only after long intervals. Applying water too frequently will force the air pockets out of the soil and drown the roots or weaken them to such an extent that they will become easy prey to rot and rot-related diseases. With clay and clay heavy soils, water deeply and infrequently.

Sandy soil. Sandy soils absorb water quickly and easily and drain it away almost as fast. With sand you must water frequently so that the soil doesn't dry out completely but for much shorter durations, since penetration is rapid and long waterings a waste of that sometimes precious substance. With sand and sandy soils, water frequently and lightly.

Humus-rich soil. A soil rich in organic matter, humus, requires less heavy watering than clay because humus aids penetration. It requires less frequent watering than sand because humus retains moisture. With a soil rich in humus, you don't have to worry about overwatering as much as you do with clay, because humus speeds drainage.

A soil with a good balance of humus, sand, and clay—the mixture that gardening books call *loam*—will require less water less frequently than poorer soils, since loam keeps the moisture plants need longer and quickly gets rid of any undesirable excess. A good, rich, loamy soil will save you water, watering time, and help you to avoid watering disasters, those caused by too much water as well as those caused by too little. A soil of this kind is, in fact, one of the best watering tools any gardener can have.

How to Water

Gardeners generally water just at ground level or just above it, in other words, by irrigation or by sprinkling. There are devices which permit you to water below the level of the soil, but for the purposes of this book and the kind of garden it's addressed to, this kind of watering is of little or no importance.

For my part, I definitely prefer overhead sprinkling to irrigation. Sprinkling distributes water evenly and gently, washes off the plants at the same time, and even knocks off a few pests from time to time. It also more closely approximates Mother Nature's way of watering.

Irrigation is more difficult and involved because it requires the digging of ditchlets and the constant channeling and rechanneling of water. If for some reason, such as the prevention of rust and mildew, you must water more selectively than you can by sprinkling, irrigation is your answer. Irrigation is also the answer if you have plants growing in close proximity whose watering requirements differ. People who live on flat ground rather than on a slope, as I do, will probably find irrigation a more practical method of watering than I find it, too.

There are special nozzles available at garden supply outlets which bubble the water gently out of the end of the hose. If you're irrigating, this type of nozzle helps to keep the soil from being washed around by the water, a factor that you have to consider when watering in this way.

There are many kinds of lawn sprinklers on the market, but I've never managed to locate one that was perfect for every watering chore. For a long time I used a sprinkler that rotated from side to side and covered a large area lightly, making it possible to ignore it for long periods without having to worry about run-off. The trouble with this kind of sprinkler is that it pours far more water to the left and the right than it ever drops in the middle.

I abandoned the rotating sprinkler in favor of a swirler which waters more evenly and heavily in what's advertized as a perfect square, although only God or someone in a helicopter could attest to the truth of that claim. The difficulty with the swirler is that it can't be left in any one place for more than fifteen minutes without creating a flood somewhere.

The swirler also leaks where it connects to the hose, a problem I haven't been able to correct with gaskets and one that compounds the flooding problem. On flat ground this problem wouldn't be nearly as serious, but since my garden, as I mentioned, sits on a slope, any water applied too heavily quickly runs off and down the sewers before it can soak in and do much good.

The next time I feel like spending the money, I'll probably pick up an entirely different kind of sprinkler and give it a try, and if it just happens to be that impossible dream, the Perfect Sprinkler, I'll rewrite this section of the book and include the brand name, the approximate price, and a testimonial that will bring tears to the eyes of the manufacturer. Let us not hold our breaths.

My years of hit-and-miss sprinkler research have taught me one thing: You almost always get what you pay for in a sprinkler. This axiom isn't quite so true if the sprinkler works on very simple principles and with few or no moving parts, but it becomes truer and truer the more complex the design and the greater the number of moving parts.

To test the effectiveness of any sprinkler's distribution, you should, as I mentioned earlier, set out coffee cans in random places in the sprinkler's path. The more evenly the cans fill, the more efficient the sprinkler, provided of course that it doesn't leak at the hose connection.

If you're lucky enough to locate a sprinkler that works fairly well for you, keep a mental note of the places it needs to be set to give you the kind of coverage you want. This will simplify matters when watering time rolls around, and it may save part of your garden for you if you can mark those spots along with their approximate sprinkling times for the kid up the street you're paying to water your garden while you're off vacationing. If you use stakes to mark the spots and the kid fails to perform his duties well, you can pull up one of the stakes and drive it through his heart.

Design for Watering

Your lawn will probably need more artificial water more often than any other part of your garden with the possible exception of such rain forest natives as fuchsias, azaleas, rhododendrons, camellias, and ferns. Because of this, it's bad policy to set plants near the lawn—or if you're on a slope, below it—which prefer their soil on the dry side.

If you're starting your garden from scratch, you can save yourself a lot of future headaches, heartaches, and time by placing plants with similar watering requirements together and by keeping those with very different requirements apart.

When you're introducing a new plant into an already established area, it's good practice to check first and see if the watering requirements of the new plant are similar to those of its future neighbors. Changing the watering schedule to accommodate the foreigner may cause the established residents some problems.

Your nurseryman will know just how much water any plant needs and how much it will take. If you're in doubt, ask him, and if you can't meet those needs in the place you want the plant, don't buy it or, if you do, put it in a place where you can meet them. This point, obvious as it is, is an important one because more new plants are lost to the gardener through improper watering than through any other single cause, or so I'd be willing to bet.

Watering the Lawn

We've already discussed lawn watering at some length in the preceding chapter, the gist of that discussion being that you shouldn't ever let your lawn dry out but keep it always on the moist side. You can usually tell if your lawn isn't getting enough water if it starts to yellow and turn brown in spots or if growth is slow and weak during warm, not necessarily hot, weather.

Sometimes, especially with older lawns, water will refuse to penetrate the soil beneath the lawn because the soil has become too firmly packed. If you suspect that this might be your problem, give your lawn a thorough soaking. A healthy lawn should feel spongy and springy after a good watering. If the ground still feels firm and hard, you've got soil problems.

Soil Loosener

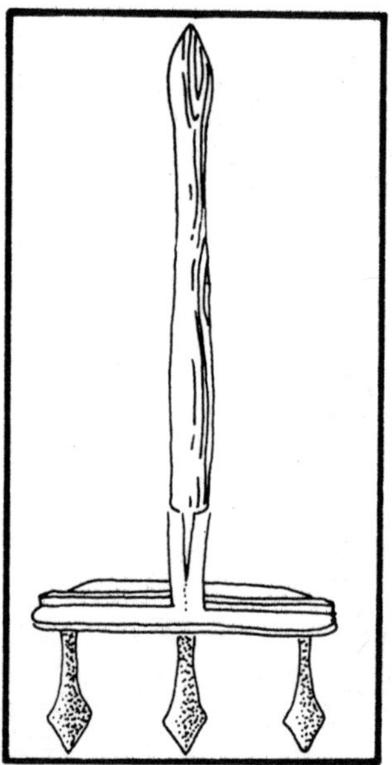

Soil problems of this kind can be corrected in a number of ways: (1) By applying special chemicals, which I don't particularly approve of and won't discuss here beyond mentioning that they exist. (2) By cutting the packed area into neat little squares with a straight-edged shovel, lifting the squares out carefully, and cutting off an inch of soil at a depth of four or five inches and replacing it with well-aged organic matter or loam, thus creating a soft under-cushion which will cause the packed soil above it to loosen when the square is replaced. This method is really only practical for very small areas. (3) By digging up the lawn completely, repreparing the soil, and planting a new one. (4) And through the use of a certain tool, the name of which I've never known, even though I happen to own one.

This mysterious tool is about the size of an ordinary shovel. It has the general appearance of a stubby fork, the tines of which flatten out into a diamond shape at the end. At the base of the tines is a flat guard which prevents anything but the tines from entering the soil. To use this nameless implement, you stab it into the soil and rock it back and forth on the guard with your foot. The rocking action breaks up the soil below the level of the lawn without disturbing the lawn surface.

If you happen to locate one of these soil looseners and decide to use it, make sure that your lawn is very dry when you do. Using it on a wet lawn will compress as much soil as it loosens, and you may compound your problem.

Brown spots in the lawn can also stem from causes other than insufficient water and poor penetration, and this is as good a time as any to talk about them.

One cause of brown spots is the lawn moth, which lays its eggs in the lawn during warm weather. These eggs produce grubs which feed on the roots of grasses, killing the lawn above. Brown spots caused by lawn moth grubs are generally patchy and not a solid circle of brown. If you suspect that you might have this problem, keep a watch on your lawn around sunset when the moths can be seen fluttering above it. The abundant presence of birds, blackbirds in particular, on the lawn is also an indication of lawn moth grub. They're there to eat them.

There are a number of pesticides which will "cure" the lawn moth problem temporarily and, in doing so, kill off your earthworm population as well. Earthworms are a great help to your lawn and to all your garden, because they are continually passing the soil through their bodies, loosening it, aerating it, and keeping it from getting packed.

Encouraging the visits of birds to your lawn is a partial solution to the lawn moth problem. I've also found that by working down the lawn with a steady, hard stream of water, I can force the grubs to the surface and kill them by hand or foot. If your lawn isn't reasonably sturdy, however, the hosing method may do it more harm than good, so approach it with caution at the beginning.

If the brown spots in your lawn are solid circles of devastation, the problem is probably dogs, the female of the species being the worse offender not only because she squats but also because of the superior potency of her urine.

One way to discourage the visits of dogs is to pepper the areas where you don't want them with cayenne. Cayenne explains to dogs in a harmless way that they would, perhaps, be happier elsewhere, and it will be some time before they return to sniff and squat again. To those who love dogs better than lawns, I offer my sincere apologies for this somewhat rude, if handy hint. I have myself on occasion used cayenne to explain to our cat that certain rugs and pieces of furniture aren't for sharpening one's claws, and she's one of the few cats I've ever encountered who makes frequent use of a scratching post for just that purpose.

Planters

It should be obvious, because of the speed of drainage and the amount of surface exposed to the air, that plants growing in raised beds, boxes, pots, and other containers are going to need more water more often than will their counterparts which grow in the ground.

During the summer, most plants growing in containers will need to be watered almost on a daily basis. This means that if you're planning to be away from home for even a few days at this time of year, you're going to have to get someone to do your watering for you, either that or risk losing your plants.

Moving the containers, even the ones holding sun-loving plants, into shaded, cool areas for the duration can help to forestall disasters of this order, but it's still a good idea to give some thought to this problem in connection with your traveling habits before you go off on a pot and planter binge or decide to take up the Japanese bonzai as a hobby.

Watering Schedules

Any garden will, in time, adjust to any gardener's watering schedule, even if that schedule means no watering at all. In such a case, of course, the adjustment will probably mean the wholesale extinction of certain parts of the garden, but nonetheless an adjustment will have been made.

Almost every gardener, dedicated or otherwise, will establish a watering schedule of some kind whether he actually thinks about it or not. Most of us are creatures of habit either by choice or necessity. The important thing is that, once a schedule has been established, it should be maintained. Drastic changes in it in either direction will soon produce drastic results.

If two or more people are responsible for watering, some sort of agreement should be reached to avoid giving the garden random water feasts and random water famines.

If you're planning to leave your garden in the hands of someone else for any length of time, it will be worth your while to analyze your watering habits in detail and to put some effort into trying to communicate your analysis to your stand-in.

If you can con another gardener, preferably a better one than yourself, into substituting for you, you might find your garden in better shape on your return than it was when you left it. Some gardening nuts just can't help gardening no matter where they are. With them it's a compulsive neurosis but a socially more acceptable one than, say, arson or child-molesting.

There really is nothing the least bit mystical about watering. It's all pretty much a matter of common sense, and the commonness and sensibility of it all will become progressively clearer to you the more you're exposed to it. I water when things need it, which probably isn't of much immediate help to you, but that's what it boils down to in the end, as you'll see when you get there.

11 FERTILIZERS AND FERTILIZING

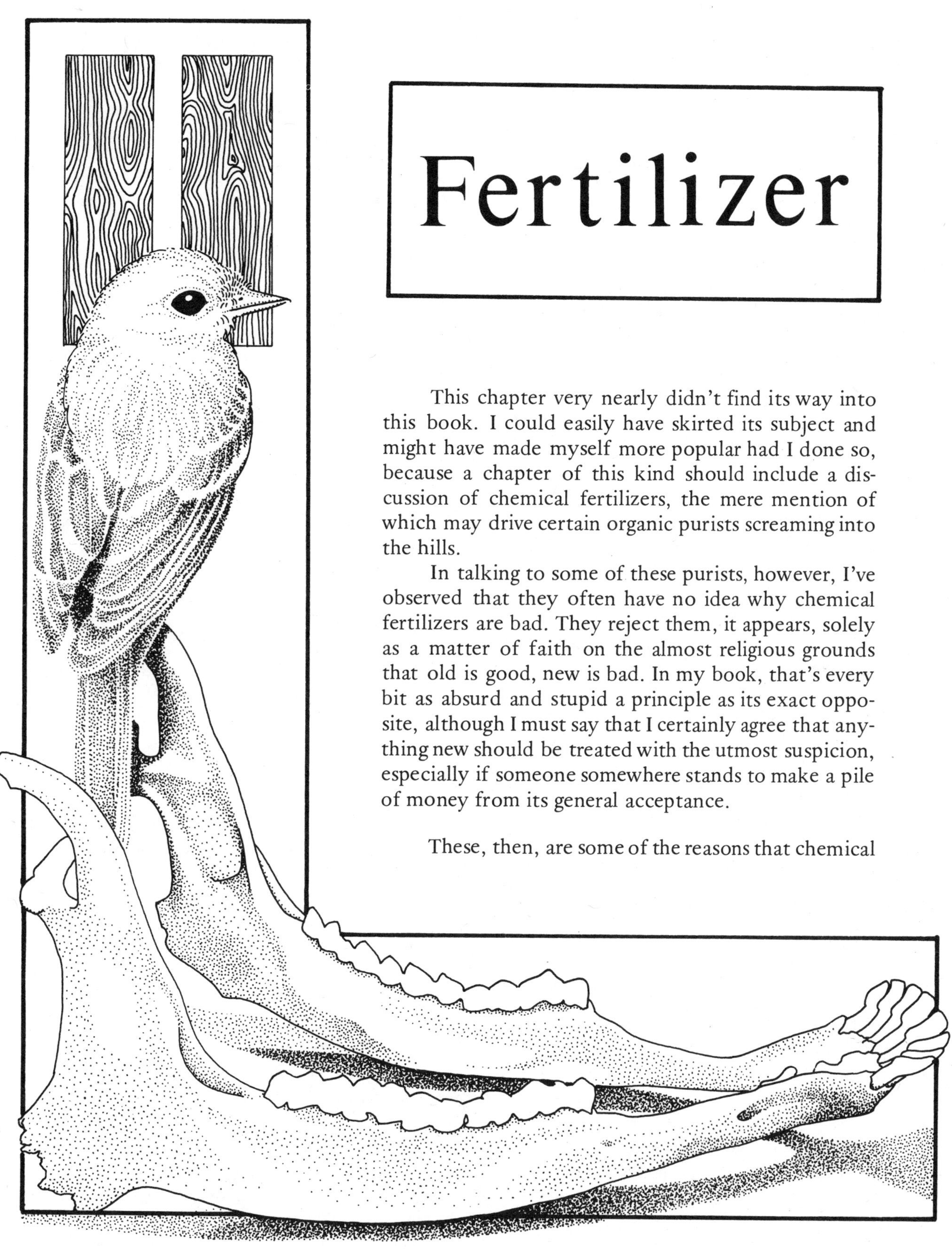

Fertilizer

This chapter very nearly didn't find its way into this book. I could easily have skirted its subject and might have made myself more popular had I done so, because a chapter of this kind should include a discussion of chemical fertilizers, the mere mention of which may drive certain organic purists screaming into the hills.

In talking to some of these purists, however, I've observed that they often have no idea why chemical fertilizers are bad. They reject them, it appears, solely as a matter of faith on the almost religious grounds that old is good, new is bad. In my book, that's every bit as absurd and stupid a principle as its exact opposite, although I must say that I certainly agree that anything new should be treated with the utmost suspicion, especially if someone somewhere stands to make a pile of money from its general acceptance.

These, then, are some of the reasons that chemical

fertilizers are bad:

1. They deplete the organic content of the soil.
2. They add absolutely nothing to that organic content.
3. They substitute nothing for organic content, which has the ability to hold moisture and air within the soil as well as to speed drainage and water penetration.
4. They eventually leave a residue of chemical salts in the soil which will poison future growth.
5. They can, if used improperly, burn root, stem, leaf, flower, fruit, and seed tissue, causing immediate, intermediate or slow death to the plants to which they're applied.
6. They force growth, growth which is far more susceptible to frost damage than is natural growth. This leads me to suspect that they may in other ways damage a plant's ability to cope with its natural environment over an extended period of time.

These are some of the reasons that chemical fertilizers are good:

1. They're cheap.
2. They're convenient.
3. They produce magic results, sometimes.

Weighing the good against the bad, those purists and would-be purists who have deigned to read this far can, it seems to me, become purists on purely practical grounds. This will make them much easier to live with for people like me.

To these practical, rational purists, I am now going to confess that I am sometimes guilty of using chemical fertilizers myself. Perhaps it might be of some use to you and to them if I explain the circumstances which cause me to sin in this way along with my reasons and rationalizations for so sinning.

Three or four times a year, I give my lawn a shot of a liquid chemical fertilizer which is high in nitrogen and which is reputed to contain a chemical that loosens and breaks up the soil. I do this in part because my lawn was over sixty years old when I acquired it and definitely showing signs of age. I also do it because I'm fond, perhaps overly fond, of rich, deep green, velvety lawns.

(Simply because a lawn is old doesn't necessarily mean that it has to show its age. Eve Muir mentioned to me that she had seen beautifully green lawns in England that were reputed to be over two hundred years old, and there's no reason to doubt that such is the case. A lawn, properly cared for, could conceivably last forever.

Proper care, again and in brief, consists of laying the original lawn on a good soil foundation, providing it with adequate moisture at all times, clipping frequently enough so that the clippings are fine enough to leave on top of it, fertilizing it organically on a regular schedule, and keeping it free of all intruders which threaten its existence.)

To compensate for the deficiencies which chemical fertilizers create in the soil, I leave the grass clippings on the lawn and give it a hearty dose of good old organic steer manure every spring. In time, I hope, I should be able to phase out the chemical fertilizer altogether and still produce the kind of lawn I want. At any rate, the lawn seems to be moving in this direction.

I also use a chemical fertilizer on many of the plants that I have growing in pots. Plants in pots, especially those growing in the house, have so many strikes against them that I feel they need the something extra that chemical fertilizers can give them. The organic richness of potting soil easily compensates for the dilatory effects of chemical fertilizer, and by repotting the plant, the soil can easily be replaced when its ability to compensate is depleted.

Anyone wishing to remain a purist even where potted plants are concerned can make a tea out of steer manure and use the tea instead of its chemical counterpart to fertilize potted plants. The tea is made by steeping steer manure in an equal amount of initially hot water for about twenty-four hours and then running the brew through a strainer to remove the solid matter. The tea can be used full strength once a month or half strength every two weeks.

I wouldn't be too surprised to find my ever-growing guilt turning me into a faithful brewer of such teas in the not too distant future. I might even be doing it today if I weren't so damned resistant to change. (For instructions on the care and feeding of house plants, see Chapter Nineteen and page 226 specifically, where we'll discuss fish emulsion as a substitute for chemical fertilizers.)

Fertilizer Analysis

Most all commercially packaged fertilizers, whether they're chemical or not, contain somewhere on their label a series of numbers reading something like 5-10-6, 12-8-4, 0-16-1 and so forth. These numbers refer to the percentage of nitrogen, phosphorus, and potassium, in that order, which the particular fertilizer contains.

These three chemical elements—nitrogen, phosphorus, and potassium—are absolutely necessary for plant growth and can be found in varying degrees in all soils, even the most virgin ones. These chemical elements are not evil in themselves. They're as natural as rain and sun and birds, and they can be added to soils deficient in them in natural, harmless, and highly organic ways. In modern times, these ways have been passed over in favor of chemical fertilizers largely because the old ways are more time-consuming, involve more work, and cost more money.

Nitrogen

Nitrogen is not a mineral and is not naturally present among the mineral content of the soil. Nitrogen is a gas and it finds its way into the soil from the air. It's beaten in by rain, brought in along with decomposed organic matter, cultivated in, and finally, incorporated into the soil by bacteria which get it from the air pockets within the soil itself.

Natural sources of nitrogen available to the gardener are *well-aged* organic matter and blood meal, the dried and packaged blood of animals which have been slaughtered for other purposes, such as food and leather.

Nitrogen deficiency is easy to detect. Plants growing in nitrogen poor soil will show vigorous new growth, but the older growth will be yellowish and may even drop completely off the plant. (House plants exhibiting these symptoms may simply be suffering from too much water.) Nitrogen rich soil, on the other hand, produces lush, verdant growth.

When adding organic matter to the soil, it's important that it be well decomposed. If it isn't, the bacteria which help to decompose it will steal the nitrogen they need to do their job from the nitrogen supply of neighboring plants. For this reason, it's not a good idea to add sawdust, ground bark or other "raw" forms of organic matter to any soil that you plan to plant right away. Age the sawdust or bark away from the soil first.

Phosphorus

Phosphorus is available to the gardener in natural form as bone meal, the crushed and ground bones of slaughtered animals. Since bone meal is a relatively expensive product, it's not economical to work it generally throughout the soil. Instead, it should be added to the immediate area when putting in a new plant or worked into the soil around plants which are suspected of suffering a deficiency.

Deficiencies in phosphorus content aren't easy to detect, because they show up mostly in slow or retarded growth, a symptom that can be caused by any number of other factors. In general, however, if your soil is neutral or alkaline, you won't have to worry about supplying additional phosphorus. If it's acidic, you may.

If you suspect that you may have a serious phosphorus deficiency, have your soil analyzed by a soil chemist before you put yourself out of pocket at the bone meal store. Should it happen that you actually do have such a deficiency, the sanest and by far the cheapest solution might be the addition of some dreaded superphosphate or ammonium phosphate. You can salve your organic conscience by viewing your foul deed not as fertilizing but as soil amending.

The pure organicist can resort to burying bones around his garden as well as pieces of old bone china. Actually, this solution isn't as silly as it sounds. The only problem is that bones and bone china take a very long time to decompose, so it would be quite some time before the garden derived much benefit from them. If a convenient way could be found to pulverize kitchen bones and bone china before burying them, the results would of course come more quickly.

Potassium

Potassium, called potash by gardeners, is available in the form of wood ashes from the fireplace. To obtain some, if you don't have a fireplace of your own, you might volunteer to clean out a neighbor's, after you've ascertained, of course, that he doesn't burn a lot of trash between his logs.

Other Minerals

Iron, magnesium, calcium, zinc, and manganese are also necessary for plant growth. These trace elements generally find their own way into the soil without the gardener's help and consequently don't have to be worried about.

And by this time, I fear that you may be worrying aplenty. What I've probably done in this chapter is made you see your garden as some kind of starving cripple, crying out piteously in a language you can't understand for things you don't know how to get or how to give it.

If that's the case, I'm sorry, and stop worrying. Unless your soil is an extremely rare case, you can satisfy all of its needs and those of the plants that grow in it with a little elbow grease and a good, old-fashioned compost pile into which you throw bones and wood ashes from time to time.

In fact, I suspect that much more fertilizing is done by the home gardener than needs to be done. We live in a society that at all levels pumps pills, medicines, and drugs into itself to make it feel better and be better. If we love our gardens, we want to give them medicines, too, and of course it's those little packages of powders and bottles of liquid at the local garden supply outlet that look like garden medicine to us. Don't play doctor with your dirt unless you're sure you know what you're doing.

We'll take up the compost pile, nature's surest remedy for poor soil, in Chapter Fourteen.

12 PESTS AND DISEASES

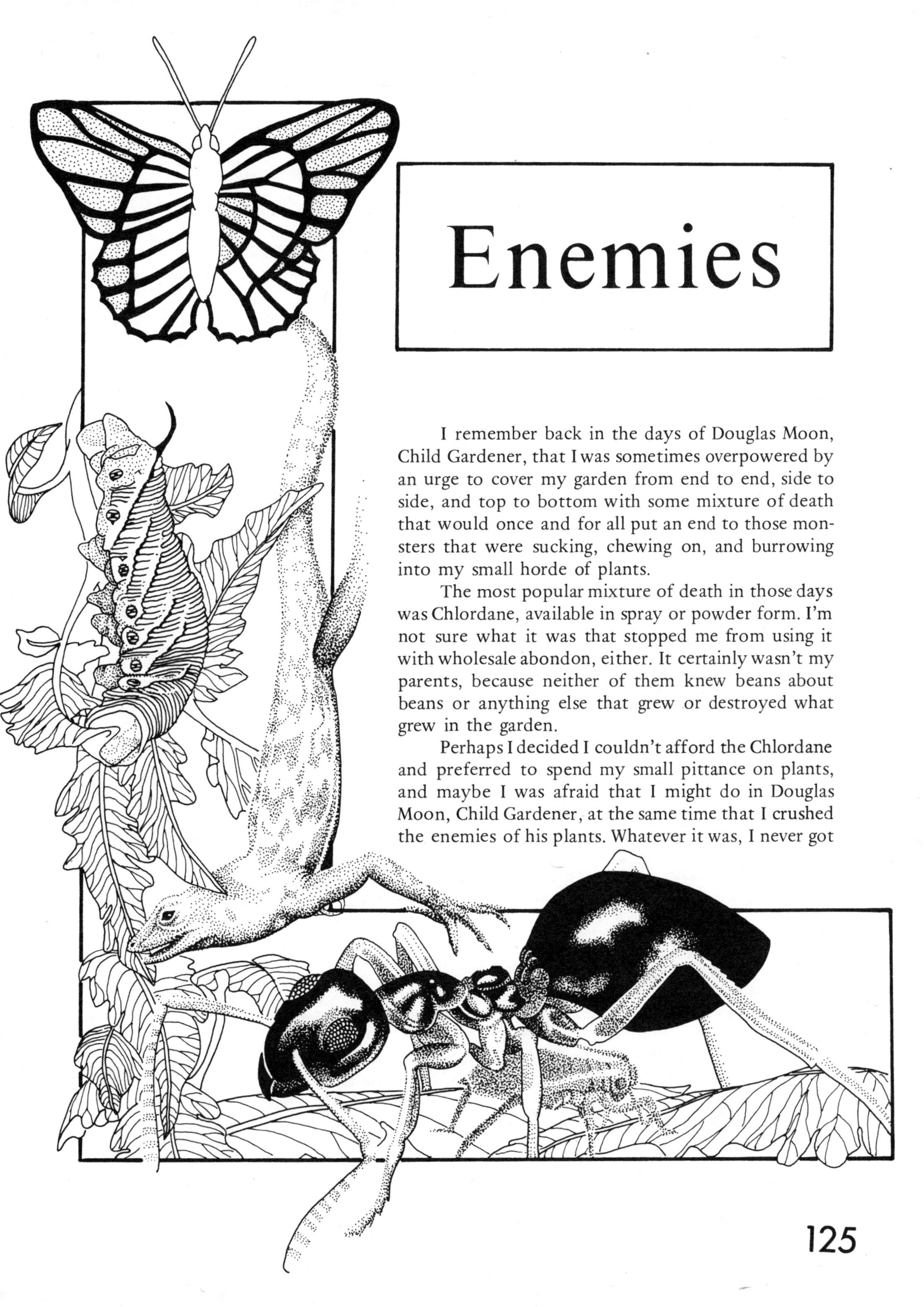

Enemies

I remember back in the days of Douglas Moon, Child Gardener, that I was sometimes overpowered by an urge to cover my garden from end to end, side to side, and top to bottom with some mixture of death that would once and for all put an end to those monsters that were sucking, chewing on, and burrowing into my small horde of plants.

The most popular mixture of death in those days was Chlordane, available in spray or powder form. I'm not sure what it was that stopped me from using it with wholesale abondon, either. It certainly wasn't my parents, because neither of them knew beans about beans or anything else that grew or destroyed what grew in the garden.

Perhaps I decided I couldn't afford the Chlordane and preferred to spend my small pittance on plants, and maybe I was afraid that I might do in Douglas Moon, Child Gardener, at the same time that I crushed the enemies of his plants. Whatever it was, I never got around to succumbing to the Chlordane urge.

Other, more mature gardeners, I suspect, did. Those were the Fabulous Fifties, probably the ten most sanitized years of the American experience. A country free of Communists, and a garden free of pests. What could be merrier? What did it matter if the soil bacteria went the way of the aphids and the six or so living Americans possessed of original ideas went the way of the Communists? We and our All-American roses would be safe however sterile the American soil had become.

Happily, in the garden at least, those days seem to be over. We've come to realize that too much sanitation breeds sterility and that sterility breeds nothing at all. Television seems to be keeping the clean freaks occupied with their own armpits and the chemical treatment thereof, leaving the garden and its wonderful dirt to the rest of us.

We are again learning to see the garden as a part of nature and nature as process, or series of processes, that is disturbed, subverted, and even destroyed by chemical sprays. We've also come to see the sprays themselves for what they really are, not garden tools, but garden cosmetics, the cosmetic benefits of which are often short-lived compared to the long term and very real damage they can do.

I will now climb down off yet another of my soapboxes and turn to a case in point. I recently heard a professional rose-grower complain that, after spraying his roses for four years with Malathion, a "safe" insecticide, he managed to develop a strain of aphids which were bigger and more voracious than their predecessors and which, more importantly, were totally resistant to further applications of Malathion.

The upshot of the story is that the nurseryman was forced to risk his entire stock of roses by pruning them almost to the ground in June, the worst month for such a pruning, in order to starve out the new breed of aphids long enough to give the roses a chance against them if and when the roses grew back. The story, fortunately, has a happy ending. The roses did grow back, the aphids didn't, and the nurseryman stopped using Malathion.

Pest & Predator

Many garden pests, such as aphids, are relatively uncomplicated, strictly vegetarian creatures. Generally short-lived, they reproduce rapidly and in great numbers, among which, because of natural mutations, there are bound to be a few individuals which can stand up against one or more chemical insecticides.

These resistant individuals, because of the speed at which the species is able to reproduce itself, will soon fill the places left by those the chemical killed. A new chemical will be needed to kill the new breed, and the cycle will start all over again. The final result will not be the destruction of the species but instead, as we've seen with the rose-grower and his aphids, the creation of a master species equipped to withstand almost anything, perhaps eventually even their own natural predators.

I remember reading a story some time ago about a man who worked in a factory near Riverside, California. The factory produced a number of poisonous chemicals, various forms of arsenate among them, if I remember correctly. One day the man, a long time employee of the company, was bitten by a rattlesnake. The man survived, but the snake died, presumably because over the years the man had built up a tolerance to arsenic and was at the time of the bite so loaded with it that the snake was poisoned.

Who knows, the story may even be true. Arsenic tolerance is a favorite ploy of English murder mysteries. Over the years, Mrs. Smith, a long-range planner, doses herself daily with a tiny bit of arsenic. One day, she liberally spices the Smith family dinner with the stuff and serves it to herself and Mr. Smith. She survives, but Mr. Smith, an unpleasant drunk who's beaten her nightly since the day they were married, keels over on his plate. Since Mrs. Smith has partaken of the same meal that killed her husband, his death is judged to be an accident, and she goes scot-free and remains so until very clever Detective Inspector Legerdemain pays her a visit and notices certain things about her physiognomy that indicate long term arsenic consumption and, *voilá*, Mrs. Smith is in the pokey.

Back to the garden, where it isn't too difficult to imagine a newly arrived ladybug biting into a Malathion-proof and Malathion-soaked aphid. The ladybug dies of Malathion poisoning, the aphid from the bite, and all the other aphids, all those the late ladybug might have eaten, survive to continue their dastardly work unmolested.

All things being equal, of course, a chemical spray has the same effect on pest and predator alike. It kills them both. But all things aren't equal, and the predator, as a species, is at a disadvantage. The predator, since it must break down animal rather than plant matter in order to survive, is by necessity biologically more complex.

This complexity means that the predator's chances of producing a successful mutant, poison-resistant strain are from the start far less than those of the pest. This complexity also means that the predator will usually reproduce fewer, albeit longer lived individuals, less often than the pest, so even if a mutant strain is created, it will be a long time before its numbers are great enough to make a dent in the mutant pest population.

In the long run, then, insecticides seem to have the opposite effect from the one intended. They create a super breed of insect pests on the one hand and on the other weaken nature's capacity to cope with those pests naturally. If any species are ever completely killed off, it will almost certainly be those of the more complex and vulnerable predators, leaving us to cope with the pests alone, us and our surely finite number of chemicals, and it's even possible that we might not be around to cope with anything, since we're much higher up on the food chain even than the insect predators, especially if we're carnivorous.

A lot more could and has been said about the far reaching aspects of pesticides, so I'm going to drop the subject here and go on to suggest some ways to handle your garden without resorting to chemical poisons, the long run effects of which, if they're known at all, look very, very gloomy.

The Best Pest Defense

The best defense against an onslaught of pests and plant diseases is an already healthy plant. It's as simple as that. We've already talked quite a bit about how to keep a plant healthy in terms of such things as proper watering, soil conditioning, fertilizing, and so forth. Another way to protect the health of plants is to keep the garden clean.

Dead leaves and other garden debris should be picked up, carted away, destroyed or, preferably, relegated to the compost pile. Left on the ground, garden debris makes ideal breeding places for all manner of garden pests and diseases, many of which will be killed off in the compost pile by the heat generated by decomposition.

Any plant that's heavily infested with something and any plant that dies suddenly and for no apparent reason should be quickly removed and destroyed, burned if possible, to prevent further infestation. Sometimes this may prove a difficult, soul-rending procedure, but trying to save a badly infected plant may end up costing you the lives of many other healthy ones.

If only a portion of the plant is infected, you can sometimes save it merely by cutting off and destroying the infected part. If you decide on this course of action, keep a close watch on the plant for further signs of trouble.

Insect Predators

Probably the most common insect predators—insects which eat other insects—are ladybugs and lace wings. Everyone, I imagine, is familiar with ladybugs or ladybirds, as some people call them. They're those charming, colorful little beetles that fly away home because their houses are on fire and their children about to be burned. They're also, for some strange reason, one of the few members of the insect world which many children and adults will allow to crawl freely on their persons.

Ladybug: Adult, pupa and larva

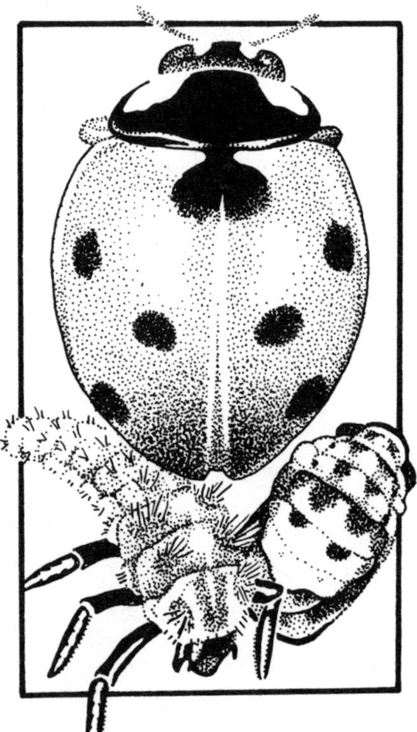

Not so many people recognize ladybugs in their larval stage when they're equally beneficial. In this stage, ladybugs are about a quarter of an inch long and look something like a cross between a beetle and a wormlet. Their heads are black, and their colorful worm-like bodies dotted with little black circles. If you run across something that looks like that in your garden, leave it alone. It's eating the things that are eating your plants.

Lace wings are easily identified by their delicate and filmy, rounded wings. Lace wings are about half an inch long and either light, bright green or light tan in color, depending on what they've been feasting on.

Another garden predator, one which isn't native to Bay Area gardens, is the praying mantis. The mantis grows to a full five or six inches in a season and will tackle caterpillars, worms, and other insects which are too large for ladybugs and lace wings to handle as well as those insects which aren't. Like the lace wing, the mantis is either green or brown in color, depending on its food supply.

If you're interested in acquiring any of these predators or in augmenting your natural supply, you can usually find them advertized in garden magazines and journals and in some seed catalogues, Burpee's, for example.

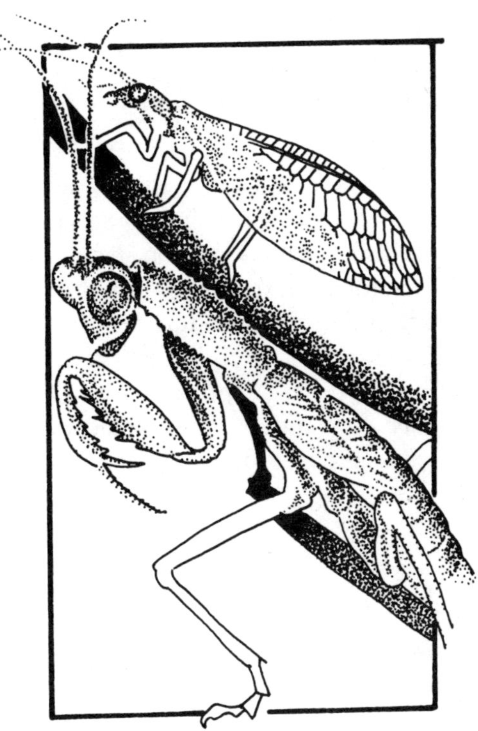

Lacewing and mantis

It's worthwhile, I think, to order a few mantis egg cases if for no other reason than to get a first hand look at a real live mantis. Mantises are extremely elegant, if somewhat grosteque looking, and it's quite a thrill when you stumble on one of these slow-moving, seemingly fearless creatures in the garden. They are, I understand, the only insect which can turn its head from side to side, and they will, too, just to get a look at you with a pair of the strangest, most beautiful eyes I've ever seen.

If you become attached to mantises, which is a distinct possibility, you'll probably have to order new egg cases every year, since mantises can survive only the mildest winters.

Spiders

The common garden spider, as well as its multitude of cousins, is also an insectivorous creature. For some reason, one that I can't easily understand, few people harbor kind thoughts about the lowly spider, one of man's better smaller friends. Perhaps this distaste has something to do with the unpleasantness of getting caught in spider webs or with the ugly reputation of the black widow, an unaggressive little lady, except where her husband is concerned, who rarely finds her way into the garden, preferring, as she does, the undersides of houses, basements, garages, wood piles, and the confines of the local dump.

If you're one of the spider-hating set, try to restrain your murderous instincts the next time you run across one. Tell yourself that your goals and the spider's, in regard to insects at least, are pretty much the same. That's reason enough, I think, for a permanent truce, however uneasy you may find it.

The Ambiguous Butterfly

As the gardener should love the spider so should he probably hate the butterfly. That beautiful creature flitting so gracefully from flower to flower is, of course, depositing vast numbers of eggs on and around those flowers, all of which eggs have a chance of becoming voracious caterpillars, and the larger the butterfly, of course, the bigger and hungrier the caterpillar that produced it and the caterpillars it will itself produce.

I am not myself a lepidoptricide, although I've been known to step on a caterpillar from time to time. If the caterpillars make it past me to the cocoon stage, I leave them alone. Contrary to popular opinion, however, butterflies are not free. They take their toll of the garden's greenery on the way to earning their wings.

Ants & Ant Cows

"Ant cow" is a name sometimes applied to aphids. The reason for this name is that aphids produce honey dew from plants which is in turn milked from the aphids by sugar-loving ants in much the same way as a man milks a cow. If the aphids aren't milked, they will explode and die, so one method of controlling aphids is to control ants.

There are numerous ant poisons on the market, most of which contain arsenic, but so little of it is needed to wipe out a hill and what's needed is used so selectively by the ants themselves that I doubt that using these poisons could be considered detrimental to the environment by anyone.

Ants aren't, however, totally without value to man. Since they sometimes attack termite colonies, they help to keep termite populations down, and termites, from a human standpoint, do much more damage than aphids.

Reptiles & Amphibians

Toads, frogs, lizards, and snakes consume large quantities of insects of all sizes and are, for that reason, a great help to the gardener. If you're lucky enough to have any one of this group around, don't do anything that might convince it to move on to more hospitable territory.

No one that I know of is yet marketing any of these animals as natural insecticides, but the toad, if he's shippable, seems an ideal candidate. The toad is unobtrusive, appearing usually only at night, as well as undemanding, since all he needs, except for insects, is a cool, dark place in which to spend the day. If you happen to know of anyone who's giving a toad away, take it off his hands.

Birds

Birds are a mixed blessing. They're an outright nuisance if you're about to harvest a crop of fruit, if you've just planted a vegetable garden or seeded a lawn, or if you're nurturing some tender leafy vegetables such as lettuce or spinach.

If you're not involved with any of the above projects, birds can be a great help, since certain birds, not all, live mostly on insects and grubs. There's no way I know of to encourage the insectivores without encouraging the seed-eaters as well. In fact, if you do want to encourage worm fowl, as Chaucer called them, the only practical way of doing it is to encourage the seed fowl first. Birds tend to feel safe and comfortable where there are other birds, and seed-eating birds at a bird feeder will decoy other kinds of birds into a garden.

A bird bath will also bring birds into the garden, give the garden some character, and provide some mild amusement for the gardener. So will bird houses, although I've never set one out myself since, in this area, it would almost surely be occupied by a family of sparrows, seed-eaters that I don't particularly want to encourage.

If you do decide to install a feeder or a bath, it's important to keep them well-stocked at all times so long as there are birds around. The birds which use them will soon come to depend on them for food or water and may starve if they find them empty and no other food or water is available to them. This is particularly true in the fall and winter months when the presence of food in a feeder may actually keep some birds from migrating south where a supply of food would be available to them independent of the whims of man.

Slugs & Snails

Here is where I climb humbly down off my ecological high horse and own sadly up to the fact that I poison slugs and snails, of which I have far more than my fair share, in the most derelict and commercial way—with metaldehyde. To date, no specific ecological horrors relating to the use of metaldehyde have reached my ears, but since I'm hooked on the stuff, I may not have been keeping my ears as open as I might have.

Whatever the case, I'm fully aware that using metaldehyde is contrary to the spirit, if not necessarily the principles, of organic gardening. In my own defense, frail as it may be, I must add here that I only bait for snails and slugs when I reach my wit's end and all other methods have failed me, when the destruction these beasts are wreaking becomes so horrendous that I lose my perspective on things. Unfortunately, this happens much too often, as you might suspect, given the phenomenal amount of damage one lone snail can do in one night.

Metaldehyde aside, the most effective action against snails is the Midnight Snail Hunt. You wait until late in the evening—a wet one when the temperature is between fifty and sixty degrees is best—and stalk through your garden, flashlight in hand. In a way, this can be fun, a Transylvanian Easter Egg Hunt, of sorts.

When you find one of the offending monsters, you either crush it underfoot or, if you're squeamish, deposit it gingerly into a coffee can or a plastic bag which can later be tossed into the garbage. Snails quickly find their way out of paper bags, untied plastic bags, and unsealed cans right back into the garden. Stepping on them is the best and easiest solution, and doing so returns to the garden, in a totally different form of course, all the goodies they've taken out of it.

To those who think that the snail has every bit as much right to the garden as the gardener, I'll have to say, "Nonsense!" Snails were introduced to this country, to San Jose, California, by an immigrating Frenchman who fancied them as food. It appears that he was tasteless as well as brainless, since he imported a variety that no self-respecting gourmet would touch, the kind the peasants eat, in other words. Perhaps we should be grateful for this gustatory *faux pas*, since the gourmet variety of snail grows considerably larger than its country cousin and, I suspect, can put away a lot more greenery in so growing.

I conjecture that, if the snail problem were to be handled in the most ecologically pure manner, it would mean collecting the culprits, packaging them humanely, and sending them back to their homeland, a solution which would soon prove impractical, prohibitively expensive, and one which the French government might come to view with alarm, considering the spectacular success of our friend from San Jose. We could, of course, learn to eat them ourselves.

In truth, if snails constituted the entire problem, it could readily be kept under control by occasional midnight hunts. Slugs present the real difficulty. They're generally smaller than snails, except of course for banana slugs which, like one I recently found, can reach ten or more inches. There are a lot more of them, too, it seems. They're harder to spot, and they're much more unpleasant to handle. Slugs also don't appear to be attracted to the usual brands of snail pellets, which only seem to kill them if they accidentally happen to crawl over one.

Because of this, I've given up using pellets entirely and turned to Corry's Slug and Snail Death. Corry's is considerably more expensive than its competitors, but it lasts much longer, and it does seem to draw slugs to it. And, no, I don't have any connection at all with Corry and Company. This isn't even a solicited testimonial, just an ordinary one.

For those wishing to avoid metaldehyde and other poisons entirely, there are a few other methods of combatting slugs and snails which are worth mentioning here. A mulch of sand will retard their wanderings and keep them out of places where you don't want them to go. Slugs and snails find sand undesirable and difficult, if not totally impossible to negotiate, but it won't, of course, kill them.

A mulch of wood ash will do even more than sand, if it's kept dry. Wood ash is a desiccant, and prolonged exposure to it will dry out a slug or snail enough to kill it. Salt, of course, will do the same thing much more quickly, but it will also kill any plant which comes into contact with too much of it.

A lot of people, I understand, have lately been setting out pie tins filled with stale beer into which snails and slugs are supposed to crawl, get drunk, and die. I can't imagine anything uglier than a garden bespotted with such contraptions, and if it ever comes down to pie tins and beer, I'll opt for snails and slugs.

I also have some doubts about the ecological merit of this practice. Beer with its content of alcohol, a poison of sorts for man and beast, is a poison totally for plants, something you might remember the next time you pour your drink demurely into someone else's potted palm or invite a tempting virgin into your conservatory and start plying her—or him—with champagne.

It would be interesting, I think, if someone who was scientifically inclined did a study on the comparative merits of metaldehyde and alcohol in the killing of snails and slugs. It might just turn out that metaldehyde did less ecological damage than the equivalent amount of stale beer, and then again it might not.

The slug and snail problem can't ever be solved entirely. It can only be handled. Even if you succeed in getting rid of every last slug and snail in your garden, others from your neighbors' gardens will soon find their way in to take their places. God bless the little man from San Jose.

The Newspaper Trick

If some of your tender young plants start dying or disappearing overnight and you've ruled out slugs and snails as the probable cause, take an old newspaper, dampen it, roll it into a fairly tight cone or cylinder, and leave it on the ground near the battle field. In the morning, unwrap the newspaper carefully and see what's inside. Among other things, you may find earwigs, nasty looking, elongated, beetle-like creatures equipped with a formidable set of pinchers at the rear.

To get rid of earwigs, you simply repeat the newspaper trick every night until, hopefully, one morning your newspaper will be empty. Periodic checks with the newspaper will keep you informed about further developments on the earwig front. The newspapers should be burned or otherwise disposed of so that the earwigs don't find their way back into the garden.

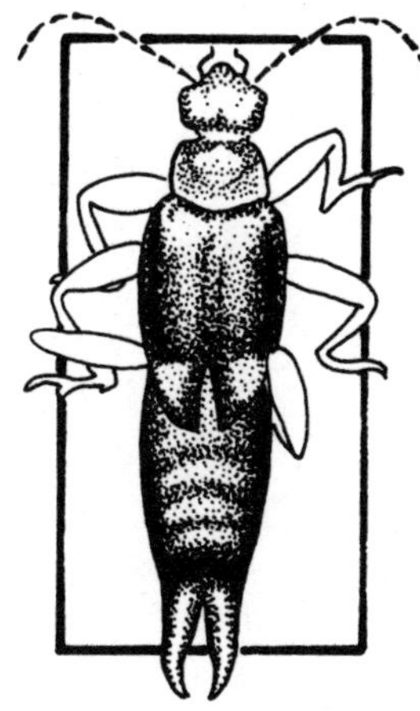
Earwig

Night Inspections

Besides earwigs, snails, and slugs, a great many other garden pests feed mainly at night. If you find that something is eating your plants but you can't discover what it is, make a sojourn into the garden late in the evening with a flashlight and take a look. You'll probably solve the mystery then and there, and once you've solved it, the solution to it may be relatively easy. There's nothing harder to fight than an anonymous enemy.

Scavengers

Back in the days of Douglas Moon, Child Gardener, I'm sure I remember that some slug and snail baits also proclaimed that they were equally effective against sow bugs, those little grey creatures that look as much like armadillos as they do pigs and which we sometimes called rolly-pollies because, when touched, they would curl themselves up into a protective little ball.

For years, I thought of sow bugs as enemies and killed them every time I had a chance. Since I've had my present garden, however, and taken to prowling it at night with a flashlight, I've come to doubt very strongly that these creatures are enemies at all. In fact, I'm now quite sure that they're just the opposite.

My garden is loaded with sow bugs, but I've never in the course of a night prowl seen one of them feeding on a living plant. Instead, they're always crowded around and busily at work on some dead vegetable matter. This leads me to suspect that sow bugs are, in fact, scavengers and that their function in the natural cycle is to return dead vegetable matter quickly to the soil so that it will again be ready for use by living plants. Sow bugs are, in other words, living compost machines.

The same seems to be true of the thousands of millipedes I find. Their feeding habits appear to be identical to those of the sow bug, and both kinds of creature—necessary and desirable as they seem to be—are, I'm sure, just as susceptible to pesticides as the real pests those chemicals are directed at.

All this goes to show, I suppose, how little one should take on faith. It also helps to demonstrate that insecticides are really nothing but cosmetics of the worst kind, cosmetics which might make a pretty face for a time but which do so at the expense of a healthy body, and no face on an unhealthy body can be pretty for very long.

There also doesn't seem to be a shred of evidence that snail bait has any effect at all on sow bugs, and this in spite of the rash claims of those fools from my youth.

The Garden Hose

One of the most successful and certainly most organic tools for fighting pests is the garden hose, especially one equipped with an adjustable spray nozzle. Many small insects and some larger ones can be knocked off plants and killed or severely incapacitated by a good strong blast of water.

For more delicate plants which can't stand up against that kind of blast, the type of nozzle I'm talking about also has a fine spray adjustment which is forceable enough to knock pests off but mild enough not to tear the plant to shreds in the process.

Some "Safe" Sprays

Rotenone and pyrethrum are by reputation organically safe pesticides. I've had no occasion to use either of them myself, since except for snails and slugs, I have my insect problem under satisfactory control, and for that reason, I can't recommend them. Before using them, however, I would first like to know what, if any, effect they have on such microscopic organisms as those beneficial soil bacteria which take nitrogen out of the air and put it into the soil, but that's a job for the laboratory, not the garden.

Homemade sprays can be concocted in the blender from weeds and other plants, like onions and garlic, which insects normally leave alone. Sprays of this kind don't actually kill insects, however. They lie to them, convincing them that a plant they normally dote on is really something they wouldn't touch with the insect equivalent of a ten foot pole.

To make such a spray, place the undelectable plant or weed along with some water into the blender and blend. Strain the mixture through cheese cloth and apply it to the plants with a hand sprayer. The kind of sprayer that attaches to the hose will dilute the mixture way beyond its ability to have any effect.

Planting Against Pests

An onion growing at the base of a rose bush will go a long way toward warding aphids off the roses, and a border of marigolds around a vegetable garden will keep off a number of pests including, I've heard, rabbits.

If you don't want onions in your rose garden, you might take a look around your garden and see what other plants you have that don't have insect problems and use those instead.

It's conceivable, if not really practical, that a garden could be arranged in such a way that most insects would find it an altogether unattractive experience and move on to happier hunting grounds in someone else's garden.

I imagine that a lot of lore of this kind has found its way into the grave with the people who knew it but couldn't pass it on to their children because their children were convinced that modern science had found all the proper solutions and that what granddad knew or thought he knew was so much myth and superstition.

At this point, I'll leave this subject to the folklorists and anyone who's got the time and energy to do some innocent experimentation along these lines.

Some Bigger Predators

Because of my slug and snail problem, I've sometimes thought about acquiring a duck. Ducks love snails, slugs, grasshoppers, worms, and a multitude of other pests, but I'm not sure that I could love a duck. They're noisy, messy, surely in violation of some local city ordinance against live stock, and I'm certain I've seen them nibbling away at tender plant growth when they're tired of snails or just too bored to look for more.

Our cat, I'm also convinced, wouldn't go for a duck at all, except to eat a small one, and for her part, she does in enough grasshoppers, cicadas, moths, and mice to earn her keep, some respect, and the peace of mind an adult duck would surely ruin.

Another great lover of snails, slugs, lawn moth grubs, and the like is the racoon, an attractive denizen of the forest that I used to love abstractly from a distance, what with its quaint habit of washing its food before it eats, its appealing little opposable thumbs and, as it turns out, its rather impressive mental capacity and remarkable adaptability. Why, they're just like people, as Aunt Gladys used to be fond of saying. Yes, indeed, they are, and I think we'd better keep an eye on them for that very reason.

Racoons, which used to confine themselves to the forested parks over the hills from our house, have decided that they can cohabit nicely with man in a residential urban environment and have moved in with us, feeding on our garbage, the fruit of our trees, the vegetables from our vegetable gardens, and on those snails, slugs, and grubs they can find among our shrubs and flowers and in our lawns.

The trouble with the racoons is that they don't really care what they do to a garden to get what they want out of it. I've awoken many a morning to find my lawn a field of sizable divots and my plants rolled over, squashed, and broken where two racoons apparently decided that they wanted exactly the same snail at the same time.

In desperation, I was finally reduced to purchasing a harmless trap in hopes of returning a few of these soon unwelcome guests to the parks, where I know in my heart they'd be happier. Somehow they managed to remove the bait from the trap without bothering to spring it. In retaliation, I wired the bait, fresh chicken parts, to the trap. They retaliated by going to work on my lawn again and ignoring the chicken altogether, leaving it to the neighborhood cats, some few of whom I found ensnared in the morning, unhurt, of course, but not a little distressed and embarrassed.

For the moment, I've abandoned the trap, mostly because the racoons have, for the moment, abandoned my garden. I have no idea why, but I suspect it might have something to do with their seeing and appreciating the significance of the cats I've trapped.

(Since this writing, the racoons have returned to my garden in ever increasing numbers, all of whom have studiously avoided my trap and my intentions of returning them to some distant and more natural environment. In their pre-dawn quest for food, they've climbed some of my young trees and broken down the branches. They've removed plants and rocks from my retaining walls, and they've smashed other plants completely to the ground. They also seem to have eaten virtually every slug and snail my garden contained and thereby reduced a once horrendous pest problem to nothing.

I can now see where in gardens less delicate and precise than mine a racoon or two might be a real asset, but I hesitate to recommend acquiring one as a pet, since a pet racoon would almost certainly come to prefer the food his master would provide to that which he could scrounge for himself in the garden.)

Conclusion

The totally pest-free garden that some gardeners once envisioned and were encouraged to try to create by the vendors of pesticides is, we now know, both impossible and undesirable. Man can't pick what he likes from nature and kill off what he doesn't. The whole package, man included, comes all wrapped together, each part dependent on all the others, and no part, even the miserable mosquito, I'd be willing to bet, dispensible.

The only real cure for the pest problem is, I suppose, some form of Buddhism, an acceptance of the right of all living creatures to continue to live and, when conflicts arise, letting the principals fight it out between themselves without interference from man.

Many of us, myself included, aren't quite ready to take that step into Buddhism, but by learning to handle our pests in a natural way, I have little doubt that we are taking a step in the right direction. A little effort, some attention, the willingness to experiment and to sustain a few losses can go a long way toward achieving a garden where there are some pests but not enough to create serious problems.

In vegetable gardening, the competition between man and bug is fiercer, because we're competing for food, but in ornamental gardening, the kind of gardening this book is primarily addressed to, we have greater leeway. If you are bothered by pests and don't like killing them or the means used to kill them, build your garden with plants that aren't bothered by pests or are hardy enough to support a few without showing the damage.

Your nurseryman, again, can be of great assistance here, so before you acquire a plant, ask him what's going to attack it and what kind of damage the plant will sustain from the attack. Then decide whether you want the plant or not.

13 WEEDING

Weeds

Someone once said that a weed was just a flower for which no one had yet found a use. Weeds have other characteristics beside uselessness, and viewed another way, they're not only useless, they're harmful.

Weeds take nutrients out of the soil which would otherwise go to feed those plants that you're actively trying to grow. If weeds are allowed to grow large and numerous enough, they can easily crowd out and even strangle to death their more desirable cousins. And sometimes, of course, weeds are just plain ugly.

Another characteristic of weeds is that they have virtually no enemies—except the gardener himself. Snails, aphids, and all the rest of the horde of garden pests pass them right by. If they didn't, we might be able to view the snail and the aphid in a slightly more favorable light.

Weeds are also notoriously unparticular about soil conditions, light, water, and the like. I've never tried killing them with kindness, but it's a thought.

Weeds also produce flowers and seeds in great profusion and much more quickly than most of their respectable competition. Weeds are, in other words, geared by nature and circumstance to survive under the most adverse conditions. I once heard a story from a reputable source about a weed seed that sprouted after fifty years, a remarkable feat, considering that many seeds lose their fertility after only a year.

The weed problem, like the pest problem, isn't totally soluble either. Some weed seeds, the dandelion's, for example, are borne by the wind, so even if you get rid of all your dandelions, seeds from other dandelions can, under the right wind conditions, find their way into your garden from as far away as a mile or more, and your neighbor's dandelion seeds don't have to wait for the right wind conditions. A slight gust will do the trick.

Some weed seeds are carried in and dropped by birds, and you yourself, if you're not careful, might bring in a new species of weed along with a new plant or even on the cuffs of your jeans.

Still, with a little effort and some vigilance, you can reduce your weed problem to relative insignificance. I inherited my present garden in a pretty run-down condition. In many parts of it, the weeds had been having a field day for five to ten years. In two years, I had the problem down to normal proportions, and four years later, I seem to have succeeded in eradicating some species altogether and have the rest under such tight control that I no longer devote any gardening time specifically to that odious task called weeding.

Weeding

Probably the most discouraging thing about weeding is that you can spend an entire back-breaking day digging weeds out of the ground, leave the area beautifully weed-free, and return again in a week or so and find the whole place as thickly populated with weeds, albeit young ones, as it was before you started.

Unfortunately, that's something you should learn to expect—at least for awhile. Any area that has long been left to the weeds is going to be teeming with invisible weed seeds that are just waiting for the bigger competition to be removed so they can have their day. There are ways, however, of making their day relatively unsuccessful. One of these ways is mulching.

Mulching

A two or three inch mulch of compost, leaf mold, peat moss or ground bark over a freshly weeded area will keep many weeds from sprouting, and of those that do sprout, only a few will ever see the light of day. Those few that do make it up through the mulch will arrive in a weakened state and can easily be spotted and removed.

If you don't happen to have any mulch handy, you can simply leave the weeds you've just pulled on top of the soil. This weed mulch isn't as attractive as some, but it will be just as effective. Many of the seeds contained in the weed mulch will sprout away from the protection and nurture of the soil if you wet the mulch down from time to time. Because of those seeds which will remain unsprouted in the mulch, however, I would recommend removing the mulch to the compost pile rather than digging it in when planting time comes so you don't run the risk of adding unnecessarily to your weed problem. The heat of the compost pile will kill many of the seeds which haven't yet sprouted.

Plastic Mulch

A clear plastic drop cloth, or portions of one, can be used in place of an organic mulch to discourage and kill young weeds. After you've weeded, dampen the ground before you lay the plastic down to insure that there will be enough moisture underneath to sprout the weeds. The plastic tarp will have a greenhouse effect in forcing the seeds to sprout, but after they've sprouted, the heat contained in the small air spaces between the tarp and the ground will cook and kill the young weeds.

Hoes & Cultivators

A small hoe or cultivator is also a very effective tool against young weeds, when any disruption of the soil around their roots will almost surely kill them. Hoes and cultivators are somewhat less effective against more mature weeds because their root systems are considerably larger and more complex. In some cases, using a hoe or cultivator may actually compound your weed problems, since they may cut the roots into small pieces from each of which new weeds may sprout.

When & How to Weed

The best time to weed is when the soil is damp. If the soil is very dry or very wet, it's more difficult to extract all of the weed's root system, and it's often necessary to get the root system in order to get the weed.

In weeding a large area, I've found a pitch fork to be the most effective tool. A pitch fork is less apt than a shovel to pack the soil, and the tines are helpful in breaking up the dirt clods so that the weed can be removed nearly in tact.

A large part of my garden, when I first acquired it, was overrun with a thornless variety of berry, the roots of which ran down to a depth of two feet. Since any piece of those roots, if left in the ground, would soon have produced a new plant, I would have been at a serious disadvantage in going after those berries if I hadn't had a pitch fork.

For smaller weeding jobs, a hand trowel is probably the most effective tool. You simply insert the trowel up to its handle an inch or two from the base of the weed, bend the handle back, and the weed pops up, hopefully with its roots and all.

Resting

The longer you can leave a freshly weeded area unplanted, the easier it will be to control the growth of new weeds for the simple reason that weeding around plants is an especially delicate, tedious, and time-consuming task.

Because of this, if you're thinking about planting a certain area with flowers in the spring, prepare the bed the previous fall and leave it fallow. Many of the weed seeds will sprout and can easily and quickly be removed before it's time to put the flowers in. During this rest period, you can also make effective use of organic or plastic mulches to kill weeds, something that it will be much harder to do once the bed is planted.

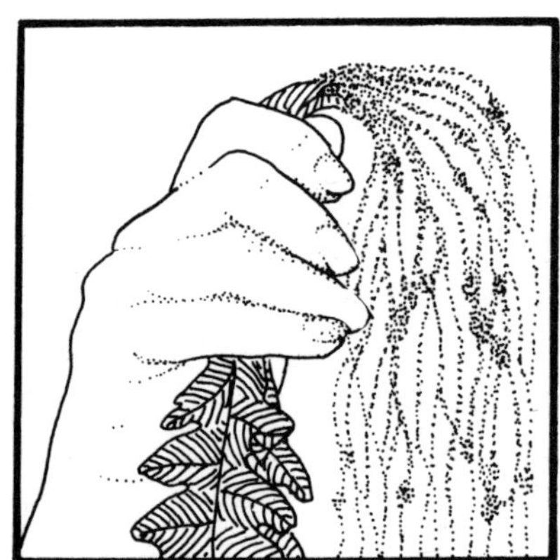

Maintenance

So far we've talked mostly about serious weed problems and how to handle them. Once the serious problems are under control, the rest will be fairly easy. Any time you spot a new weed, bend over and pull it out right then and there, even if it means leaving the pulled weed laying on the ground. Don't wait for that Saturday sometime in the future when you're going to take care of all the weeds at once. The weed you pull today won't produce five hundred more tomorrow, but the weed you leave in the ground until you're better dressed for weed pulling may.

Getting to Know Your Weeds

I've heard some amateur weeders, especially unwilling ones, complain that they can't tell the difference between the weeds and the flowers. The most important thing about these people, after you've found out whether or not they're telling the truth, is not to employ them to pull weeds. If you have the same problem yourself, or think you do, a little time and some observation should soon clear the matter up for you.

Most gardens of the kind we're talking about probably won't have more than about ten different kinds of weeds, and those ten will soon become recognizable to anyone who pays even the slightest attention to them. It might even be interesting and profitable for you to make a survey of your weeds. Some day, when you have a little extra time, collect one of every kind of weed you have, study them, familiarize yourself with them, and then introduce them to anyone else in the family whose responsibility it is to keep them under control. Weeds are, in many ways, just as interesting as more respectable plants, and getting to know them and their habits makes it considerably easier and very definitely more interesting to handle them.

I have one particular weed, the name of which I don't know but should find out, which has turned out to be the most active of my ten weeds. It pops up everywhere and with great regularity, and at first I had a hard time spotting it, especially in a concentrated mass of greenery.

This particular weed has a soft look uncommon to most weeds, and its color is somehow wrong, too healthy and bright a green, perhaps. Now, however, because I'm used to it, I can spot a new one out of the corner of my eye at twenty feet after sunset, a feat which might lead me into a chapter on the phenomenology of gardening, but which won't because I have vague plans of some day finishing this book.

Is It Really a Weed?

Some day and somewhat reluctantly, you'll have the dubious pleasure of showing your garden to a friend whom you happen to believe knows a great deal more about gardening than you do. Suddenly, this friend will ask you why you're letting all those weeds grow over there, and you'll wince and try to explain that you didn't know they were weeds, that they came with the garden, and that you kind of like them. And you'll promise yourself and your friend that you'll get rid of them the next day.

Don't. Not unless you really don't like them. What may be a weed to your friend may not be a weed to you, and if it isn't a weed to you, it simply isn't a weed. A weed is something that you don't want in your garden, something that's in the way, something that's useless, harmful, ugly or too aggressive. If it isn't any of these things, it isn't a weed, and well-meaning friends be damned.

Chemical Weed Killers

I have plenty to say about chemical as opposed to human weed killers, things that would burn the ears off those who survived the chapter on pesticides. Suffice it to say that no chemical can ever with any amount of practice learn to distinguish between a weed and a flower. To chemicals, they're all weeds. Suffice it also to say that many of the available products of this type were developed as weapons of war against the garden that once was Viet Nam, and suffice it finally to say that most of these products are produced by those same oil companies who have done so much to besmog and pave over the gardens of America. Poop on weed killers.

14 COMPOST AND MULCH

Compost

Until very recently, most composting was done only by your grandfather and other quaint, old-fashioned people. Your father, if he thought about composting at all, probably pooh-poohed the idea. It was too messy, inconvenient, and a waste of time. It was also a lot easier to set out the lawn clippings, prunings, and dead leaves for the trashman to cart off to the dump.

At the same time, your father was probably laughing at the blind ignorance of the Oklahoma dust bowl farmers who farmed their once rich prairie literally into the sky. He shouldn't have laughed. He was himself stripping his land of its organic matter, depleting his soil, and sending it on its way to becoming a wasteland which would eventually support little or no plant life. If what he was doing was less noticeable than what happened in Oklahoma, it was only because it was happening more slowly.

Things now are beginning to move in the other direction, and we're beginning to realize that granddad wasn't so much quaint as he was wise. It's dawned on us again that if we harvest a carrot, the value of the soil we harvested it from is decreased one carrot's worth and that if we want to maintain the original value of the soil, we're going to have to put that carrot back into the soil in one way or another.

Returning the carrot—or the plucked rose or the faded annual—to the soil can be done in a couple of ways, the most common of which has been to purchase organic matter from the local nursery and dig it in, organic matter in the form of—and this must be starting to sound like a litany by now—leaf mold, peat moss, ground bark, and steer manure.

Organic matter acquired in these ways has the advantage of being neatly packaged, reasonably unrepugnant to the squeamish, and ready for immediate use. It has the disadvantage of being expensive and, if purchased in large quantities, of turning the hapless gardener temporarily into a stevedore.

The second method is, as you may already have guessed, making and using your own compost. Composting, and we may as well face it from the start, isn't the most attractive or enjoyable aspect of gardening. It's messy, your father was right. It does take time as well as some space, and it can be smelly, very smelly indeed.

Still, composting is just as much a part of the whole gardening experience as planting seeds or picking roses, and I personally find a handful of my own sweet-smelling compost as rewarding a prospect as the reddest, fullest rose or a freshly picked, garden-ripe tomato, but I'm a gardener and gardeners are weird.

Making your own compost is also cheap, often to the point of being free, and it can even save you money. You won't be laying out quite so much money at the nursery on the one hand, and on the other, you won't have to pay the trashman for hauling your prunings and clippings to the dump anymore.

The Compost Pile

The simplest way to compost is to dump all your fresh organic matter in a heap and leave it there to rot. This is also the least sightly way and the way that takes the longest. You can speed up the process of decomposition by keeping the pile moist, by turning it frequently with a pitch fork, and by covering it with a black plastic tarp.

The tarp aids decomposition by absorbing heat from the sun and by retaining moisture in the pile, and it will also help to keep flies away, which makes the pile more endurable and less of a neighborhood liability.

When one pile has reached a convenient size, a second pile should be started to allow the first one to break down completely. Any pieces in the first pile which fail to break down can be screened out and added to the second pile, and so forth into a third pile.

You can make a compost screen by knocking the bottom out of a wooden box and replacing it with one inch wire mesh or by attaching the wire mesh to a framework made from scrap lumber. Old two-by-fours would be more than adequate for this purpose. You can, of course, change the grade of the compost by either increasing or decreasing the size of the wire mesh.

The Compost Pit

The compost pit is a hole in the ground approximately a foot deep and two by four feet square, depending, naturally, on the needs of the individual gardener. Because the compost in a pit is kept at near ground level, it's easier to keep moist and will therefore decompose a little faster. The pit is more sightly than a pile if only because it's harder to see, and like the pile, the pit can be covered with a plastic tarp to absorb heat, retain moisture, and retard flies.

Rather than digging a new pit when the old one is full, the usual practice is to add fresh organic matter only at one end and gradually work the material down until it's ready for garden use at the other. To make a compost pit practicable, you have to have one large enough to meet your needs exactly or it will soon become a pile and have to be treated like one.

Plastic Bags

Perhaps neither the compost pile nor the pit is ideal for a garden the size of the one this book is addressed to. Both require considerable space, space which you might prefer to grow things in, and both run the risk of offending neighbors, who might decide to take their complaints about flies and the smell of rotting garbage off to the authorities.

To escape these possible urban consequences of trying to be a more natural man, I have turned for help to a very unnatural product, the plastic bag. I use two kinds, the large ones available from the supermarket for lining garbage cans and the smaller ones that steer manure is sold in.

I prefer the steer manure bags because they're much tougher, because they last indefinitely, and because they come free along with the steer manure. Into these bags, I put any relatively soft organic material such as tender prunings, weeds, dead leaves, and departed annuals. When the bags are jammed full, I moisten the contents, tie the ends, and put the bags in some out of the way corner of the garage, basement, or garden.

In six months or less, depending largely on the temperature and time of year, the contents of the bags will have broken down fairly well, but often only fairly well. The smaller the plastic bag, the more apt its contents are to turn into a wet, gooey, smelly mess rather than into dark, crumbly, sweet-smelling compost.

If and when this happens, the gooey mess, which will have become less than a quarter of its original size, should be dumped somewhere inconspicuous in the garden, hosed down to help kill the smell, and possibly covered with plastic. In a very short time, nature will finish the decomposition, and you'll have your dark, crumbly, sweet-smelling compost.

The Garden Cycle

If all the debris from your garden is returned to your soil in one of these three ways, pile, pit, or plastic bag, the organic value of your soil will remain constant. If, however, you're doing any vegetable gardening or bringing flowers into the house which find their way into the trash or if you're removing large and virtually uncompostable trees and shrubs, the organic value of your soil will decrease accordingly.

To offset this loss, you can bring in additional organic matter from the nursery. You can also make good use of a number of different kinds of table and kitchen scraps, saving them in a convenient container and adding them to your compost pit, pile, or bags when the container gets full.

I've been surprised from time to time when people asked what the large jar on the kitchen sink was for and, if they helped in the kitchen, what could and what couldn't be added to it, so I suppose it might be worthwhile to go into some detail in that regard for others who might have doubts.

You can add to the compost:

1. Anything or any part of anything that's ever grown in the ground or out of it: Carrot tops, potato peelings, rotten tomatoes, apple cores, and so forth.
2. Egg shells.
3. *No* fats, oils, grease, or anything that's been cooked in or contains them.
4. *No* meat or cheese scraps. These will breed a horde of flies and in other ways sharply increase the odds of breeding diseases, human diseases.
5. Nothing that contains salt or has come into contact with salt in cooking. Ordinary peanut shells are fine, but salted ones are not. Salt is a plant poison.
6. Clean bones, but remember, however rich they may be in desirable phosphorus, they're extremely durable and you'll be finding them again and again on the wrong side of your compost screen.
7. Unfiltered cigarette butts, ashes, wooden and paper matches, and used wooden toothpicks.

Trees & Shrubs

Tremendous amounts of valuable organic matter can be removed from the garden in the form of sizable prunings, parts of trees and shrubs, and even whole ones. For a couple of years, in order to prevent this loss, I studiously cut up what debris I had of this kind with pruning shears and even spent hours working over the larger branches with a hatchet.

I cut and swore, chopped and moaned, and cut and swore some more. No job, save one in an assembly line, could possibly have been more tedious, and none of my other gardening chores was nearly as time consuming.

I was reaching the dangerous point of not pruning when pruning needed to be done and of swallowing my principles and calling in the trashman. It was about this time that composters came on the market at prices I couldn't possibly afford, and I was one of the first to buy one. I've never been sorry.

Composters

At this writing, most composters sell for somewhere around two-hundred dollars, and I doubt that they will decrease much in price even if they achieve the popularity I think they deserve. If you decide to get one, it will probably be the single biggest investment you ever make in your garden, unless you've got a deluxe power mower, and only you can decide whether such an investment will be worth it to you in the long run.

To me, it's been worth it already, certainly in terms of the hours I've saved chopping up branches, branches which, if put through the composter twice, produce an esthetically pleasing, immediately usable mulch, one which can be applied directly to the ground without putting me to the trouble of having to decompose it first.

In time, your composter will pay for itself in terms of the real dollars that would otherwise have gone to the trashman to cart off your debris. I calculate a total of four years of thirty gallons of debris a week, which is about normal for a lot the size of mine, before the composter pays for itself.

In this figure, however, I haven't included the value of the compost itself or the money you will have saved in the meantime on organic matter at the nursery. I also haven't included the cost of the gas and oil it takes to run the composter, but that cost is fairly negligible, since the composter will run for hours on a gallon of gas, and the oil, one and three-quarters quarts, need only be changed every twenty-five hours.

Shredders

Composters come in two general types, shredders and grinders. Mine is a shredder, the six-horsepower Sears model, lest I leave you unnecessarily in the dark. This model consumes anything up to and including a two-inch branch with awe-inspiring speed and viciousness and throws out nothing much larger than a fifty cent piece.

I recently pulverized all but the thickest part of the trunk of a small—and dead—tree in about a quarter of the time it would have taken me to turn that same tree into a bundle that the trashman would have found acceptable enough to deign to cart away.

For a time, I had trouble getting wet or partially decayed matter through the composter, but I solved this problem, at least partially, by feeding the hopper more slowly and by hosing the compost through before it could clog the works. This produced a sort of compost pudding, but the excess water soon drained out, leaving a residue suitable for bagging and storing.

On second thought, I'm not too sure that I can fully endorse the hosing method. The last time I tried it, I burned a big hole in an expensive rubber hose when it accidently came in contact with the composter's muffler, and that's a very poor way to save money.

Besides accepting soggy and decayed matter reluctantly, the shredder type of composter cannot handle dirt, and rocks will damage the blades severely, big ones at least. I've also given up entirely trying to feed the sword-like, highly fibrous leaves of my yucca tree through the composter. When I've done this, I always end up with a tight mass of strings wrapped around a set of immobilized blades, a mess it takes me a good hour to untangle.

If most of the things you'll be composting are dry or freshly cut and if you don't have an abundance of yucca trees, however, the shredder is the ideal composter for you.

The Bagging Attachment

The Sears shredder comes with an optional bagging attachment which is designed to put the compost directly into heavy plastic bags that are suitable for storage. Unfortunately, the sharpness of some of the shreds coupled with the speed at which they exit often tears the bags and soon makes them unusable.

To save on plastic bags, I concocted a bag of identical size out of light-weight cotton. This bag has been able to withstand any and all onslaughts from the composter, and it's no trouble to transfer its contents to a more delicate plastic bag once the shredding is done.

Grinders

The second type of composter is the grinder. The grinder also breaks down organic matter mechanically, but it does so less efficiently, producing pieces larger than those produced by the shredder, pieces which will naturally take longer to finish breaking down organically.

The chief advantage of the grinder is that you can feed soil through it as well as wet and decayed organic material. This comes in handy if you're breaking up hard, compacted earth and if you're adding organic matter to the soil and want it done thoroughly.

For the kind of garden we're talking about here, however, a shredder is probably the better bet, but if you're thinking about turning your entire back yard into a vegetable garden and farming it, you might consider a grinder. The garden-rich and garden-greedy will, of course, have one of each.

A Handy Hint

If you've got a couple of good friends or some respectable neighbors who are interested in gardening or simply have an organic trash problem, you might consider investing in a composter together.

A cooperative composter would dramatically reduce the initial cost to the investors, and no one would be greatly inconvenienced, since the composter isn't a tool that anyone would be using on a daily or even a weekly basis.

Composters are a little on the heavy and bulky side, too, so it might be worth your while to make a quick friend of someone strong who owns a truck.

Some Disadvantages

As you may have already guessed, a composter produces some smog. Taking into account the small size of the motor and the relative infrequency with which you'll be using it, it won't produce much. For those who wish to avoid the smog problem altogether, some makes of composters are available with electric motors.

I learned recently, however, that some commercially sold electricity is now being produced by burning gaseous and liquid hydrocarbons, so the electric motor may not really be the anti-smog alternative it seems to be but merely a matter of producing the smog somewhere else and producing more of it, too, since it will take more gasoline to produce the electricity to run an electric composter than it will gasoline to run the gas model directly.

There's also no escaping the fact that the composter, the gasoline driven one at least, is noisy. Mine sounds pretty much like a motorcycle with a little model airplane motor whine thrown in for character. If you have noise-sensitive neighbors, you might take this unhappy fact into account. So far, my neighbors haven't complained or even commented, but I haven't had the courage to ask them for an unbiased opinion, either.

That composters are dangerous can't be denied, but the full extent of the danger may not become apparent to you until you've actually used one yourself. The mere idea of a hand or a cat, ours in particular, dropping into the hopper turns my spine to glass. Luckily, the cat hates the thing and disappears like magic any time I use it. Hands, mine and yours, are a different matter, unfortunately.

The last problem with composters that leaps to my mind is a bit fantastical but perhaps worth the mention nonetheless. I wouldn't, you understand, want one to fall into the hands of a gadget freak. Composters are, in their own inimitable way, fun to operate, and I can all too easily picture one of our gadget-loving friends standing bashfully beside fifty plastic bags full of compost and pointing sheepishly back at a desert of his own creation.

Using Compost

Glorious compost can be used in exactly the same way and for exactly the same purposes that you would use any organic material you purchase from the nursery, peat moss, leaf mold, ground bark, and the like. If it's sieved finely enough, you can even use it on your lawn as a substitute for steer manure. If it's not sieved finely enough, however, small pieces of undecomposed twigs will get caught in the mower and make mowing an even more dismal task than it already is.

If you're planting a vegetable garden or preparing a flower bed, dig as much compost as you can spare into the soil, and dig it in to a depth of at least nine inches. You can accomplish this task more easily and efficiently with a pitch fork than you can with a shovel.

When you're planting a shrub or a small tree, fill the bottom of the planting hole with compost and work some more of it into the soil that will surround the root ball. This will serve to lighten the soil, making it easier for the roots to grow out away from the ball as well as giving them something to feed on while they're doing it.

Compost also makes a perfect mulch. We've talked some about the various benefits of mulching in scattered parts of this book, and now might be a good time to summarize those points and add anything to them that might have been left out.

Mulching

Mulching is one of the most beneficial things any gardener can do for his garden as well as one of the aspects of gardening, in California at least, that is most often overlooked, ignored, and avoided by gardeners.

Mulching—the application of a layer in varying thicknesses of organic matter to the top of the soil—accomplishes the following things:

1. It holds moisture in the soil, keeps your water bill down, and makes more efficient use of any rain you happen to get.
2. It dramatically retards the growth of weeds and weakens those that do grow.
3. It keeps roots cool and protects shallow roots from damage by the sun and wind.

4. It feeds the roots of shallow rooted plants such as camellias, azaleas, and rhododendrons which will not tolerate having organic matter cultivated into the soil around their roots.

5. It provides protection against frost damage.

6. It's a painless way of returning organic matter to the soil, leaving the spade work to the rain and the normal procedures of gardening.

7. It refuses, unfortunately, to mow your lawn, feeling that it's done quite enough already.

Mulching, although it may sound like a slightly artificial practice, is really in perfect accord with nature's methods. In a natural environment, leaves, branches, dead flowers and so forth fall to the ground and are left there to decay and return to the soil where they will again become part of the growth cycle.

Composting and then mulching with the compost is the gardener's way of imitating nature. The gardener's way has the advantage of speeding up the process, of making it more sightly, and of lessening the chances, through the heat generated in the compost pile, of breeding pests and diseases.

What is truly contrary to nature's way and the natural cycle is cleaning up all the fallen and dead debris and throwing it away like so much dirt vacuumed off a rug. The housekeeping analogy doesn't apply in the garden. The rug doesn't need the dirt, but the garden needs its debris. If it's systematically deprived of it, a garden of diminishing vitality and beauty will be the result.

An Interesting Story

We modern inhabitants of America are really a strange breed of people. No book on gardening should have to contain any discussion at all about the value of organic matter and the desirability, if not the absolute necessity, of keeping it rather than throwing it out with the beer cans and plastic bleach bottles. That's something we should *know*, and we may be the first—and the last—people on earth not to have known it or, having known it, to have forgotten it.

I always sort of knew it. My grandfather, a suburban gardener and a good one, kept a compost pile. I tried to do the same, but my youthful and overly delicate sensibilities were offended by the sight and smell of decay, and I gave up the idea in disgust and joined my father in loading our organic treasure into the weekly trash barrels.

When I acquired a garden of my own six years ago, I started a compost pile almost without thinking about it. I'm not really sure exactly why I did it. Perhaps it was only because I was faced with dismantling and disposing of a jungle, and we were so house poor at the time that disposing of it in the conventional American way, via the trash can, would have put us in another house, the poor house, to be exact. I'd like to think not, that I was, in truth, thinking organically, but I'm not sure.

In any case, the true significance and value of organic matter was brought home to me loud and clear a couple of years ago in a book I was reading on Japan written by an American who spent some time there in the middle of the last century when Japan was still thoroughly Japanese.

Japan has for centuries been poor in organic matter of all kinds. That I knew, but I didn't know just how poor. In discussing Japanese toilet facilities, our compatriot of the 1800's mentions that most Japanese houses were then equipped with indoor toilets under which was a box that could be pulled out from the street and emptied.

This was done on a weekly basis by sewage workers and, as you might expect, it involved an exchange of money, but not, I'm willing to bet, the exchange you would expect. The sewage worker paid the householder for the contents of the box, and not the reverse, and he paid pretty high, too. He paid enough so that five students living in the same room could pay all their rent with what they got from him.

How disgusting, comes the chorus of voices from those of us who flush for everything, and what strange, perverse people the nineteenth century Japanese must have been. Not so, say I. In a way, they were more civilized than they are now and certainly a great deal more efficient.

You see, the sewage worker, in turn, sold the sewage to the farmer, the farmer turned it back into food and sold the food to the students, who ate it and sold it back to the sewage collector. A perfect organic cycle, an endless chain without waste.

I doubt very much that in this cycle there was any real concept of waste or any real distaste for any of the products along the chain. This hypothesis of mine gets some support from the fact that the Japanese have no dirty words as we know them and no imprecations, in the last century at least, based on natural functions and products.

Since the supply of organic matter anywhere is by no means infinite, we might do well to keep our hands on our own grass clippings, especially if we're really attached to the pleasures of the flush toilet, an organically unsound device at best—unless, of course, they get busy at the other end, and in some places they already have.

In San Francisco, I understand, reclaimed sewage is available for use in the garden. This leads me to a story about the wonderful ability of tomato seeds to survive almost any amount of processing, the details of which I'll leave to your imagination.

Footnote

The book on Japan that I've been talking about is by Edward S. Morse and is called *Japanese Homes and Their Surroundings*. It's available in paperback, at the time of this writing, from Dover Press. I recommend it highly to anyone interested in houses, gardens, carpentry, tools, art, Japan, nineteenth century America and to anyone who, like me, dotes on unselfconscious charm. In his own way, Mr. Morse belongs with Sir Thomas Browne and Samuel Pepys.

Mr. Morse trying to convince his Victorian readers that there's really nothing indecent about Japanese communal bathing is alone worth the price of the book.

15 PRUNING

Pruning

Pruning is held by the uninitiated to be one of the great mysteries of gardening. It isn't a mystery, and it isn't mysterious. It's difficult primarily in that it often involves art—and that's art in the strictest sense of the term, the shaping and modeling of forms, in the case of pruning, the sculpting of plants.

If you're not artistically inclined, if you don't have much faith in your artistic ability, or if you don't think you know how plants ought to look, the solution to your pruning difficulties is to prune slowly, very slowly, stepping back from your creation after every cut, appraising and examining your work from all sides before making another cut, and then repeating the process until you're satisfied with the appearance of your creation.

The Cardinal Reason

The cardinal reason for pruning is a simple one. *You prune to get rid of something that you don't want to be there.* Your reasons for not wanting something to be there may vary. These are some of the more important ones:

1. The plant is simply too big and you want to make it smaller.
2. The plant is becoming too leggy and you want to make it more compact.
3. The plant is becoming too dense and you want to open it out.
4. The plant is becoming top heavy and you want to restore its balance, to give it some symmetry, and to keep it from breaking at undesirable points.
5. Some of the growth on the plant is weak, unsightly, or dead and you're tired of looking at it.

The Cardinal Misconception

Most people, I suspect, back away from pruning—and sometimes the mere thought of pruning—because they think that plants need to be pruned for their health, like a dog's nails may need to be clipped or a parrot's beak shaved or trimmed.

The plant, they feel, is somehow in desperate need of a surgeon, suffering, as it must be, from some unseeable and unrecognizable form of plant appendicitis, and perhaps even on the very brink of death. They think they could save the plant if only they knew what, when, where, how, and why to make the proper cuts, but they don't.

This attitude is patently and grossly absurd. In only a very few cases can plant pruning be considered medicinal, and of those few cases, only one or two really are medicinal. The others are matters of engineering, and we'll talk about both as we go along.

If you're somewhat relieved by these assurances but still entertaining some doubts, turn back to page 68 and review the ways in which nature prunes. You'll note that all of them are extremely crude, ill-timed, and grandiose. One doesn't get the picture of Nature, the tender mother, carefully meeting each and every little need of each and every one of her little plant babies. Instead, the picture is one of storm, holocaust, and wholesale destruction. Man the gardener, even at his most ignorant and destructive worst, is gentle and harmless by comparison.

Pruning for Size

Most garden pruning consists of keeping plants from getting out of hand, of keeping bigger, hardier specimens from choking out their smaller, weaker neighbors, and of keeping all of them out of the way of man when they start for the sidewalks, the lawn, the patio, or toward the house, where in combination with the wind, they may do structural damage.

Pruning for size is the horticultural equivalent of a haircut, not an appendectomy, and it should be done for the same reasons: when and if the hair gets too long, gets in the way, becomes troublesome, or starts splitting at the ends. Just as some people like their hair long, some people prefer their plants big. Others may prefer short hair and like keeping their plants small and in abeyance. It's largely a matter of personal taste.

Pruning of this kind can be done at any time of year. If something is getting out of hand or beginning to bother you, get rid of it now. There are, of course, times to prune that are better for the plant than others, and we'll talk about why they're better later on, and you can decide whose needs are more important, yours or the plant's. In the meantime, keep in mind that your chances of killing or even seriously damaging a plant by pruning it at the "wrong" time are almost nil. Plants are tough, and even the delicate orchid, in its natural environment, is a critter to be reckoned with.

After You've Pruned for Size

Once you've pruned out what was in the way or what was too big, you should focus your attention on the plant itself. Getting rid of parts of a plant will almost certainly throw the whole out of balance, and some additional cuts will be necessary to restore the plant to some kind of symmetry.

For six months or so after a major trimming, keep an eye on the plant. Your recent pruning efforts will have a decided effect on the general growth thrust of the plant, and a few more cuts may be necessary from time to time to make sure that the thrust is headed in the direction you want it to go.

Pruning for Compactness

In time, some plants may become leggy or rangy. Some branches may have grown too much while others have lagged behind, and the plant will have come to resemble nothing so much as a gangly and awkward teenager. With animals, a few additional years will correct this condition. With plants, they will only exaggerate it.

To correct legginess, get a general picture in your mind of the profile you'd like the plant to have, and by this I mean a loose circle that will encompass the outermost dimensions of the plant as you want it to be. Remove all those parts of the plant that reach beyond your hypothetical circle and all those inside it down to within two-thirds or less of the center. I'm not, of course, suggesting a perfect circle unless what you're after is a perfectly spherical plant.

In most cases, a plant that has been pruned will put out two smaller branches from the leaf buds just below the cut and possibly more from the leaf buds just further down, eventually creating a denser, fuller whole. For greater density and fullness, you simply repeat this operation again after the new growth has established itself until you get exactly the effect you want. If performing this task makes you nervous, take it slowly, starting with a bigger circle than the one you eventually plan to end up with.

An extreme example of pruning for compactness is the clipped, formal hedge, where the final shape is in reality a geometric surface, usually, but not always, a plane. In creating a formal hedge, the gardener always keeps the exterior outlines firmly in mind and prunes, or clips, accordingly.

To create a formal hedge, the gardener first clips deep within the final outline, and he does so in order to build up a network of under branches which will be able to support the desired structure when the hedge is mature. The hedge is then gradually allowed to reach its final proportions and, when it does, it's kept to them with weekly trimmings during the growing season. When the exterior becomes woody, as it may in time, the hedge is pruned back severely and allowed to grow out again.

Not all plants lend themselves to such formal definitions, but many do, among them the privet, boxwood, pyracantha, as well as and surprisingly enough, the Monterrey cypress, California redwood, and to a certain extent, the lemon, although these latter two lend themselves better to slightly less formal structures.

Some perennials also benefit from this kind of pruning, and with chrysanthemums, for example, it's really a necessity. Mums virtually disappear into the ground every winter. In the spring, they begin to shoot up again, and if they're left alone, they will be so spindly when they bloom in the fall that the weight of the flowers will topple them to the ground, and you'll be faced with the tedious task of staking and tieing them.

To prevent this from happening, pinch out the centers of the stems from the time the mums are six inches high until late in the summer when the buds begin to form. Some staking may still be necessary, but if the plant is large enough, the density you will have created within it should be great enough to support the plant without staking it. Pinching in this way will also greatly increase the number of flowers the plant will produce.

Pruning for Openness

Openness is the opposite of compactness, and plants are opened out, made less dense, for a variety of reasons. One of these is purely artistic. It may occur to you that a particular plant has an attractive network of trunks, branches, and stems and that the appearance of the plant could be improved if parts of that network were made more visible.

Another reason for opening out a tree or shrub is to let in light. You may want more sunlight to filter through a tree to those plants growing below it or to the side of it, or you may want more light to reach into the tree itself, either to encourage the production of fruit within the tree or to improve the interior health and vigor of a tree which has become dead and unattractive looking from the underside.

Opening up a tree, especially a young and vulnerable sapling, will allow the wind to pass more easily through it and may, in the course of a severe windstorm, actually save its life by keeping it from being blown over and uprooting or snapping at the trunk. Decreasing the wind resistance of vulnerable plants is one of the psuedo-medicinal—or engineering—aspects of pruning that I referred to earlier in this chapter.

Another engineering aspect of pruning is the removal of cross branches, those branches which grow into, toward, or through the center of a tree rather than outward from the center. When it's windy, cross branches will rub against the main structure of the tree, like a bow across a violin, and may knock off ripening fruit and do permanent damage to the real structure of the tree.

Deciding whether cross branches are desirable or not isn't always easy. I'm currently involved in a tacit dispute along these very lines with a neighbor of mine with whom I share a common hedge, privet by name. On my side, I try to keep it clipped along formal lines. She, from her side, reaches all through the hedge and cuts out cross branches and a great deal of lateral growth.

The difference in our two approaches lies in our different goals. I'm after density and my neighbor is after height. I don't want to see anyone at all on her side of the hedge, and she apparently wants to see everyone on my side vaguely, everyone up to fourteen feet tall. I'm prejudiced in my own favor, of course, but then we have so few people among our friends who are much above ten feet that I can't help but feel that I have right on my side.

Generally speaking, cross branches are undesirable in fruit trees, in trees which have a single trunk system, and in all plants whose growth pattern is naturally or by design open and outward. Cross branches are very desirable in hedges, however, because cross branches are what make a hedge, neighbor.

To open out a tree, you first tentatively select a branch for removal and you follow that branch to the center of the tree or to a spot as close to the center as you can get without removing something you don't want to remove. But don't cut yet. Before you do, make sure that you know exactly the extent of the branch in question.

I have, on occasion, become hurried and made such a cut too quickly, removing to my great surprise and horror a lot more of the plant than I ever intended to, and once you've done that, there's nothing you can do but weep and wait a few years until the plant fills out again.

It's particularly easy to make this kind of mistake when you're working with a plant that has a complex structure of twisted and intertwined branches. To avoid making it, follow your branch in and out a few times, shaking and bending it back and forth and up and down to determine its true extent and contents and to get a reasonably clear picture of what the plant will look like without it. Then make your cut.

Before we go on, let's return for a moment to those chrysanthemums we were so studiously making dense and compact a few paragraphs ago. Perhaps your goal isn't density and self-support at all. Instead, you may be after extra large, very showy flowers. To get them, leave the mums alone and let them grow as they please. Instead of pinching out the center growth, get rid of any side growth that forms, and be ready to stake the plants at the first sign of top heaviness. When the buds begin to form, pinch out all but the main bud on each stalk. You'll have a lot fewer flowers following this course, but those you do have will be gigantic.

To summarize: *Pruning is often strictly a matter of your goals for the plant.*

Openness & Compactness

Those peoples, like the French and the Japanese, who have made a real art out of gardening often employ both of the pruning techniques we've been talking about on the same plant in order to achieve some very sophisticated effects.

The Japanese will, for example, take a tree or a shrub, the natural shape of which is more or less conical, and open it out, exposing the trunk and branch structure to view. They will then clip the leafy growth that remains into compactness, creating a layered arrangement of tufts at the ends of the branches, the final product bearing little or no resemblance to the original shape of the shrub.

The formal gardeners of France, using the same two techniques, produce many non-natural forms in their gardens, plants which are often shaped along lines similar to those of the traditional French poodle cut. The Mexicans, following the French tradition, have in Guadalajara's Parque Azul arrived at plants in the exact form of animals.

The chief difference between the French and Japanese styles is one of symmetry. The French prefer to make perfectly symmetrical shapes from asymmetrical plants, while the Japanese, at their virtuous best, will take a relatively symmetrical plant like a spruce and make it studiously asymmetrical. Horticulturally speaking, however, the methods they use to achieve these different ends are the same.

Top-heaviness

This is the last aspect of pruning that belongs strictly to the engineering category. Many plants, particularly young ones, may put out more growth at the ends of their branches than those branches can comfortably support. If something isn't done to correct this in time, the extra weight may cause the branch to snap at the base, leaving you with a much smaller, considerably less attractive, and often badly damaged specimen.

Top-heaviness can be compensated for by securely tieing or staking the troubled branch until such time as it's able to support itself. This is a time-consuming operation, one which the plant may all too soon outgrow, as well as one which, if not done correctly, may result in breakage anyway.

The surest, safest method of correcting top-heaviness is to prune slowly down the branch until all symptoms of excess weight disappear. If you make your first cut too close to the center of the plant, you may find that you've cut off more of the plant than was either necessary or desirable.

By the time the branch has grown out again, it may be strong enough to support itself, but if it isn't and it starts drooping once more, this operation should be repeated until it's clear to you that the branch is able to support all of its own weight unaided.

Around picking time, the branches of fruit trees, if too heavily laden with fruit, are in imminent danger of breaking. Since back-pruning at this point will mean the loss of much valuable fruit, another method should be found to protect the branch from breakage. The best solution to this problem is a long, forked stake placed between the branch and the ground with the branch resting securely in the fork. After the fruit has been harvested, the stake can, of course, be safely removed.

Weak & Dead Growth

Weak, dead, or dying growth can and should be removed as soon as it's detected. Removing it is partially a cosmetic measure, but it has its medicinal value as well, since it reduces the chances of disease breeding in the plant and of disease spreading if it already exists there.

Dead wood is usually stiffer, harder, and less flexible than living wood, and it will not respond to the wind in the same way. For that reason, removing dead wood will decrease the chances of wind damage to the plant.

From a purely cosmetic standpoint, getting rid of dead and weak wood can produce startling results. I have on occasion taken a large, spindly, unhealthy looking plant and reduced it in a matter of a few minutes to a smaller, fuller, healthier looking specimen. To people who are naive or timid about pruning, this can look like magic, and if you're part ham, as I am, you may not be able to resist helping your friends with their pruning chores once you get the knack of it. Before you start helping them, however, make sure that it's clear that they're the ones who'll clean up the mess.

The one exception to the dead growth rule is growth which has been killed by frost. Frost-killed growth should be left on the plant until all danger of further frosts has passed, preferably until new growth has begun to assert itself and you can get a clear picture of what's really dead and what only seems to be. Frost-killed growth acts as a kind of sky mulch, protecting the living growth further down from damage from later frosts. Removing damaged growth too soon, however desirable cosmetically, may result in the death of a plant that might otherwise have been saved.

I should probably mention here that we're talking only about a certain group of plants, those vulnerable individuals that will withstand a normal winter with little or no frost damage but which a bad winter, which everyone gets from time to time, will blacken and defoliate. We are not talking about those hardy, deciduous individuals which normally lose their leaves in the fall and pass the winter in a barren, dead-looking state. This type of plant is best pruned in the dead of winter when it's in its most dormant stage.

In the Bay Area, the fuchsia is the classic example of winter vulnerability. During a mild winter here or if they're grown very near the ocean, fuchsias rarely sustain any frost damage at all. Under these conditions, they're essentially evergreens. The harsher the winter, the further from marine influence, and the higher the elevation, however, the more vulnerable fuchsias become, but nowhere in the Bay Area are they considered to be ungrowable.

We live about three miles from the bay at an elevation of about six-hundred feet. Come January, most of my fuchsias are spindly and sparesely leaved and the tips of their branches are dead. After the Great Freeze of December, 1972, all of my fuchsias appeared to have been killed to the roots. By late February to my great surprise, a few hardy individuals had begun to put out new leaves almost at the tips of the branches. Leaves soon began to appear on others further down. Some others produced no leaves at all on the old wood but grew up again from the roots. Only one, and a very young one at that, proved to have been completely killed.

Had I responded to the Great Freeze by running out and pruning all my fuchsias to the ground, as I was sorely tempted to do, considering how ugly they looked, I would only have compounded the frost damage, and I might even have succeeded in effecting a significant reduction in my fuchsia collection. In the case of the Great Freeze, the lazy, procrastinating gardener did better than his ambitious, do-it-now brother, a rare event in the annals of gardening.

Shaping

We've already talked quite a bit about shaping plants through pruning, and perhaps enough has already been said to make this section unnecessary. Still, some garden pruning is done for no other reason. No question of legginess is involved, the plant isn't too big, it isn't in the way of anything, and there's no danger of its being dangerously resistant to the wind. It just needs a little pruning here and there to improve its general appearance.

Unfortunately, I know of no way to communicate the difference between a handsome shrub and one that's not so handsome. What may look good to me may not appeal to someone else. I, for example, have never really been taken by complicated and ornate espaliers, although I have great respect for the skill, the patience, and the time it takes to create one. That I happen to prefer a more natural look is merely a matter of personal taste, and there's no way to convey taste or, really, to prove that someone's taste is truly superior to anyone else's.

If you're in doubt about your own ability to improve the appearance of a plant by pruning it, about the only advice I can give you is to experiment slowly. What you are, essentially, is a neophyte sculptor faced with his first block of marble, holding for the very first time a hammer and chisel in his hands. The block of marble, like the shrub, has a number of "perfect" shapes contained within it. It's your job to determine what those shapes are and to come up with the one among them that best suits you. Shaping a plant, like chiseling into marble, is a series of small compromises that you make with the material you're working with. That a plant is living tissue is only a secondary consideration when you're shaping it.

In pruning, as in sculpting, it's important to keep in the mind that your subject is three dimensional. A cut that may look good from one angle may mar the appearance of the plant from another. Any plant that you're pruning for shape should be pruned from all sides or from every side that's visible from any point in the garden. This may involve walking around the plant with your thumb extended artistically in front of you, which may cause some raised eyebrows among your neighbors. If this happens, simply explain that you're practicing to become a gardener and that gardeners are weird. No further explanation should be necessary.

If you're dubious about your ability to prune for shape, it's best to stick to the general outlines of the plant as it grows naturally, since the more the pruner works against the natural contours and growth habits of a plant, the more apt he is to get himself and his subject into trouble. This shouldn't keep you from experimenting, however, but when you decide to experiment, always experiment on a plant that you feel you can afford to lose.

Like people, some plants are more flexible than others. The relatively inflexible rose bush can be trained into a small tree by selecting a single upright cane and pruning out all the others. On the other hand, a rose bush can never be trained to be a climbing rose. A climber is genetically a slightly different animal from the very start.

The highly flexible privet makes a perfect formal hedge, an informal hedge, a screen, and an individual privet can be turned into a small tree simply by removing all those parts of it which aren't part of small-treeness. A person who tried to make a formal hedge out of a planting of birch trees would, on the other hand, be damned from the start. The birch is always and forever a tree. Nothing you can do to a birch will keep it from saying "Trunk!" loud and clear.

The wisteria is an example of extreme flexibility. It will vine gracefully over an arbor and it will happily climb a tree. It can be trained along a wall, formally espaliered, made into a shrub and, with a lot of hard work, it can be turned into a full-fledged tree, a formidably sized one of which can be seen in the Japanese tea garden in San Francisco's Golden Gate Park, a living tribute to the master-pruners who engineered it.

When to Prune

There are certain times of year that are better for pruning than others. Except for frost damaged plants and in a few other situations which we'll talk about later, the best time to prune is in the dead of winter when plants are in their most dormant stage.

The reason for this is simple. When a plant is dormant, it will be less apt to lose vital fluids from a major cut, the cut will have time to heal before the juices start to flow again, and diseases which might enter the plant through the cut are least active when the weather is cold.

Another advantage of winter pruning is that it gives you a skeleton look at the structure of deciduous trees and shrubs. Without the leaves, it's much easier to tell what the true shape of a tree is, where the undesirable cross branches lay, and what can best be done to correct any deficiencies in the tree's structure or its overall shape.

We now come to that famous, horror-inspiring fiat typical of so many gardening books, which goes something like this: Fruit trees should be pruned around the end of January. The novice gardener reads this and panics. My God, he thinks, I've got this apple tree out in the back yard, and I love it, and it's out there crying out to be pruned, and I don't know what to do about it. What he does do about it is arm himself with a pair of pruning shears and march timidly toward the tree. He timidly lops off a few branches, which makes him feel even worse than he did before. He cuts off one more branch and walks back into the house a confused and bewildered mass of jangled nerves. He's certain of only one thing now, that real gardeners aren't only weird but a different breed entirely, a Martian import of sorts to whom the apple must speak in a secret language, "Cut me here, dear, cut me here."

"Fruit trees should be pruned around the end of January" doesn't mean that anymore than "Your hair should be cut when it's wet" means that you're duty bound to cut it every time you wash it.

What it does mean is that come January you should take a close look at your apple tree, sizing it up from top to bottom and side to side, to see if it needs any restructuring. The secret language involved goes something like this, and this is you, not the tree, talking: "There's a cross branch I'd better get rid of. And another. There's a branch that hits me in the head every time I walk under it. That one better go, too. The tree's too thick here and I'd better thin it out a little. The tree's getting a little bit too high for its girth, so I'll just lop off these top branches. It's out of balance now because of the cuts I've made, so I'd better cut off this branch and shorten these to make it a more harmonious whole."

It's possible, although not terribly likely, that the only thing you'll say after your apple tree inspection is, "Well, it looks fine to me. Guess the best thing to do is leave it alone until next year."

Some Exceptions

Unfortunately, there seem to be few hard and fast rules in gardening. All of the rules should make sense, and so should the exceptions. If they don't make sense to you, I wouldn't bother with them until they do. If a gardening book tells you not to prune your lilacs, camellias, rhododendrons, and azaleas in the dead of winter, as I am now telling you not to do, ask why or find out for yourself. The rules and the exceptions to them aren't nearly as important or as informative as the reasons behind them.

The reason for not pruning these particular shrubs at this particular time is a simple one. All of these shrubs form their buds on the previous years growth. If you remove that growth by pruning it out in the dead of winter, your shrubs won't bloom the following spring. Nothing horrible will happen to them. They won't die. They just won't bloom again for a year.

Shrubs of this type should be pruned while they're in bloom in conjunction with cutting flowers for the house or just after they've finished blooming in conjunction with removing the faded flowers. The longer you wait to prune them after they've finished blooming, the more apt you are to decrease your display of flowers for the following year.

And let me say one more time, by *should be pruned* I don't mean that they absolutely have to be pruned. I mean that this is your best opportunity to prune them if you feel it's necessary or desirable. If you don't, leave them alone for another year.

Sealing

Any pruning cut that's much more than a half to three quarters of an inch in diameter should be sealed.

Sealing does three things. It prevents loss of vital fluids. It prevents the entry of pests and diseases, and it keeps out water and moisture, which may cause internal rot and the eventual death of the plant.

Sealing compound is available at your local nursery or garden supply outlet. To seal a cut, you simply cover the entire area with compound, making sure that no part of the wound is left exposed to the air.

Where to Cut

On a branch, the best place to make a cut is just above a leaf bud. The reason for this is again largely cosmetic. If you cut just below a leaf bud, that part of the stem or branch between the cut and the next leaf bud down will die, leaving an ugly brown protruberance on the plant, one which will in time fall off anyway.

If you're removing an entire branch, cut it off as close to the main branch, or trunk, as you can. Cutting in this way makes it easier for the plant to seal the wound itself, something it must eventually do even if you've sealed it with compound. This kind of cutting also eliminates ugly, unnatural-looking stubs and stumps.

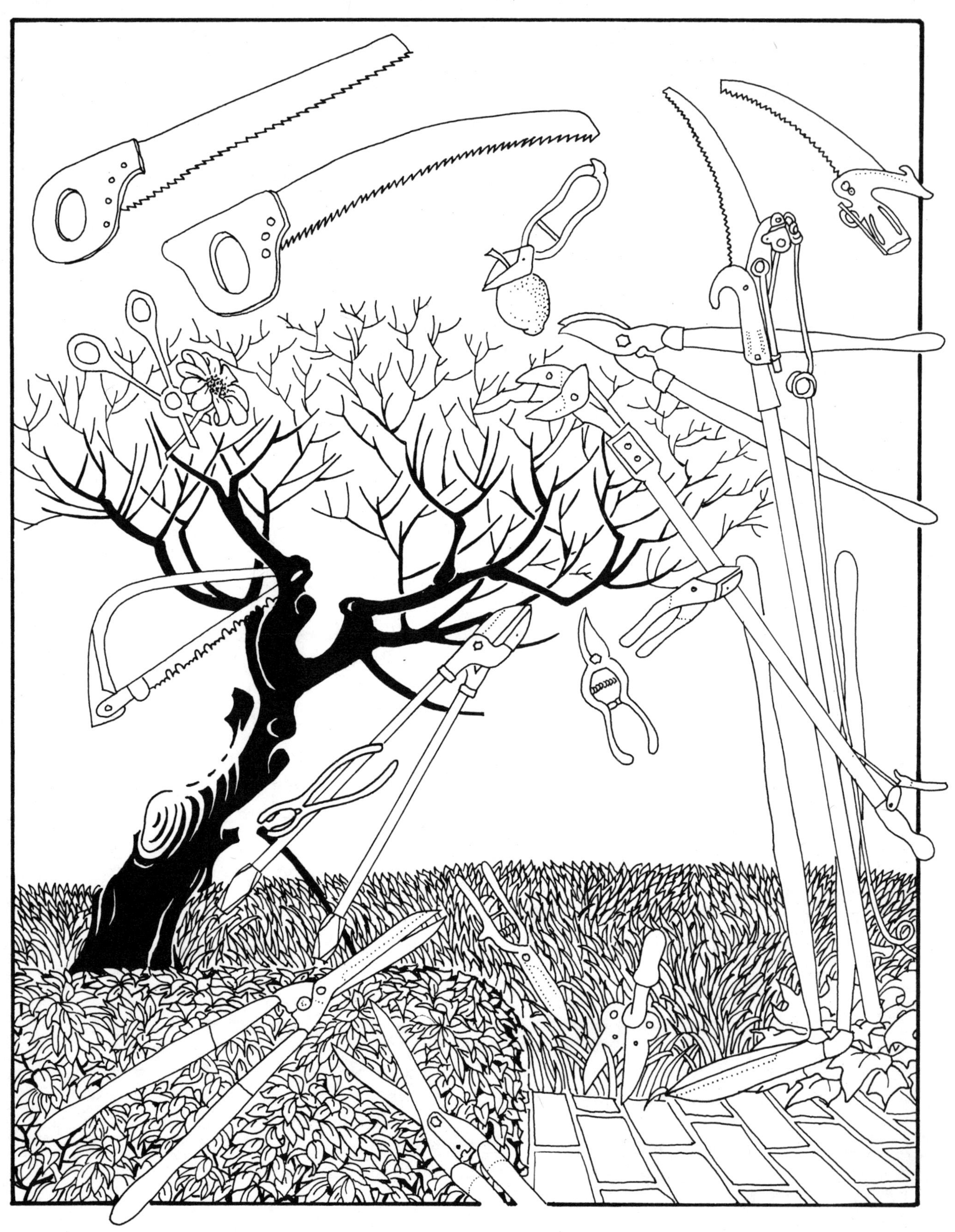

Pruning Tools

Which Way to Cut

Whenever possible, make vertical cuts. Upward facing, horizontal cuts, especially large ones, will act as trays and collect water, which spectacularly increases the danger of rot.

Smooth Cuts

The smoother and cleaner a cut, the better. Rough jagged cuts take much longer to heal and are much more apt to admit water and disease. Clean cuts also look better.

Alcohol

You can greatly decrease the chances of spreading diseases from plant to plant if you dip your pruning shears in alcohol between plants. In many cases, this precaution won't be necessary, but if one of your peach or nectarine trees has peach leaf curl, and you'll know it if it does, an alcohol dip is an absolute must. With peach leaf curl, it's sound practice to dip between cuts to avoid spreading the disease to parts of the tree which may not already be infected.

Pruning Tools

Every gardener should be equipped with at least four basic pruning tools:

1. Lawn or grass shears
2. Pruning shears
3. Hedge clippers
4. Pruning saw

Lawn shears, besides being the most effective tool for keeping the lawn out of the flower beds and for taking care of those places the lawn mower misses, are also helpful in getting rid of unwanted young and green growth. Using them on tougher growth will quickly dull them, making them useless for what you really need them for. I often, if the truth were known, find myself taxing my own lawn shears beyond their capacity and hating myself for it, making me one of those people who doesn't always follow his own advice however sound it may be.

Pruning shears come in a large variety of shapes and sizes. For ordinary jobs, the kind I find most useful, are the small ones which suggest a parrot's profile. These shears will cut quickly through a hard branch half an inch in diameter and through larger ones if the wood is softer. If you have trees to prune and dislike swaying precariously from the tops of ladders, you can avoid it by using a pair of long-handled shears or a lopper. Both of these tools are fairly expensive but a lot cheaper—and a lot more fun—than a broken leg or a fractured skull.

Hedge clippers are a tool with a limited and specific purpose. They should be used only on the softer growth of hedges and shrubs which you're trying to round. They can also be used to keep ivy off a walk or to top ivy when it begins to get too high. Hedge clippers should not be used for more rigorous pruning tasks because they're not built for it. They're also not much use when it comes to sensitive pruning jobs.

A pruning saw is a must if you're going after branches which are more than three-quarters of an inch in diameter and if you dislike the idea of hauling your carpentry tools out into the garden. Pruning saws come in a variety of shapes and sizes for a variety of tasks, and a visit to the hardware store will give you a much better idea of what you might need along these lines than I can here.

My Neighbor's Husband

My spruce-loving neighbor has a husband whom she occasionally drives into the garden to work. He obviously hates his garden duty and his work shows it. Not long ago he was apparently under orders to prune one of their orange trees, and to do it, he chose a pair of hedge clippers, of all pruning tools the least suitable for the job.

He aimed the clippers at the lower part of the tree and hacked away for a good long time, greenery flying in every direction. After he finished and had retreated to the house, I peered cautiously over the fence to view his work, a piece of spying that I've regretted ever since.

The tree looked very much like a woman with a beautiful head but from whose body all skin, fat, flesh, and organs had been removed and, as if this indignity weren't enough, it appeared that the skeletal remains had been repeatedly fired at from all sides by shotguns so that every bone was broken, frayed, and splintered.

The tree survived and, *mirabile dictu*, it's even managed to fill itself out again and cover with a new set of leaves much of the structural damage my neighbor's husband did to it. It stands, I feel, as a living testimonial to the ability of a plant to withstand not only the mistakes of a novice pruner but the onslaughts of a stupidly vicious enemy, for so his work appeared to me.

Needless to say, I don't recommend my neighbor's husband's approach to pruning. Pruning, for whatever reason it's done, is a surgical task, and it's done best when simple surgical principles are observed. I don't imagine that my neighbor's husband would be pleased to see, as they wheeled him toward the operating room, his surgeon, Dr. John Ripper, reeling drunkenly and weilding a rusty scythe, his eyes ablaze with confusion and blood lust. From our standpoint, of course, mine and the orange's, it would be poetic justice.

16 THE VEGETABLE GARDEN

6 Vegetables

During the Second World War, when I was but a wee lad, we called hamburgers victory sandwiches and wieners and frankfurters hot dogs. Hamburg, Frankfurt, and Vienna, you see, were deep in enemy territory and therefore unmentionable. Those of us patriots who had access to any land at all planted some or all of it in vegetables and called it a victory garden.

Victory gardens, we were told, would help us win the war. Whether they did or not, I don't know, but they did keep a lot of people occupied at home while others were off doing the actual fighting, and in California, at least, victory gardens helped to offset the loss of produce we experienced when we carted the green-thumbed, truck-farming Japanese off to jail.

After the war, only the hot dog survived as such, probably because its new name didn't specifically evoke the war. Everybody gets tired of war after awhile. The victory sandwich and the victory garden along with all its tasty, home-grown vegetables disappeared.

My grandmother kept hers, of course. She'd always had one, war or no war, victory or defeat, but my parents had become too sophisticated by the war itself to continue to feel comfortable about digging in the dirt after the war was over.

It's only in the last few years that the home vegetable garden has begun to make a comeback, and for several reasons, I think. There's been a general resurgence of interest in all kinds of gardening, for one thing. For another, food prices are, it seems, disproportionately high, and the produce available at the market is often of inferior quality because much of it is picked too green so that it can be shipped too far.

And then there's the question of pesticides. How heavily has the commercial produce we buy been poisoned, and what effect is that poisoned produce going to have on those of us who eat it? Pest-free produce may look lovely to those whom canned and frozen foods have taught to taste with the eyes instead of the tongue, but perhaps if no bug has deigned to nibble at, say, a head of lettuce, we might be smart to avoid it ourselves.

Vegetables are also among the easiest of all plants to grow, and they're fast. Radishes, for example, take only a month from seed packet to table, and almost no vegetable takes more than three. Because you can eat them, vegetables are great fun to grow, even for those who really don't care much for other kinds of gardening, and the difference in the taste of home-grown vegetables is indescribable. My wife and I recently sank our teeth into our first home-grown crookneck squash and found it impossible to tell where the butter left off and the squash began, a problem we've never encountered with supermarket crooknecks.

What Size Garden?

On a city-sized lot, there usually isn't room for the kind of old-fashioned vegetable garden that grandma had, unless you're willing to relinquish a large portion of your outdoor living space, something that I haven't yet been willing to do myself, although my wife, the cook, keeps pushing me in that direction.

My own vegetable garden measures approximately ten by thirty feet, an area large enough to make an appreciable dent in the food budget, to grow a variety of vegetables, some of them large ones, and to keep our palates in tune with nature and properly contemptuous of American agribusiness.

(American agribusiness, it seems to me, strives daily to decrease the quality of life in this country for the sake of yet an even faster dollar, and that's a dollar I sincerely hope the agribusinessmen—what a name for farmers—are using to feast on in France, land of small farms, resident shopkeepers, and fabulous fresh food, since it would be truly disappointing to think that agribusinessmen ate what they produced and depressing to think that they enjoyed it.

If you can't afford to hop back and forth to France, however, you can plant a vegetable plot, and call it a victory garden. There are all kinds of wars, and that's about the size of it.)

There's no real reason, except general convenience, that you have to confine all your vegetables to one area of your garden. Vegetables can be mixed in with your flowers and ornamentals, and some vegetables are ornamental in their own right and can be planted for beauty as well as food.

The artichoke, for example, has dramatically ornamental gray-green leaves and is an attractive addition to any garden where it will grow. Asparagus spears if left to mature, as some must be if you want to maintain your planting, look like giant ferns and make a beautiful background for smaller plants. Pepper plants are indistinguishable from small ornamental shrubs, and even carrots, which have attractive fern-like foliage, would make an acceptable border display or an interesting—and edible—mass planting.

I've seen some gardens, especially ones whose proprietors were of Italian descent, that mix vegetables, flowers, shrubs, and trees indiscriminately and to good effect from an artistic standpoint. Such gardens are, in fact, often downright charming as well as being productive and profitable.

We have some young friends who recently planted their first vegetable garden this year in an area not much more than seven feet square, and from it they've harvested an unbelievable amount of produce, including cucumbers, which they vined up over steeply sloped lath trellises so that the vines would take up less room and the fruit would be less apt to rot on the ground, something I plan to do myself next year.

Size, it seems, when it comes to a vegetable garden, is of little importance compared with interest, ingenuity, and imagination.

Where to Plant

If size isn't of great importance, however, location is. All vegetables need sun, some more than others, but generally speaking, the more sun the better. In the city, sun is sometimes hard to come by. There's always a fence, your neighbor's garage, or your own favorite tree blocking out some of it during different parts of the day.

When selecting a site for your vegetable garden, choose the sunniest spot you can find, the spot that gets the most all-day and year-round sunlight. If it comes to a choice between only morning or afternoon sun, choose the afternoon sun. It's hotter.

Plant as early in the year as you can so that your garden will get the full benefit of the long June days and the June sun, which is directly overhead and consequently less susceptible to garages, fences, and tall trees. This may mean that you'll be planting in relative shade in March or April for the May, June, and July suns and harvesting in late July or August before the shade starts to creep back.

If part of your vegetable garden is sunnier than others, give the sunniest parts to beans, chard, corn, cucumbers, melons, peppers, squash and tomatoes. These vegetables need as much sun as you can give them, and they absolutely thrive on heat.

Root vegetables (beets, carrots, parsnips, radishes, and turnips), members of the cabbage family (broccoli, Brussels sprouts, cabbage, cauliflower, kale, and kholrabi), members of the onion family (chives, garlic, leeks, onions, and shallots), as well as lettuce, peas, potatoes, and spinach don't require as much sun, and most of them actively dislike heat.

All the vegetables mentioned in the last paragraph should be planted early or late enough in the year to avoid the hottest parts of summer. If they're confronted with the heat of summer, they go to seed almost immediately, depriving you of much or all of your possible harvest.

Another way of compensating for a dearth of sunlight is to make sure your soil is in excellent condition, loaded with organic matter, quick draining, moisture-retentive, and free of dirt clods and rocks.

What to Plant

The first consideration in selecting which vegetables you want to grow is to decide what vegetables you're willing to eat. I suspect that many first time vegetable gardeners, caught up in the excitement of their forthcoming adventure, have planted, say, parsnips only to find when the parsnips reached the table that no one in the family could stomach them.

Here is a list of the most commonly grown garden vegetables:

Artichoke
Asparagus
Beans
Beets
Broccoli
Brussels sprouts
Cabbage
Carrots
Cauliflower
Celery
Chard
Corn
Cucumbers
Garlic
Leeks
Lettuce
Melons
Onions
Parsnips
Peas
Peppers
Potatoes
Radishes
Rhubarb
Rutabagas
Spinach
Squash
Tomatoes
Turnips

Cross out those vegetables that you aren't willing to eat, just as I have omitted eggplant, which I loathe, which I wouldn't be caught dead growing, and about which I proudly insist I know nothing. I do know, however, that the eggplant is a cousin of the potato, which I admire heartily, and that both are cousins of the deadly nightshade, sometimes called belladonna, the potato being, in my book, the only respectable member of the family.

Plant Size

The following vegetables require considerable growing room and, if your garden is by necessity a small one, you might want to eliminate them from your list.

Artichoke
Asparagus
Beans
Corn
Cucumbers
Peas
Potatoes
Squash

Peas and beans don't require a lot of room on the ground, but the trellises and poles that they're usually grown on occupy a lot of air space and may create undesirable shade for lower growing vegetables nearby. The same is true of corn. You can partially avoid the height problem by ordering your garden in descending steps of east-west rows with the tallest vegetables at the north end of the garden and the lowest growing at the south.

If height is a consideration in your garden or you simply don't want to bother with trellises and poles, low-growing, bush varieties of lima and string beans are available, as are several dwarf varieties of peas which still require trellises but shorter ones. A stroll through a seed catalogue such as Burpee's will help to determine which varieties are best for you.

Tomatoes

Because of their size and ranginess, tomatoes belong on the above list. I have omitted them partly because they're so easy to grow but mostly because of the tremendous difference in taste between a vine-ripened and a store-bought tomato. If you're growing any vegetables at all, no matter how small your garden, I don't think you can afford not to grow tomatoes.

Like pole beans and peas, tomatoes require some sort of artificial support, since the natural inclination of the tomato vine is to place every last one of its fruits squarely on the ground, where it will start to rot just as it starts to ripen.

Staking—pounding sizeable stakes into the ground and tieing the vines to them—is the usual method of supporting tomato vines. Another, newer method is to grow the vine inside a cylinder made out of heavy gauge wire mesh twelve or so inches in diameter. The fruit is harvested from the top of the cylinder or through a door cut into the wire mesh. Trellises are another possibility, but whatever method you use, make sure it's a sturdy one. Tomato vines are fast-growing, aggressive, and extremely heavy when laden with fruit.

Tomatoes come in a seemingly endless variety of sizes, shapes, and even colors. If for some reason you're tired of red tomatoes, you have the option of growing yellow, orange and pink ones. There are varieties of tomatoes, such as the Frisco Fogger, which do well in cool summer areas where tomatoes usually do poorly.

Your local nursery, if it's a reputable one, will stock the varieties that are best for your area, and you should be able to get them either in seed or seedling form. If you're experimentally inclined, you might find a look through a seed catalogue interesting and rewarding. Burpee's catalogue alone offers more than thirty different varieties of tomato.

Asparagus, Artichokes & Rhubarb

In the case of asparagus, I haven't followed my own sage advice. Asparagus occupies a sizeable, as well as the sunniest and most desirable, part of my own small vegetable garden, a space which I might do well to turn over to other vegetables, and that's just exactly what I plan to do this winter—by incorporating an entirely new patch of asparagus into the ornamental section of my garden and removing the old patch from the strictly vegetable part after the spring harvest.

It will kill my soul to do this, and I'm really dreading it. It takes two to three years to bring an asparagus patch to full maturity, but once you've done that, the patch will continue in full production for ten to fifteen years with little or no care beyond a one-inch winter mulch of steer manure. The patch I'm going to tear out has a good many years left in it.

The problem is that the asparagus harvest only lasts for five to ten weeks out of the year, after which you must let the spears reach ferny maturity so that the patch can rebuild its root system for the next year's harvest. During the remaining forty-two to forty-seven weeks of the year, the asparagus patch is still taken up by the asparagus, although it's producing nothing at all for the table.

In putting my asparagus patch where I did, I was guilty of some very bad planning, and I'm paying for it now. If you're planning on planting asparagus, which can be done using either seeds or roots, find a spot in your garden that gets quite a bit of sunlight and make sure it's a spot that you're not going to have any other use for for the next ten or fifteen years. A spot along a west or south facing fence is ideal.

Artichokes and rhubarb are two more perennial vegetables which have attractive leaves and can be used ornamentally around the garden. Like asparagus, they both require deep, rich, well-drained soil and, if grown in a cold winter climate, a thick mulch to keep the root system from freezing. The artichoke is at its ornamental and productive best along the cool summer coasts of Northern California, but if you like artichokes and inhabit a climate where winters aren't too severe, they're still worth a try.

A dried stalk of artichoke blossoms, which resemble giant thistles, a plant they're closely related to, is a highly decorative and durable household ornament.

Rhubarb, by the way, is a kind of chard, the kind that isn't designated as Swiss. Snails are extremely fond of rhubarb, and a few too many of them can quickly lower rhubarb's ornamental value.

What's Best to Grow for Eating

Unlike the tomato, not all home-grown vegetables are as markedly superior in taste to their store-bought counterparts. Generally speaking, most cool season vegetables—root vegetables, members of the cabbage and onion families, lettuce, potatoes, and spinach—travel and store reasonably well. If you live in an area like the Bay Area where good produce is readily available commercially, you might do well to concentrate your vegetable gardening efforts on the warm season vegetables, which seem to lose their taste and freshness much more quickly.

The warm season vegetables we're talking about are corn, cucumbers, melons, peppers, squash—zucchini and crookneck in particular—and, of course, tomatoes. Peas, a cool season vegetable, also lose their freshness quickly and, apparently, are often harvested when they're too mature so that they arrive at the store tasting bitter and wooden. For that reason, peas belong in this group, too.

The members of the cabbage family demand a fair amount of growing room. Considering the relative indestructability of cabbage itself, its comparative cheapness, and the room it takes to grow it, I wouldn't recommend your planting it unless your vegetable garden is sizeable. In a small garden, the space taken up by cabbage could probably be used more profitably to grow something else.

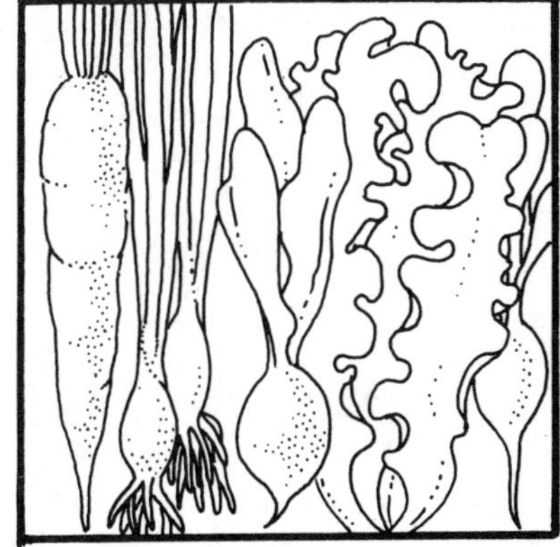

And for Size

Certain vegetables, for the amount of room they take up, deliver a proportionately large amount of produce and are ideal for the small garden. This group is comprised of members of the onion family, the root vegetables, and the leafy vegetables. Because this book is primarily concerned with small gardens, this group deserves particular attention.

The Onion Family

Of all the vegetable families, the onion family is probably the most controversial, eliciting the strongest opinions from all sides. Everyone either likes onions or dislikes them, and garlic is for some heaven on earth, while for others it's food barely fit to feed the devil. I'm particularly fond of every member of the onion family and, with one exception, I've found them remarkably easy to grow.

Onions can be grown either from seed or from onion sets, which are small onion bulbs. Seed planting is by far the cheaper method, but sets are more reliable and a better bet for the novice gardener. Onion sets are available at your nursery in the late fall and, in mild winter areas, can be planted all winter long through April. In colder climates, they should be planted just as soon as the soil is workable.

Onions are normally harvested around the middle of summer when the tops start to brown and droop. At this time, they should be pulled up, cleaned off, and allowed to dry in the sun for a few days before you store them in a cool, dark, dry place.

All my attempts to grow garlic have resulted in puny failures. I'm not sure why, but I suspect that it may have something to do with the scarcity of winter sun in my vegetable garden. I'm doubly hurt by this failure because I'm extremely fond of French garlic soup, which requires an enormous amount of garlic to make and which, in my opinion, beats the *chausettes* off its more famous compatriot, French onion soup.

No one, of course, believes me about garlic soup until they've tasted it themselves, a fact I've learned to live with and one that gives me the pleasure of being able to say I-told-you-so from time to time. As for the plant itself, stick a few cloves in the ground when you're planting your onion sets and see what happens. You can't possibly do worse than I did.

The leek is a relatively esoteric vegetable, although it happens to be the floral symbol of Wales where, I suspect, it has greater currency than it does here. Leek seeds should be planted in the late winter or early spring and the leeks harvested in the fall, which means that leeks take almost a year to mature. They can be picked before reaching maturity and used as a substitute for scallions, which they closely resemble. A bowl of leek and potato soup will teach you the true worth of the leek, if the leek is a vegetable you're not already familiar with.

Scallions, small green onions, should also be planted in late winter or early spring. They are always planted from seed and can be harvested as you need them when they're big enough to use.

At this writing, I doubt that one American in ten has heard of a shallot or, if he has, that he could tell you what one was. A shallot is about the size of a small head of garlic and, like garlic, it's composed of cloves, although the cloves are larger and fewer in number. The shallot has a mild, sweet taste reminiscent of the onion but much more delicate and complex.

Shallots have begun to appear in American markets because of the spreading interest in French cooking, in which they're used extensively. Apparently, most shallots are still imported. The prices asked for them are astronomical—more per pound now than for filet mignon—and there doesn't seem to be any real reason for these prices because I've found shallots remarkably easy to grow, a feat which helped greatly to offset my miserable failure with garlic.

If you're interested in experimenting with shallots but can't find sets at the nursery, you can do what I did and buy a few bulbs from the supermarket. Five years ago, I bought six small ones for about ten cents apiece, planted them in December (early spring, if you live in a cold climate), and by August when I harvested them, I had sixty. The following year, over the protests of my shallot-greedy wife, I planted all of those and produced enough to supply the kitchen for a year as well as enough for a substantial replanting the following winter. We're now harvesting enough shallots every year to be able to give some away, which pleases me. What pleases me even more is to look over my shallot crop and tote up its retail value in my head. Doing this makes me feel like a real farmer with a cash crop instead of the dilettante city gardener that I really am.

The great advantage of growing your own onions, garlic, and shallots is that they will keep for almost a year if they're stored in a cool, dark, dry place. This means that you won't be faced with a crop that comes ready for use all at the same time. It also means that, even with a small garden, you can fill virtually all your needs for these vegetables yourself, and that is a soul-satisfying as well as an economically sound practice.

Root Vegetables

Beets, carrots, radishes, and turnips take up very little room and are easy to grow. They should be planted in the early spring just as soon as the ground becomes workable. In mild winter areas, a second crop can be planted in late summer or early fall for harvest in the early spring. If planted too late in the spring, the heat of summer may cause these vegetables to go to seed before the roots reach maturity, and once they start to go to seed, the roots become inedible.

Beets and turnips are a double bonus for the gardener because the greens as well as the roots are edible, and you can harvest some of the greens for eating while the roots are maturing. I frankly prefer beet greens to spinach if a little vinegar is added to the water while the greens are cooking.

With carrots, you have to keep a sharp eye out for snails and slugs. I've watched a snail making its merry way down a row of carrots which had just barely begun to sprout. If I hadn't been keeping an eye on the vegetable garden, all of the carrots would have disappeared into the snail before I'd seen them come up, and I would have sworn that they hadn't come up at all and concluded that carrots were, indeed, difficult to grow.

A number of different varieties of carrots are available to the home gardener, the main difference between the varieties being that some are short and stubby and others long and thin. If your soil is loose and sandy, the long, thin, commercially grown varieties are best for you, but if your soil is heavy or rocky, you'll have much better luck and much better looking carrots if you plant the shorter kind.

Beets are a vegetable that I can't stomach canned unless they've been pickled. I also don't care for cooked beets when they come from the produce section of the market. My wife finally talked me into growing some beets of my own, and I went along with her because

I'd planned to eat only the greens. I tasted some of the beets she cooked fresh from the garden, to please her, and I now love beets—my own, that is.

Turnips, in my book, are a vegetable that should never be cooked, but if they're raw and fresh from the garden, I prefer them to most apples.

Most Americans tend to cook all vegetables far too long, which is probably why there are so many active vegetable haters among us. If you're growing your own vegetables for the first time, make it a practice to taste everything you grow before you cook it. It may change your whole attitude toward vegetables at its very roots. Even raw asparagus fresh from the garden is a taste delicacy and a splendid addition to any salad.

Leafy Vegetables

Lettuce and spinach are cool season vegetables which should be planted at the same time that you plant root vegetables. With lettuce and spinach in particular, it's a good idea to plant only a foot or two of seed every other week to help spread your harvest over a longer period of time.

You can start harvesting the leaves of these two vegetables just as soon as they're big enough to use. Just cut what leaves you need for the table from the outside of the plants, leaving the main part in the ground, where it will continue to produce more leaves until it starts to go to seed.

If you're growing head lettuce as opposed to leaf lettuce, you can harvest the looser exterior leaves until the head has reached maturity. When that happens, the head should be harvested immediately, since it will quickly go to seed, giving the whole plant a decidedly bitter and unpleasant taste.

By growing these two vegetables where they will get some shade in summer and by keeping them moist, you can prolong your harvest into the hotter months when these vegetables normally do poorly.

If you're a spinach-hater and what you hate about spinach is its metallic taste, you can get rid of that taste completely by removing the stems and as much of the veins as possible from the leaves before you cook them. This is done by placing the leaf top down in one hand and pulling the stem back and over the underside of the leaf. That's a French culinary secret and something that may not even belong in this book. M. Popeye made me put it in.

Watering

Once your vegetable garden has been planted, you shouldn't let it dry out. Vegetables grow very rapidly and in doing so must absorb a lot of water. If they're seriously deprived of the water they need, they will tend to stunt, become woody, and lose much of their potential flavor.

Some vegetables, of course, need more water than others, the warm season vegetables requiring, as you might deduce, somewhat less than their cool season cousins. The problems created by this variation in watering requirements can be avoided by growing these two different kinds of vegetables separately in different areas of the vegetable garden.

Over-watering warm season vegetables can cause some problems. It encourages some of the diseases these vegetables are prey to, and it sometimes causes them to produce a surplus of greenery and little or no fruit. Over-watering is, however, a condition that's easily detected and remedied.

Even in the hottest weather, a thorough watering every other day should be enough to sustain your vegetable garden. In cooler weather, watering once every four or five days should be adequate.

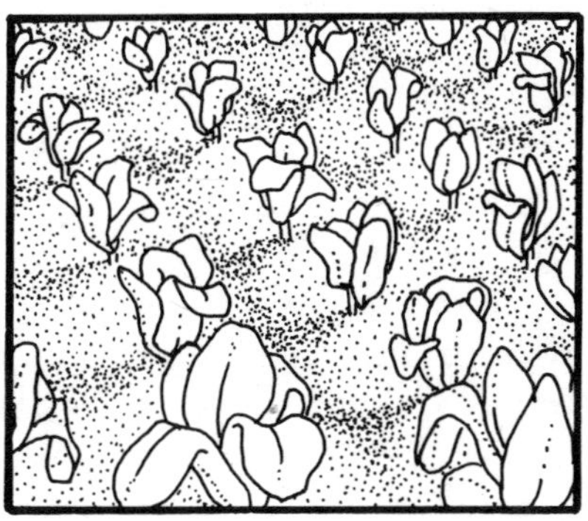

Spacing

Commercially sold seed packets give spacing directions which are ideal if you have all the room you want and more for your vegetable garden. If you, with your small garden, allow the suggested number of inches between seeds and the suggested number of feet between rows, you may find that you have room enough for only two or three different vegetables. For a greater variety, you're going to have to condense.

If there's a rule of thumb for small vegetable gardens, it's to space things about twice as close as the seed packet recommends. In some cases, this may be a little too close and in others you may be able to space even closer. A little experimentation will soon let you know what you can get by with and what you can't.

When condensing your crops in this way, it's especially important to keep a watchful eye on them. If they start to crowd each other too much, you may have to harvest part of one crop before it reaches maturity, or you may have to thin both crops here and there to open them out more. If your planning's been very poor, you may have to sacrifice one crop entirely and chalk it up to experience, the proverbial best teacher.

Vining vegetables like cucumbers, melons, and tomatoes can be brought up off the ground and placed on trellises where they will be out of the way of their earth-bound neighbors. With tomatoes, of course, this is a necessity for the reasons we discussed above.

If space is an important factor in your garden, don't hesitate to remove sagging, faded leaves and any rank, rangy, or otherwise useless growth. Such growth not only takes up valuable space, it also keeps the sun from other plants and those parts of the same plant which could really benefit from it.

The Intensive Method

Almost all seed packets recommend thinning seedlings after they're reached a certain height. This practice gives a few selected individuals adequate room to reach maturity uncrowded by any competition.

Another method of vegetable gardening, the intensive method, doesn't thin but allows all seedlings an equal opportunity to reach maturity on the assumption that the stronger will prevail and the weak die off or grow slowly until the stronger have been harvested and the weak can mature in the room the strong have left behind.

I've found this method particularly satisfactory for growing carrots. From a single intensive planting, I harvested a great number of carrots, many times more from the same space than if I'd thinned, over a period of more than a year, since the weaker seedlings remained virtually dormant until the stronger had matured and been removed.

If you want to experiment with the intensive method, there are several things you should know. First, your seeds should be scattered in rows two to three inches wide or wider rather than in one single straight line. Second, your soil should be extra rich in organic matter, and for two reasons. One, such a planting is going to be very demanding as far as nutrients go and, if the nutrients aren't there, the planting will suffer unnecessarily. Two, humus-rich soil is much less resistant than ordinary soil to root growth, and your planting will again suffer unnecessarily if it has to compete with the soil as well as with itself for root room. For this kind of planting, a mixture of half garden loam and half well-aged organic matter wouldn't be too rich.

The third and last thing to remember when planting intensively is to remove any plant that starts to go to seed immediately. Such a plant is an active liability, since it's lost all chance of ever being usable but it's still taking up valuable space and absorbing valuable nutrients from the soil.

The intensive method is, of course, not practicable with large vegetables such as corn, melons, squash, and tomatoes, all of which tend to fill up the space available to them even when planted at some distance from each other. It works best with root vegetables and small leafy vegetables such as lettuce, spinach, and chard.

Soil

In a number of places in this book, I have hammered away at the desirability, if not the absolute necessity, of having or creating for yourself rich, fast-draining, moisture-retentive soil, but nowhere is good soil more important than it is in the vegetable garden. The reasons for this are, hopefully by now, obvious. From no part of the garden will you consistently be taking away as much organic matter as you will from the vegetable garden, organic matter in the form, of course, of produce for the table.

The richness of the vegetable garden's soil must be maintained if you want to maintain the quality of your produce. If you want to improve that quality, you must continue to improve the soil. You should never plant new seeds without first working into the soil what organic matter you have available to you either in the form of compost or, if you can afford it, steer manure, peat moss and leaf mold.

If your soil is basically heavy and clayey, order a yard of river sand—or whatever amount you need to make the soil loose and crumbly—and dig it in. Happily, if you perform this tedious task adequately the first time, you won't have to do it again, since the sand won't disappear and it won't be absorbed by the vegetables, although, of course, there are those who swear that spinach actually eats sand.

I'm not going to belabor this point much further except to say that, if your soil is in good condition, you'll never have to consider using chemical fertilizers. You'll get the same "magic" results without them, and your vegetables will be strictly organic forever, unless you stoop to using pesticides, of course.

Before planting any vegetables, the soil to be planted should be turned over with a pitch fork to a depth of at least nine inches. Sand and organic matter can most conveniently be added to the soil at this time and any invading, competitive roots from surrounding trees or shrubs removed.

Don't start working the soil if it's wet. You're liable to create dirt clods that will become almost indestructible when they dry out and harden. Always wait until the soil is on the damp to dry side before you start working it.

When to Pick

The time to harvest your produce is, of course, when it's ripe, when it most resembles the produce you buy at the market. If that's not clear enough, a few mistakes in either direction will soon let you know when any particular vegetable has reached maximum perfection.

The important thing about picking home-grown vegetables, the onion family excepted, is not to pick them and store them or let them sit around if you can possibly avoid it. Doing this will cause them to lose much of their garden freshness and make them taste more like what's available to you in the markets. Pick your tomatoes when the knife is awaiting them, lettuce after you've got out the salad bowl, and corn when the water on the stove starts to boil.

This means that you'll be planning some of your meals around your garden. You won't be going to get a particular vegetable, you'll be going out to see what's ready, but that's hardly a novel idea. It was in fact the only idea until somebody told us we could have any vegetable we wanted at any time of year and presented us with the tasteless frozen mush that grows in supermarket freezers. That mush may have been vegetables at one time—the law requires that much, I think—but exactly when is a matter of some controversy.

Radishes

For the very shy novice vegetable gardener, I recommend the radish for starters. Nothing is easier to grow or matures faster—only a month, as I've said, from seed packet to table. There are a wide variety of radishes to choose from—red ones, white ones, black ones as well as round ones and ones shaped like icicles. There's even a giant radish, the daikon, which you can use to startle and amaze your friends and neighbors, and startling your friends and neighbors is an aspect of gardening that shouldn't be underrated.

Once you've seen what magic you can perform with radishes, let your enthusiasm run rampant. Vegetable seeds are cheap and vegetables grow—or fail—quickly. You can give the whole vegetable spectrum a whirl without suffering any serious setbacks to your pocket book—or soul—and in doing so, you're bound to find a number of vegetables which do well for you, vegetables that you'll be glad to eat and proud to parade before the wondering eyes of those same startled friends and neighbors.

17 HERBS AND SPICES

Herbs

Herbs as a separate class of plants belong together only in the house, usually but not always in the kitchen. In the garden, they're often as different as night and day or, more appropriately perhaps, as different as a tree, the bay, and a lowly annual, basil.

A bright student may want to get technical now and claim that a bayleaf is not really an herb at all but a spice, like the powdered bark of the cinnamon tree, and that, I suppose, is a possibility.

The dictionary defines an herb as a seed plant which doesn't develop any persistent woody tissue. If that's true, the bay most certainly isn't an herb, but neither then is rosemary or, for that matter, thyme. I've got an aging thyme plant, which is visible to me as I'm writing this, that's very definitely woody and quite assuredly persistently so. The dictionary definition of herb isn't, it seems, very satisfactory.

If I were concocting a definition for herb, it would go something like this: Any plant which because of its lingering olfactory (smell and/or taste) properties finds its way into the house where it's put to some use or other relative to those same olfactory properties. If such a plant finds its way into food, it becomes a spice. If it doesn't, it remains an herb.

I've qualified "olfactory properties" with "lingering" in order to preclude such transitory olfactory delights as roses from my definition, whereupon our bright student will, I'm sure, raise his hand to say that rose petals, when used to concoct a potpourri, take on a certain herbal aura or significance, since in the case of a potpourri, the smell of roses does linger while their visual beauties recede into the background or, more properly, into the bottom of a jar.

Since it's apparently impossible, as our bright student has pointed out, to tell where ordinary plants leave off and herbs begin as well as where herbs quit being herbs and start being spices, we'll call every plant that this chapter deals with an herb. That will fit in nicely with the fact that this is a gardening and not a cook book.

Because herbs, in the garden, are such totally dissimilar and unrelated plants, the best way to handle them is, I think, to take them one at a time, since there are absolutely no generalities that exist among—or that can be applied to—all of them. Some people may be under the impression that all herbs love sun and dry soil and that all can be grown in the same place in the garden. Many herbs do love sun and dry soil but certainly not all of them. Some can be grown in the same part of the garden, others cannot. Many herbs can't even be grown in the same part of the world.

Unfortunately, the scope and nature of this book doesn't permit a discussion of every herb or even an exhaustive discussion of any particular one. I'm omitting many fairly common herbs, and I may be omitting some that are more important to some people than the ones I mention. The herbs that I'm going to be talking about are, frankly, the ones that I'm most familiar with and those that, for various reasons, I like the best.

Basil

Ocimum basilicum

Basil is an annual and is best treated as a vegetable in the vegetable garden or grown by itself in large containers. Basil prefers rich soil, a lot of sun, and ample water. Letting it dry out completely, a risk that you always run if you grow it in containers, causes the succulent leaves to blacken and die back.

Because of my slug and snail problem, I prefer to grow basil in large flower pots. This keeps the basil up off the ground and away from all but the most aggressive and adventuresome of these pests. In late winter or whenever all danger of frost has passed, I sow an entire packet of seeds for spring, summer, and fall harvesting.

Because fresh basil is an important herb in our house, I sow a smaller pot in late summer and bring it into the house in October, where it sits in a sunny window and produces fresh basil all winter long.

To prolong your basil harvest, it's necessary to keep the flower spikes picked off the plants so they can't go to seed. By mid-summer, when the flowers start coming fast and furiously, you have to pick almost on a daily basis. The pickings can, of course, be dried on a screen in a cool, dark, and dry place for future use.

My great fondness for basil causes me to sin in an unorganic direction, I must confess. From time to time, when my potted basil begins to fade, I'm guilty of giving it a dose of nitrogen-rich chemical fertilizer. In a matter of a very few days, the foliage is once again a lush, deep and vibrant green and the plants are booming away at producing those delicious smelling and tasting leaves. Some temptations, even sinful ones, are irresistible.

Basil comes with purple foliage as well as with green, and some people use the purple varieties as border plants and in ornamental mass plantings. The purple varieties are generally milder and less flavorful than the green ones, however.

Some people hold that basil is a fly-retardant, but I've noticed that quite a few flies seem to make it past the basil pot and in through the open back door next to it. Still, I've never seen any flies actually sitting on the basil, so there may be some truth to this claim.

Bay

Laurus nobilis

This plant, the provider of that recipe classic, the bay leaf, is one of two trees on my list of herbs. Sometimes called the sweet bay or the Grecian bay, this tree grows slowly to a height of thirty-five to forty feet, which may make it a somewhat larger herb than your garden can comfortably support.

Happily, when young, the sweet bay makes an excellent container plant, and planting it in a container will, of course, help to keep it small. The sweet bay lends itself well to formal shapes, if you or your garden are classically inclined, and it will grow in almost any soil so long as it drains well. In very hot climates, the sweet bay does best if placed away from the hot afternoon sun.

Bay

Umellularia californica

Leaves of the California bay (laurel) are sometimes used in cooking to substitute for those of the true bay, the two trees being related only in the similarity in taste and shape of their leaves and in no other way.

In *haute cuisine* circles, there's some argument about whether the California bay is, in truth, a satisfactory culinary substitute for the true bay. However, it's my understanding that a reputable spice company packages and sells the local product across the board as Bay Leaves without creating a todo among gourmets.

The California bay is an exceptionally handsome tree that will grow almost anywhere and under almost any conditions. It's rarely bothered by insects, and it always presents a neat and clean appearance. California bays, for that reason, make excellent patio trees as well as tall well-groomed hedges. If you're in the market for a tree as well as a source of spice, you might consider planting one of these.

Depending on where you live, this tree is sometimes called a laurel, an Oregon myrtle, or a pepperwood. Whatever you call it, it's easily identified by crushing a few leaves in your hand and smelling them. The odor emitted is powerfully aromatic, so powerfully aromatic, in fact, that a little too much of it will quickly sicken you.

Early California settlers used the bay in their homes to ward off insects and moths. Too much of it in a small room would, I imagine, ward off an unwanted guest as well.

C(h)amomile

Anthemis nobilis

Not very many people these days drink chamomile tea, a concoction brewed from the plant's tiny flowers after they've been dried. These flowers resemble tiny, petalless daisies, which isn't too surprising, considering that chamomile is a cousin of the golden marguerite or yellow daisy (*A. tinctoria*).

Whether or not you use it in the kitchen, chamomile has a definite place in the garden. Low-growing and moss-like in appearance, it makes an excellent ground cover for small or large areas, and it can be used very effectively in rock gardens as well. Chamomile isn't particular about soil, requires moderate water, will take moderate shade, and emits a pleasant, pungent odor when stepped on or crushed.

I take a cup of chamomile tea myself from time to time. I find it a pleasant tasting beverage and a soothing one on a stomach upset by neighbors the likes of Farmer McGregor.

Catnip

Nepeta cataria

Catnip, the word, is probably a corruption of "cat mint," since the plant itself resembles mint—indeed, it's a relative—and because the plant is famous for making cats, animals of unusually great dignity, behave like fools. Some people, I'm told, make a tea for themselves out of catnip or use it to flavor other teas.

A perennial, catnip grows as a ground cover to about two feet in height. Catnip prefers light soil and full sun, and it can become invasive if it isn't watched carefully.

Chives

Allium schoenoprasum

Chives, as we learned in the last chapter, belong to the onion (*allium*) family. In this chapter, we learn that chives are an herb, a perennial herb which likes moist, rich soil.

In the Bay Area, chives are evergreen, but in cold climates, they become dormant in winter. If you live in such an area and want fresh chives all winter long, you can put a small clump in a pot and set it in a sunny window. Under the right conditions, chives will do quite well inside.

Chives have purplish, clover-like flowers and become rangy after they've finished blooming. To restore them to some semblance of order, the whole plant should be cut back to ground level after the blooms have faded. This may sound like a drastic measure, but it isn't. Within a day or two, new spears will start to shoot up from the ground as if by magic.

Unlike many herbs, chives don't lend themselves to drying. If for some reason you want to store chives, you should quick-freeze them just as soon as they've been cut and use them as needed.

Dill

Anethum graveolens

This is, of course, the famous pickling spice. It's an annual, requires a lot of sun, loves heat, and isn't terribly fussy about soil or water.

Dill grows quickly to about four feet high. During the summer, its leaves can be used for flavoring, and its seeds can be saved for use in the winter. Bringing a bunch of dill into the house will make the house smell wonderful, like a pickle factory, or wonderfully like a pickle factory, depending on your point of view.

If the Latin names which follow the English ones in this chapter are starting to rankle you, relax. There's nothing really formidable about *Anethum graveolens*, however formidable it may sound. *Anethum* is only the Latin word for "dill," *grave* means "strong," and *olens* means "smelling." Put them altogether and they spell strong-smelling dill. There's a chapter on garden language yet to come.

Anise (*Pimpinella anisum*), a close relative of dill, is grown in exactly the same way and under the same conditions. Where dill is usually considered a tart or salt spice, anise is a sweet one, although there are remarkable similarities in the smells of both plants when they're fresh.

Fennel

Foeniculum vulgare dulce

There are two kinds of fennel, common fennel and sweet fennel. Sweet fennel is sometimes called Florence fennel or finocchio. Both types are related to dill, which common fennel closely resembles, and both are perennials, although they're usually grown as annuals. Both like lots of sunlight. Finocchio does best in rich soil, while common fennel prefers its soil slightly on the alkaline side.

Some time ago, I dined at a budding French-style restaurant in Berkeley. Fennel-spiced veal and cooked stalks of finocchio comprised the main course, which led me to the conclusion that this herb can very definitely be overdone. It's possible, I suppose, that the same *entree* in more experienced hands might have been a delight.

Finocchio, an attractively fan-shaped plant, has some landscape possibilities.

Lavender

Lavandula spica, vera, officinalis

This type of lavender, commonly called English lavender, is the most widely grown variety. French lavender (*L. dentata*), Spanish lavender (*L. stoechas*), spike lavender (*L. latifolia*), as well as several dwarf varieties of English lavender are also available.

All varieties of lavender are easy to grow, provided they have plenty of sun, loose, well-drained soil, and not very much water. They all make excellent landscape plants, all have attractive evergreen foliage, either gray or gray-green in color, and all produce aromatic flowers which can be dried and used in sachets to perfume clothing and, I hear, repel moths.

Lavender plants should be pruned back after the flowers have faded or been picked to keep the plants from getting rangy.

Marjoram

Majorana hortensis

This herb is sometimes referred to as sweet marjoram, as opposed to wild marjoram—oregano—to which it bears a similarity in taste.

Marjoram is a perennial in mild winter climates. In cold winter climates, it can be brought into the house and grown in a sunny window along with chives and basil. Marjoram prefers moist soil slightly on the alkaline side and plenty of sun, although my own marjoram does nicely in partial shade.

Marjoram makes a satisfactory landscape plant if it's kept trimmed back so that it doesn't get rangy or woody.

Mint

Mentha

Mint comes in a variety of types and tastes, peppermint (*M. piperita*), spearmint (*M. spicata*), orange mint (*M. citrata*), apple mint (*M. gentilis*), woolly mint (*M. rotundifolia*), pennyroyal (*M. pulegium*), and *M. requienii*, the jewel mint of Corsica, a very low-growing, moss-like plant which makes a wonderful rock garden subject.

Mints do best in fairly rich, moist soil and in partial shade. They often, in fact, do too well, sending out a plethora of underground runners and popping up all over the place. Since a small segment of runner will produce a new plant, mint can be very difficult to dig up and get rid of. For that reason, most varieties of mint are best grown in a confined area or in pots.

Woolly mint, a non-aromatic, non-herbal mint, and the jewel mint of Corsica don't spread and invade like other mints.

Pennyroyal is reputed by some to be a flea-repellant, which should make it an attractive addition to any Bay Area garden or Bay Area home which houses pets. Pennyroyal is also somewhat less invasive than the other mints.

Oregano

Origanum vulgare

Oregano, wild marjoram, is a perennial herb which will grow almost anywhere. It does best in fairly rich soil with good drainage and, like mint, spreads by means of underground runners. Under ideal growing conditions, it too can become invasive.

Some people claim that the oregano grown in this country lacks the zest of the Italian product, but I haven't noticed any real difference myself. Perhaps the difference in taste depends on where in the United States the oregano is grown, the more Mediterranean the American climate, the more Italian the taste of the oregano.

Parsley

Petroselium hortense

Parsley comes in two varieties, curly-leafed and flat. The curly-leafed variety is best for decoration. The flat-leafed kind, sometimes called Italian or French parsley, is best for taste and in cooking.

Parsley is a biennial, but it's best grown as an annual, since the plants become woody, go to seed, and lose much of their taste the second year.

This herb likes rich soil, sun, and quite a bit of water. It's a very slow germinator, a process you can speed up by soaking the seeds in warm water for twenty-four hours before planting. Still, the seed may take as long as three weeks to sprout.

Rosemary
Rosemarinus officinalis

As a landscape plant, the rosemary is my favorite of all the herbs. With age and some pinching here and pruning there, it will develop an interesting, dramatic shape and a trunk that can't be described as anything but ruggedly picturesque. Because of their growing habits, rosemaries make excellent bonzai subjects. The needle-like leaves are evergreen, rich and dark in color, and the abundant small flowers come in a number of shades of blue, depending on the particular variety.

Rosemaries won't tolerate poor drainage, but other than that they're not terribly fussy, putting up with poor soil, no summer water, and hot sun. My own ancient plants do very well in damp soil and in partial shade. They have even survived being torn up almost by the roots and transplanted on a very hot day when I was in the heated throes of installing a patio and too full of beer to be nearly as careful as I should have been.

I'm convinced that everyone should have at least one rosemary, be it a bush variety or one of the prostrate kind, which will trail gracefully over a wall, down a slope, or serve as a ground cover in a limited area.

Sage
Salvia officinalis

This is traditionally the most popular herb in America as well as being the only spice, except for pepper, that one of my grandmothers ever went near, and she went near it for, you guessed it, turkey stuffing, using quantities of it to my great delight.

Sage likes poor soil, demands excellent drainage and, it seems, requires much less water than I seem to be able to give it. To correct this problem of mine, I planted some sage in a pot and set the pot in the patio where I assiduously avoided watering it. The sage grew beautifully for a time. Then, when my back was turned, it shot a number of roots out through the hole in the bottom of the pot and drowned in a miniscule puddle of standing water. This may be the first case of plant suicide on record, and I was fortunate enough to have it in my own back yard.

Sage is, as you might have guessed, an excellent addition to a cactus garden or in any other arid spot you might happen to have around. Purple and variegated sages are available if you're looking for variety.

Tansy

Tanacetum vulgare

Tansy is a relatively rare herb with a long and ancient history of medicinal use. It isn't used for medical purposes today, but its coarse, fern-like leaves make it an attractive addition to the garden, and that's mainly why I keep it around. One of these days, though, I'm going to brew myself some tansy tea and try it, since my faith in modern medicine is ever waning just as my belief in ancient practices proportionately grows. I would, at any rate, rather die at my own hands than at those of some sanctimonious, over-paid quack however many diplomas he happens to have hanging on his walls.

Tansy can reach as high as four feet, and it can become invasive. The patch I'm growing under an apricot tree stays well below a foot in height and is spreading very slowly. Sniffing a leaf now and then seems to help clear up my sinuses, and that alone makes tansy a welcome guest in my garden.

Tarragon

Artemisia dracunculus

Tarragon likes sun, medium rich soil on the dry side, and good drainage. It's a perennial that disappears into the ground during the winter in all climates, and some people find it hard to grow. I've had good luck growing it, but I've never been able to make it produce an aroma to match that of commercially available tarragon.

My tarragon seems to reach its aromatic peak in June, at which time I cut off a sprig and stick it in a bottle of white vinegar to improve the vinegar's flavor. From the standpoint of my particular palate, tarragon is a spice that's easily overdone. Just a little too much of it and I can't taste anything but tarragon.

Tarragon is a cousin of common wormwood (*A. Absinthium*), the mind-rotting oil extract of which is a chief component of absinthe and which caused absinthe to be taken off the market, something I didn't know when I first visited France but might have guessed from the horror-sticken face of the bartender I ordered it from.

Thyme

Thymus

The most commonly grown variety of thyme is *T. vulgaris*, which is called, appropriately enough, common thyme. Common thyme is a low-growing, perennial shrub. Mother-of-thyme or creeping thyme (*T. serpyllum*) has a similar flavor but is a ground cover as is *T. herba-barona*, which is called Caraway-scented thyme because of its taste and smell.

As a garden plant, lemon-scented thyme (*T. serpyllum vulgaris*) is my favorite of the thymes. Lemon thyme has dark green leaves edged in yellow and makes a striking perennial ground cover. Of all the lemon-scented herbs, it's the most lemony, and a sprig of it in a cup of boiling water makes a delicious herb tea.

Woolly thyme (*T. lanuginosis*) also makes an attractive ground cover or rock garden plant. It forms a low mat of undulating woolly gray leaves that appears at first glance to be rock. Woolly thyme has no particular taste or smell and isn't of any use in the kitchen.

All varieties of thyme like sun, light soil, and not too much water. If you plant every kind of thyme, you and your friends can play that fascinating horticultural guessing game, "What thyme is it?" Planting the various thymes around a sun dial will add yet another dimension to this ever-popular lesson in pronunciation.

Woodruff

Asperula odorata

To the best of my knowledge, sweet woodruff is used only for flavoring May wine, which doesn't make it a must for every kitchen garden. Its strikingly beautiful leaves, however, are highly reminiscent of the woods, and if you have a moist and shady spot in your garden, it's well worth it to have woodruff around just to look at.

Woodruff grows to a height of about eight inches, spreads rapidly in rich soil, and emits a sweet, hay-like aroma. Since it isn't a very common herb, it may prove hard to find, but the rewards are great if you persevere.

That about concludes what I have to say about particular herbs. As a group, no other plants have excited as much interest throughout history, and no other group has been as much written about and discussed. The Middle Ages produced elaborately designed and executed herb gardens and attributed mystical as well as culinary and medicinal significance to the plants that grew in them. It was, in part, the quest for new herbs and spices that brought on the Renaissance and awakened the interest of Europeans in lands other than their own.

New books on herbs are appearing every day to take their places in libraries and on book shelves next to ancient herbals. No culture is without an herbal tradition of some kind, and lately we Westerners have begun to take a second look at our tradition, even to looking into the medical value of certain time-honored herbs, which modern doctors, the only titled Americans, have pooh-poohed.

There is something strangely special about herbs, something that becomes more apparent to you with every new one that you add to your collection. I'm not really sure what that something is, but I do know that having herbs around awakens and stimulates your sense of smell and taste and that that alone makes the whole of gardening a more pleasant, interesting and, finally, educational experience. Herbs connect you to your garden and to the land in a way that flowers and even vegetables can't.

18 THE ROSE GARDEN

Roses

For those fearless creatures who weren't frightened away from roses by my description of some of the problems they create for those who try to grow them (page 39), I'm now going to describe in some detail just what's involved in the installation and maintenance of a rose garden, one from which you might expect to achieve some measure of success and now and then a few acceptable roses for the house.

LOCATION

Step one in your progress toward a rose garden is to stake out a large, sunny area in your garden. An ideal spot would be one which received full sun in the winter, spring, and fall and light, filtered shade in the summer, a very hard spot to come by in most gardens. Roses produce best in the relative coolness of the spring and fall and suffer badly from the heat in summer. In the hot glare of the summer sun, a rose bud will open, burn, and drop its petals all in the course of a single day. If your roses are growing in light summer shade, you have a better chance of retrieving them and getting them into the house before this happens. In very hot summer climates, an area which receives only morning sun might be a partial answer to this problem.

The area you choose shouldn't be smaller than ten feet square. If you're tempted to scatter your roses randomly around your garden, resist the temptation. Bush roses really aren't landscape assets, except when arranged in some sort of official rose garden, and they're also much easier to take care of properly if they're all planted together.

Tree roses and climbing roses are a slightly different matter. Both have some landscape potential, but they should be planted and cared for in the same way as bush roses, except when it comes to pruning them. We'll discuss pruning further on.

Preparation

After you've staked out your rose garden, remove everything that's already growing there, shrubs, ground covers, bulbs, weeds, perennials, annuals, as well as the wandering roots of nearby plants, and remove those down to a depth of at least a foot. Roses don't like competition of any kind.

You can remove roots while you're turning over the soil and working in steer manure, other kinds of organic matter, and sand if your soil is heavy and clayey. You'll need at least two-hundred pounds of steer manure for every one-hundred square feet of ground, but the more steer manure and organic matter the better. It's doubtful that you could ever add too much.

For the next two months, keep the area moist and turn it over every two weeks, adding more organic matter if you've got it, digging it in to the depth of a foot, and further breaking up the soil. Your soil will have reached perfection when a moist handful of it forms a loose, crumbling ball. Keep working until your soil reaches that stage.

Selection

While you're preparing the soil, you can start to think about selecting your roses, and this is a job that should be done with the greatest patience and care. If you're in doubt about what varieties to plant, and you certainly should be, and if you're lucky enough to have a municipal rose garden handy, visit it as often as you can. Roses, as I mentioned above, are at their best in the late spring and early fall, so plan to time your visits accordingly.

During your visits to the rose garden, compile a list of the ten or so varieties you like best, considering such things as color, fragrance, size, shape, number and durability of the blossoms, and the general appearance of the plant, its compactness, the color and density of its foliage, its height, and its resistance to pests and diseases. Each time you visit the garden, check out the roses you've selected and make notes on any changes in them for the better or worse.

When you're convinced that the ten roses on your list are indeed the ten best for you, try to corner one of the caretakers and ask him what he thinks about the roses you've chosen. Are they really good performers? Do they require any kind of special attention? Do they bloom over a long period of time? How well do the flowers hold up? How susceptible are they to mildew? And most important, how does he think they will behave in your particular area? If a caretaker isn't available or doesn't prove helpful enough, take your questions to a nurseryman, one whose specialty is roses—if that's possible.

In a rose garden ten feet square, you'll have room for nine roses planted three feet apart, and you shouldn't plant them too much closer than that. If your object is largish bouquets made up of the same kind of roses, you probably shouldn't select more than three varieties from your list of ten and plant three bushes of each. If, on the other hand, all your roses will end up singly in bud vases, you can afford to plant one bush each of the nine varieties you choose.

Kinds of Roses

Of the roses that are planted today, the most popular are the hybrid teas, the grandifloras, the polyanthas, and the floribundas. Of these, the hybrid tea class offers the greatest number of varieties, and most of the roses available from the nursery will belong to it.

The hybrid tea is the rose best suited for the type of rose garden we're talking about and, along with the grandiflora, the best rose for cutting. The grandifloras are somewhat larger and more vigorous plants than the teas, but the line dividing the two is so fine that some varieties have been switched from one class to the other.

Chrysler Imperial, Tropicana, Tiffany, Peace, Chicago Peace, and Sutter's Gold are among the best known of the hybrid teas. Queen Elizabeth is probably the most popular and most planted of the grandifloras, and deservedly so, too. Many varieties of hybrid teas are available as climbers and trees as well as bushes.

Polyanthas are smaller bushes which produce masses of small flowers. Some are available as climbers. Cecil Brunner is probably the best known member of this class.

Floribundas produce clusters of blossoms larger than those of the polyanthas but smaller than the hybrid teas. If you insist on using roses as landscape plants, the floribundas are the best bush roses for this purpose.

For a rose garden, however, you should only be considering hybrid teas and possibly grandifloras.

Grades of Roses

Roses come in three grades: No. 1, No. 1½, and No. 2. They are graded for performance and beauty, if they carry an AARS tag, after having been watched carefully for two years. Buy No. 1 AARS plants if you can find them. They'll cost you more, but they'll be worth it in the long run. Rose gardening is difficult enough without starting out with inferior plants.

Bare Root Stock

One of the advantages of compiling a list of roses in advance during visits to a rose garden is that, come winter, you can buy exactly the roses you want and at considerable savings in bare root stock.

In the late fall, rose growers dig up their two year old plants, package them soil-free, and ship them out to be sold. In the spring, those plants which haven't been sold have to be replanted in cans by the nursery, the cost of which will, of course, be passed on to the customer. If you know what roses you want in January or February without having to see them in bloom, you can save yourself the cost of the replanting operation, and you'll also have a bigger choice of varieties and of individual plants, since bare root stock doesn't take up much room and a nursery can handle much more of it than it can of canned stock.

Buy your bare root stock from a reputable nurseryman if you can. If you buy it from a supermarket, a drugstore nursery outlet, or a mail order house, the chances are greater that the stock will have been mishandled somewhere along the way, and you may find, come spring, that you've acquired a dead plant. It will be difficult for you to prove that you weren't responsible for the plant's death and, even if you do succeed in getting your money back, you'll have to wait another year before you can take advantage of bare root prices again.

Planting

Before planting bare root roses, soak them overnight, roots, tops and all, in a solution of one tablespoon horticultural vitamin B-1 per gallon of water. This will help to revivify the plants and give them a head start toward spring growth. After you've dug out the planting hole, work a little bonemeal into the bottom of it before you set the rose in.

When the weather warms up, add a two to three inch mulch to the entire rose garden. Leaf mold, peat moss, finely ground bark, and well-aged, soil-free compost are fine for this purpose. Mulching will, as we've discussed before, help to retain moisture in the soil, keep it from baking hard in the sun, cut down on your weed problems, and keep the soil cool in summer and warm in winter. When mulching, be sure to keep the mulch off the crown of the plant and below the level of the graft line.

In the late fall, mulch again, this time with about two inches of steer manure, and then continue the spring and fall mulching for the life of the garden, working the old mulch into the soil before adding the new one to it. Mulching in this way should satisfy most of the garden's fertilizing needs, but additional applications of rose food won't hurt unless, of course, it hurts you to use chemicals.

If you're planting roses from cans, you should wait until the weather is cool and do your planting early in the evening if possible. Work some bonemeal into the hole before setting the plant in, and once it's in, water it with the same vitamin B-1 solution we talked about above. This will help to minimize the shock of transplanting. After the canned roses are in the ground, they should be treated in just the same way as bare root stock.

Watering

Roses appreciate a good deal of water. If you live in a cool summer climate, it's best to irrigate them deeply once a week. Irrigation helps to prevent mildew. To make sure the water stays where it belongs, form a basin of dirt around each plant. The basin should be about the same diameter as the plant itself.

In hot climates and during hot weather, roses benefit from overhead sprinkling. It washes the dust off the leaves and helps to freshen and cool the foliage and flowers, but you should still keep an eye out for mildew, a disease to which red roses are particularly susceptible. With the first sign of mildew, all overhead watering should come to a stop.

Newly planted roses require less water than established plants, and too much water on new roses will keep them from taking a firm hold.

Pruning

Roses should be pruned during the winter when they're most dormant, and it's a certainty that every rose is going to need some pruning at this time. How they are pruned will depend on whether they're bush roses, tree roses, or climbers.

Bush roses. As a rule of thumb, a bush rose should be cut back to about sixty percent of its pre-pruning size. If it has more than three or four canes (trunks), the oldest and woodiest canes should be completely removed. Old canes will have lost their productivity, and they'll only be in the way of newer, more vigorous and productive growth.

After these operations have been performed, the bush should be shaped. Any side branches which jut out and throw the bush off balance should be cut back or removed completely and, finally, the entire bush should be returned to some sort of symmetrical, generally rounded whole.

Tree roses. The same general rules apply to pruning tree roses except that with tree roses you shouldn't prune the foliage ball down to less than twelve inches in height. The foliage ball is that part of the tree which begins where the tree starts to branch out and ends at the tree's top.

Climbers. How climbers are pruned will depend in part on what they're climbing on and on how you want them to continue to climb. Misguided shoots which are too stiff to be redirected in the way you want them to go should be removed. Old, woody canes should be cut out at the base of the plant to make room for newer ones.

There is no particular reason to reduce the size of a climber unless you happen to want a smaller plant. If you want the plant to spread out more along a fence or wall, you should remove some of the shorter growth so that the plant will put its energy behind the longer canes.

Suckers

None of the roses that we've been talking about grow on their own root stock, which is usually of too poor a quality to support a healthy, vigorous plant. Commercially marketed roses are grafted onto other, hardier root stock, usually the roots of wild roses. At times, this root stock will attempt to put out some growth of its own, and this growth is known as suckers.

Suckers are fairly easy to identify, since they shoot out from below the graft line. If the graft line isn't easily distinguishable, as it won't be on some plants, sucker growth can be identified by its unusual strength and vigor. It shoots straight for the sky and it shoots fast.

Suckers and suspected suckers should be removed as soon as you see them and removed completely, which means that during the spring and early summer you'll have to watch your roses carefully. If the suckers are allowed to bloom, the grafted stock—the rose you paid for—will never again be more than a mere shadow of its former self. If this happens, it's best to dig the rose up, throw it away, and plant a new one in its place.

Picking Roses

The best time to pick roses is in the cool of the morning or evening. As soon as they've been picked, they should be placed in warm water, which is easier for them to absorb than cold.

Roses which have opened fully on the bush won't last very long in the house and are best left where they are. Instead, roses should be picked in the mature bud stage and left to open in the house. If allowed to do this, they often manage to keep their shape and their freshness longer than they would have on the bush.

Pests

As well as being the favorite flower of many people, the rose is also a favorite food of many garden pests and diseases, which makes growing roses a particular headache for the organic gardener.

Unorganically speaking, the best pesticides ever developed for the rose grower were the systemic ones. Systemic pesticides are dug into the dirt around the roots of the plant and absorbed into it along with water, making the whole plant pure poison for anything that tries to eat it. Needless to say, systemics produced some beautiful flowers and some remarkably healthy-looking plants.

The organic gardener will, I'm afraid, have to be satisfied with knocking the aphids off his roses with the spray from the garden hose and resign himself to sharing part of the beauty of his roses with some of nature's smaller creatures. In dire straits, he might try rotenone or pyrethrum, which are reputedly safe and ecologically sound, and now and again in a real crisis, he might even find himself stooping to using Malathion, which, they tell me, breaks down and disappears in six weeks.

Anyone who is both a serious rose grower and a serious ecologist is going to have problems.

An Old Wive's Tale

I'm particularly fond of old wive's tales, and I happen to know one about roses which I'll pass along to you and which you can treat as you like. The tale involves an old lady, naturally, someone my grandmother was supposed to have known, who had remarkably beautiful, pest-free roses, roses that were, if I remember correctly, the envy of an entire village.

When asked what she did to produce these miraculous roses, the old lady answered that she did nothing at all—except that every evening, when she was finished with the dishes, she took the dishpan outside and dumped the dishwater over the tops of her beautiful plants.

It should be remembered, if you're tempted to try this experiment, that the old lady washed her dishes in real soap and not in dish detergent, which will kill pests, diseases, roses, and even old ladies if they drink it. I've never gotten around to testing the tale myself. I've never been brave enough, really, but I have gotten as far as buying a box of Ivory Soap with that project in mind. What stops me is the fear that that lying old lady may have had such beautiful roses because she was the only one in town who *wasn't* poisoning her roses with soap.

A Theory

Another theory that I've never gotten around to testing, one that would almost surely work, is my theory of rose garden rejuvenation. The soil in a rose garden which has been established for five or more years is bound to have become densely packed and largely depleted of many of its nutrients, especially those down around the roots where the plants really need them.

Given this, it seems to me that, during the winter when the roses are dormant and about two weeks after their winter pruning, it might be a good idea to dig them up and give the soil a thorough reworking, pouring in steer manure and a lot of organic matter and otherwise preparing the soil as if for a new garden.

While the roses were out of the ground, they would of course have to be submerged in a solution of B-1 (see above) to prevent their drying out and to minimize the shock of treating them in this rather rude manner.

One of the reasons that I haven't tested this theory is that the soil is usually at its wettest and most unworkable worst at the only time of the year that this operation could feasibly be undertaken. Still, it's a nice theory as theories go, and come some dry January, I might actually put it into practice. Lord knows, my rose garden—the one I inherited with the house, mind you—could use something.

The Moral

The moral of this chapter is that if you decide to go into rose gardening, go into it whole hog. Don't skimp, don't economize, and be prepared to work and work some more. If you're not prepared to work or if life tempts you to cut corners and accept second best at a price reduction, grow something else and buy your roses from the florist—or from innocent, rose-growing old ladies who happen to be witches.

19 PLANTS IN THE HOUSE

House Plants

There is no such thing as a house plant. Somewhere in the world what you're absolutely certain has to be a house plant is growing in a vacant lot. If you happen to be there and ask the local inhabitants what they call it, they'll tell you that it doesn't have a name, that it's just a weed.

A friend of mine groans every time he sets eyes on a piggy-back plant (*Tolmiea menziesii*) that his wife is tenderly nuturing. Piggy-back plants grew wild where he was raised, and part of his early gardening duties included ridding the family property of them. Having one in his house is for him rather like putting your garbage in a safe deposit box.

Another friend of mine who lives on Maui has to stifle her hysterics every time she sees one of my dieffenbachias. To her, my dieffenbachias are puny, miserable specimens of a plant that, even at its vigorous best, hardly belongs in the house. She sees them as you and I would view a sparrow in a canary cage, but to me and by mainland standards, my dieffenbachias are brilliant and beautiful successes.

For my part, I can't help snorting a little at the potted geraniums I've seen being treated like visiting royalty. I don't bother with geraniums in the garden, and I wouldn't be caught dead bringing one into the house. They're simply too easy and uninteresting to grow, too much like weeds.

On the other hand, I was bowled over on a recent visit to Mexico by the sight of a variegated split-leaf philodendron (*Monstera deliciosa*) which had climbed twenty-five feet up the trunk of a coconut palm and was still climbing vigorously. I confined my appreciation of this wonder to my fellow countrymen, however, because I knew that the locals would have further impugned gringo sanity had they discovered that any of us had a smaller version of this monster as a permanent house guest, taking up room that might otherwise have been given over to something more practical, like a pig.

There's a lot of silly snobbery attached to the growing of house plants, in particular to what plants are truly worthy additions to the sacred confines of the human abode. It's harmful snobbery because it scares timid people away from plants which are reputed to be exotic as well as keeping others from enjoying plants that are thought to be too easy to bother with.

Up until the 1930's, sansevieria and aspidistra were common house plants, but one rarely sees them anymore. Their hardiness and durability apparently killed them. They grew for people who couldn't grow anything else in places where nothing else would grow, and consequently, they came to be thought of as common, which is particularly sad in the case of the aspidistra, a handsome plant which will grow in very little light, something few other plants are willing to do.

I'm a victim of house plant snobbery myself. I still can't look the common philodendron in the face because, in the 1950's, every house I went into had one growing out of a lamp base and another one emerging from a ceramic black panther with either a red or a green rhinestone eye. Sometimes the panther was a lamp, too, and when it was, it sat on top of the television set as a Television Lamp, a breed now vanished from the face of the earth.

My own eye might not have become jaundiced, yellowed but not rhinestone, if any of these illuminated philodendrons had been healthy, but they rarely if ever were. They often sported no more than one or two green leaves attached to several yards of barren, straggly vine wrapped around the lamp, the panther, or the panther lamp. They spelled failure, and I've always wondered why more people didn't throw them away sooner.

In spite of the philodendron craze and its dismal conclusion, a real house plant boom began in the late 1960's, a boom that I still have mixed feelings about. On the one hand, I like rooms filled with greenery. They're more alive, like a room with a fish tank in it or one with a bird in a cage. On the other hand, the house plant boom sky-rocketed the price of house plants, which were a relatively cheap form of entertainment for those of us who were aficionados before the boom began.

I probably shouldn't complain. A high price is a small price to pay for a room full of greenery, I guess, and I would like to see plant life become a permanent part of the American home. One way to help to insure that it does is for us to rid ourselves of our snobbery, to learn to tolerate and even enjoy easy plants, because they'll be there to tide us over when we fail with the more difficult ones.

Another way for us to insure our success with house plants is to realize from the start that the house, any house but the greenhouse, does not provide a very congenial atmosphere for any plant. There are, however, certain things you can do for plants to make it easier for them to accept the uncongenial atmosphere and certain things you can do, if you're willing to, to make the atmosphere more congenial.

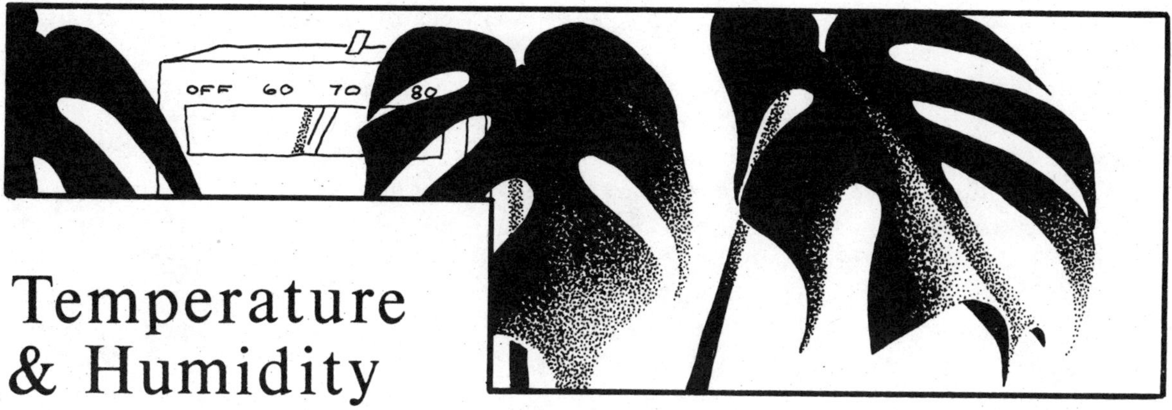

Temperature & Humidity

It would be nice if we could talk about temperature and humidity separately, but we can't. As far as plants are concerned, they're inseparably correlative, as we'll see.

Most house plants prefer a steady temperature somewhere between sixty-five and seventy degrees, given the moisture content of the air in most houses. If the temperature rises much above seventy-five, artificial moisture will have to be added to the air or the plants will start to suffer.

If you keep your house up around eighty degrees in winter, you'd better give up the idea of growing house plants altogether, because to do so at that temperature would mean that you'd have to provide a degree of humidity equivalent to that of a greenhouse, a degree of humidity that would make your plaster fall, rot out your wooden windows, and spawn mildew like mushrooms after a rain. In time, you might even get a few mushrooms.

If you want to grow house plants, learn to live with the thermostat set at seventy-two degrees or lower, or keep your plants in rooms where the temperature won't exceed that. (Since this chapter was drafted, we've all been hit with the energy crisis. If people do follow the ex-President's advice and keep their thermostats set at sixty-eight degrees, they're going to be surprised at how much better their plants will do. In gratitude, I feel that all good Republicans should buy a philodendron and name it Nixon in honor of this inadvertent bit of White House green-thumbery.)

During the summer, when air from outside is allowed to circulate through the house, higher temperatures aren't as dangerous because Mother Nature will most likely be doing some correlating of temperature and humidity on her own. If you have air-conditioning of the type that removes moisture from the air, however, you're going to be in trouble again, and you'll either have to find a way of replacing some of that moisture or make sure that the air-conditioner is cooling your rooms to seventy-two degrees or below.

On the other end of the temperature scale, you'll run into problems of a different kind. Since many house plants are native to the tropics and subtropics, they won't tolerate low temperatures. The minimum temperature that they'll endure will, of course, depend on where they originated. Generally speaking, however, you should never let the house get below forty-five degrees. At forty degrees, you'll start to lose any number of plants.

Moisture Compensation

There are several ways of compensating for insufficient moisture in the air. Perhaps the easiest and most effective one involves adding an inch or so of pea gravel to the saucers or trays underneath the pots. The gravel allows water to remain in the saucers out of the way of roots, water which will slowly evaporate upwards toward the leaves, where it will become available to the plants as airborne moisture.

If you don't have gravel or something like it in your saucers or trays, remove the excess water from them after you've finished watering. Letting the bottom of the pot stand in water will drown the roots, deprive them of the oxygen they need from the air, encourage root rot and, if done frequently enough, insure the death of the plant. Any moisture that might happen to find its way into the air through this negligent practice is going to be of little consequence compared to the damage the water will do.

For removing excess water from saucers and keeping the water below the level of the bottom of the pot, I've found a plastic meat-basting syringe to be an ideal tool. Using a syringe saves carting the full saucer and a dripping pot off to the nearest sink, and it also saves cleaning up the inevitable splashes and splatters afterwards.

Another way of getting moisture to the leaves of a plant is to use one of the various misters available in plastic, brass, and glass. Misting, unfortunately, isn't a terribly selective business, and fussy housekeepers may object to mist falling on surfaces which want nothing less than to be dampened. Housekeeping considerations aside, you can mist a plant as often as you like, and the more often the better, cacti excepted.

A third method of moisturizing a plant is to take it outside or into the bathroom where you can give it a shower or let it absorb the benefits of a warm, gentle rain. If you take the plant outside, keep it out of the sun or you're sure to burn it. If it's raining, set the plant somewhere where a sudden gust of wind can't knock it over.

I stupidly lost a beautiful schefflera in just that way. While it was enjoying a shower outside, the wind blew it over and it fell four feet to the ground, but since the pot wasn't broken or the plant very much dislodged from it, I thought I was home safe. I then had the painful experience of watching my prize specimen die very slowly over a two week period and die from what could only have been shock.

Dousing my shocked schefflera immediately with a solution of vitamin B-1 might have saved it, but I was too stupid to think of that at the time, too certain that nothing really serious had happened, and only vaguely aware that plants could be concussed. Perhaps it wasn't really the fall that killed it so much as the plant-wilting strength of my language on discovering that it had fallen. That's no way to talk to a plant, young man.

Another way of getting around the moisture problem is to grow your plants in groups. In this way, they can each take advantage of the moisture which the others create and together produce a much moister mini-climate than any of them could produce if grown alone.

If your house is exceptionally dry, you can use standing trays of water to evaporate moisture into the air. In Germany—where house plants have long been very popular and steam heat, which is extremely dry, very common—ceramic trays are placed on top of the radiators and kept constantly filled with water in order to create an atmosphere moist enough to support plants. In this country, you may have noticed bread and cake pans sitting on top of gas floor furnaces for presumably the same purpose.

To be effective, trays and pans filled with water don't have to be placed on top of a heater. They could as well be placed on window sills where the sun would help to evaporate them or anywhere else, for that matter, where plants were growing.

It's virtually impossible to create an atmosphere in your house that's too moist for plants. That you don't have to worry about. What you do have to consider is that the atmosphere may become too damp for the health of the house itself as well as too damp for the health of its human inhabitants. As with temperature, some sort of balance has to be achieved which is acceptable to plant and animal alike.

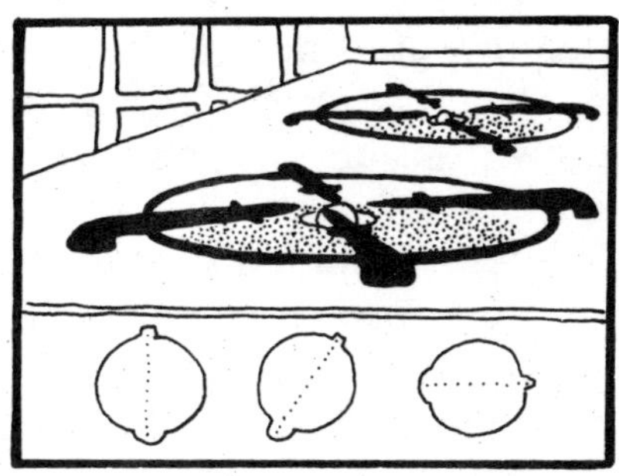

Heat Considerations

As you've almost surely guessed by now, plants aren't particularly fond of heat and are especially averse to most kinds of artificial heating methods. Because of this, they should always be kept as far away as possible from heaters, furnaces, fireplaces, stoves, and heating vents and ducts. Plants should also be kept out of drafts and drafty areas because of the sudden changes in temperature which drafts often bring.

Since heat rises and the temperature of a room is always higher toward the ceiling than it is around the floor, some thought should be given to the height at which a plant is placed. Ivy, for example, which likes it on the cool side, might thrive on the floor in one place in the room, while placing it five feet directly above that spot on, say, a bookcase might cause it to languish and die.

There are no hard and fast rules about height placement, but most plants will do better if they're kept away from the cold and drafts of the floor and the more stagnant hot air of the ceiling. An ideal height, if there is one, would probably be somewhere below your eyes and above your waist when you're standing—or neither above nor below the windows in a room.

In summation, the factors to be considered when placing a plant are how much heat or cold the particular species will tolerate, how much light or sun the particular spot gets, how hot the room is, how much moisture the air contains, and how often the plant will be watered. If a hanging plant, any plant placed high in a room, a fern, or an ivy starts to show signs of withering, it would be a very good idea to lower it.

Some windows, especially south and west-facing ones, can also prove dangerous for plants, especially if they're set too close to the glass without benefit of an intervening curtain to filter the light and stave off the heat. Most ferns wouldn't last a summer's day in such a spot. On the other hand, there might not be a better place for a cactus, provided it wasn't put there after having spent some time in a darker corner of the house.

Water

More house plants are probably killed by water than by any other of the number of horrors which living in a house threatens them with, and they don't die from too little water but from too much of it, from too much love and attention, if you can call it that.

The tendency is—and I'll own that I've passed through this stage myself—to pour on the water just as soon as the plant starts to look the least bit weak, when the chances are about ninety percent that the reason it started to weaken in the first place is that it's been given far too much water already.

I've discovered after ten years of growing house plants with moderate success that I don't need to water them more than once a week, and that's once a week in August as well as in January. About the fifth day, of course, I start keeping an eye out for sagging foliage, especially with plants in small pots, which expose a greater surface area to the air than do larger pots and, for that reason, tend to dry out faster, but by and large, the once a week rule seems to be a hard and fast one.

Soft-nosed person that I am, I am of course willing to grant that there may be some exceptions. I do, I admit, live in a cool summer climate, and although we have some summer days which climb up over a hundred degrees, we never have more than three or four such days in a row. If we did, I might have to water a little more often than I do.

Plants which grow in hanging containers will need more frequent watering than other plants if they're placed high up in a room and if the containers they grow in don't have saucers to catch and help redistribute the water that isn't absorbed by the soil the first time through. Plants which grow in sunny windows, particularly if the sun lingers on the soil, may also need more frequent watering than plants which don't.

Still, I doubt that any plant anywhere in the country in any part of any house will demand water every day or even every other day. Restraint when watering is the lesson, and it's a hard one to learn, particularly for the novice and especially if you love plants, want to succeed with them, and feel that you must constantly be doing something, anything to show that you really care.

Letting a plant go limp from lack of water is much easier on the plant than drowning it. The surest sign of over-watering, when the lower leaves start to yellow and drop off in number, is the sign to watch for. If and when that starts to happen, steel yourself and keep your watering can away from the plant for at least a week or until the loose soil at the top of the container is absolutely dry to the touch, which is the surest sign that the plant might appreciate a drink.

Soaking

Now that I've scared you off watering entirely, I'm going to turn around and tell you to plunge your pots into water over their tops and let the pots sit in the water for a couple of hours. If you've got big pots, the bathtub is a perfect place for performing this puzzling act, an act which you should perform once every six months or so, excusing from the performance any plants that you suspect might be suffering from overwatering already.

There are two reasons for plunging and soaking your potted plants. One of them is to leech out harmful mineral salts which build up in the soil and in the pot itself, if it's an unglazed clay one, in the course of normal, everyday watering and fertilizing, particularly if the water in your area is hard.

The second reason for soaking is to make sure that water applied in the normal way will reach all of the soil in the pot. After six months of normal watering, channels may develop in the soil which drain the water through the pot before it can moisten all the soil and reach all the roots. Soaking the pot will help to eradicate these channels and insure that future water is evenly and adequately distributed throughout the pot.

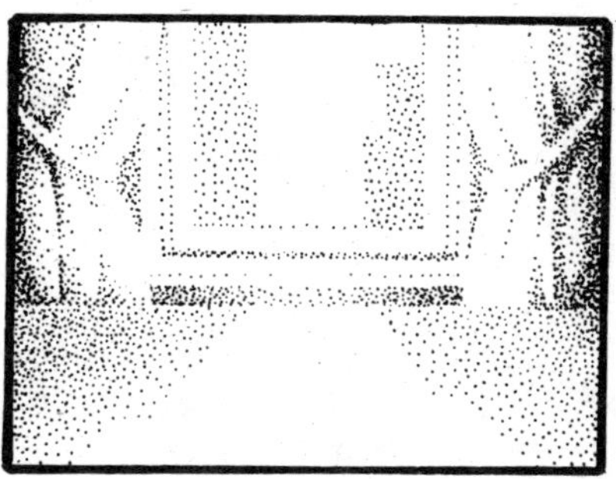

Light

Most house plants prefer strong, indirect light. This makes a large, north-facing window or the area beneath a skylight an ideal location for growing plants. An east-facing window, which gets only morning sun, is also a good location.

With west and south-facing windows, you start to run into problems, since these windows generate and hold a great deal of heat and because the sun's rays through them can easily burn foliage if those rays are allowed to reach it unfiltered by a curtain. Afternoon sun is, simply, stronger and hotter than morning sun.

Sunburnt foliage is easily recognized and further damage to the plant can be prevented by moving the plant out of the sun. On the other hand, plants which aren't getting enough light produce foliage which is paler in color than normal and growth which is straggly and elongated in appearance. Any plants exhibiting these latter symptoms should be moved by degrees into stronger light. They should not, however, be placed immediately in direct sunlight, which would quickly finish them off in their already weakened condition.

How much direct sun, if any, a plant will take and how much light it will do without depends, of course, on the species in question. If you're acquiring a species that's new to you, it's always a good idea to inquire into its lighting requirements and to keep a close eye on it until you're satisfied that it's satisfied with the location you've given it.

Because plants tend to grow toward the light and because few rooms are evenly lighted from all directions, you should turn your plants from time to time to keep them from becoming lop-sided or developing strongly defined fronts and backs—unless, of course, a plant with its back to a wall is what you're after, and in some instances that may very well be the case.

Moving

Unlike furniture, plants cannot be moved about the house with impunity. Every spot in your house will vary somewhat in the amount of light it gets and in its temperature range. A plant which has sat for awhile in one spot will have made certain adjustments to that spot, and moving it elsewhere may affect it adversely. That's why you should think first before moving any plant, especially one that's doing particularly well where it is.

On the other hand, if a plant is doing poorly where it is, the best thing for it might be to move it somewhere else, especially if you've already ruled out over-watering, improper soil, and so forth as the probable causes of its poor performance.

The Plant Hospital

One of the rooms in our house, the guest bedroom, has gradually evolved into a kind of plant hospital. Our guest room is the lightest room in a fairly dark house as well as being the room furthest removed from the evil influence of a gas furnace, both of which attributes make it the best room in the house for growing plants.

Any plant which starts to show signs of distress gets sent to the guest room where it remains until it dies or until it's completely recovered from whatever house malaise it's suffering from as, happily, is most often the case. Of course, I always keep a few robust specimens in this room, too, so that guests won't think I'm dropping subtle hints about the durability of their welcome.

In most houses, the bathroom would make the best plant hospital—if it's light enough as well as big enough for both people and plants. Because of showering, bathing, face and hand washing, and even flushing, a great deal of moisture gets into the air in a bathroom, moisture which can't help but benefit an ailing plant and help to save it if it can be saved.

A plant hospital is also a good place to put a new plant for awhile before introducing it into the less accommodating parts of your house. Doing so will help it adjust to the rigors of life in the house, which is of particular importance if its former home was a greenhouse.

Schizophrenia

A lot of plants die of schizophrenia, their owner's not their own. A plant is usually purchased because of its decorative value and often with a particular spot for it in mind. The plant, however, may not like that spot at all and may refuse to flourish there. The owner then becomes torn between his interior decorating and his horticultural instincts. The decorator in him says, leave it there, it'll learn, and the gardener says, move it and save it. If the decorator dominates or if the gardener is too slow in asserting himself, the plant usually loses.

Everyone who grows house plants faces this dilemma from time to time, and everyone has to work it out for himself. I mention it here only to say that if your decorating priorities are very strong, plants may present you with more difficulties than you're willing to put up with and that you might be better off doing without them altogether.

Soil

As a grower of house plants, you may not have much latitude when it comes to heat, humidity, light, and temperature, but you do have complete control over the soil your house plants grow in, and through soil, you can help your plants to overcome many of the disadvantages growing inside presents them with.

There's absolutely no excuse for using poor soil. The best soil is dirt cheap compared to the value of the plant. If you're tempted to use soil straight from the garden, forget about it. Garden soil may be fine for plants whose roots are free to search at will for the nutrients they need, but it's not good enough for plants whose roots are confined and, by necessity, overcrowded in a pot.

The best soil for house plants is, generally, one that's rich, light, fast-draining, and moisture retentive. You can buy potting mixtures ready-prepared at a nursery outlet which will meet these requirements or you can make your own. Commercially prepared potting mixes are expensive, considering the real value of their contents, but if you do relatively little potting, their convenience may be well worth the price to you.

Recipes for potting soil vary somewhat for different species and among certain gardeners. A good standard recipe is one part river sand, one part leaf mold, one part peat moss, and one part good, rich garden loam. Another good recipe is one-third river sand, one-third organic matter (peat moss, leaf mold, or thoroughly aged, finely sieved compost), and one-third loam.

If you're potting cacti, a mixture of half sand and half organic matter is probably best, since it more closely approximates the soil in which cacti normally grow than do either of the above recipes. Ferns, on the other hand, will appreciate a superabundance of organic matter and very little clay in their soil, because such a mixture more closely approximates the top soil of a rain forest floor.

Even better than sand for everything but cacti is vermiculite, a commercially available mineral product that's popped into light-weight kernels which, unlike sand, retain moisture in themselves as well as speeding drainage and keeping the soil light and loose. Vermiculite also adds very little weight to the mix, which isn't true of sand, and like sand, it affects only the physical and not the chemical make-up of the mix.

Adding a tablespoon of blood meal and one of bone meal to every gallon of potting mix will insure that it's rich in nitrogen and phosphorus. Adding an equivalent amount of pure wood ash, if you've got it, will supply beneficial potassium.

Fertilizing

I mentioned in the chapter on fertilizers that my organic and ecological principles don't extend to using chemical fertilizers on house plants, and I gave my reasons for this on page 118. If your principles do extend that far, you can get around the problem by making a brew out of steer manure according to the instructions on page 119 and using it in place of chemicals.

Another way of avoiding the chemical problem is to fertilize with fish emulsion—if you can get it. I've seen some chemical products labeled "Fish Emulsion" which really aren't but which have a chemical analysis similar to that of the real thing. If you're in doubt about whether it's the real thing or not, untwist the cap and smell the contents of the bottle. Real fish emulsion smells like real and somewhat rotten fish. The chemical product won't, unless some unscrupulous shyster has devised a chemical fish smell to entice the conscientious unwary. If that's the case, examine the liquid itself. It's the real thing if it's thick, dark brown, and generally repulsive. If it's clear and green, it isn't.

The labels on most chemical house plant fertilizers instruct you to use so much of their product once a month on your plants. You'll be better off using half the suggested amount every two weeks. More frequent applications of a weaker solution are less apt to burn delicate root hairs and ends. For the same reason, avoid over-fertilizing. Chemical fertilizers are strong medicine, and a little too much of a good thing will be a bad thing for almost all plants.

The only plant I ever owned which positively doted on overdoses of chemical fertilizers was a prayer plant (*Maranta leuconeura*), and the particular individual I'm talking about, and still own, is a peculiar plant indeed. For a couple of years, it became deciduous, something marantas aren't supposed to do. The first year it did this, I thought it had died and threw it away, retrieving it as soon as I'd dumped it out and noticed the abundant tubers at the bottom of the pot.

The plant, as I thought it might, grew up from the tubers the following spring and again died back completely the next fall. After three years of this kind of erratic behavior, I got tired of fooling around with the plant and put a whole teaspoon of powdered chemical fertilizer in its saucer. It was sink or swim for that plant as far as I was concerned. The plant swam, returned to the circles of the evergreen, and I've yet to see a maranta, even in a greenhouse, that can touch this one for size, vigor, and lushness of growth.

Repotting

There are three reasons for repotting a plant:

1. Its root system has outgrown the pot.
2. It's depleted the nutrients in the soil.
3. It's become top-heavy and it needs a weightier base to keep it from toppling over.

Top-heaviness is easy to diagnose. You merely have to look at the plant or wait until it falls over to know that it's top heavy. Nutrient depletion and root crowding are somewhat more difficult to diagnose, but they usually happen with some degree of simultaneity, and they show themselves in the production of slow, weak, small, and inferior growth.

On the average, a plant in a six-inch pot—the diameter of the pot at its top—won't have to be repotted more than once a year. Plants in larger pots will have to be repotted less frequently, and plants in smaller pots more frequently, just how frequently depending on how fast they're growing.

The best time to repot, unless the plant is definitely telling you that the time is now, is in the winter or early spring when the plant is most dormant and before it starts to put out its new growth.

Before repotting, give the plant a thorough watering and let it stand for a day or two so that the soil is moist but not wet. Very wet soil, because of its weight, may tear away during repotting, pulling valuable roots with it, and very dry soil may crumble away, leaving the roots unnecessarily exposed to the air and causing them to become compacted when the plant is set into its new soil.

You remove a plant from its pot by gently turning it upside down, poking your finger or some other instrument into the hole at the bottom of the pot, and tapping the top of the pot lightly on the edge of a table or bench. When performing this act, make sure that you've got a firm hold on the trunk of the plant so that it doesn't go crashing head first to the floor. If the plant proves to be unusually stubborn, set it upright again and go around the inside of the pot very carefully with a table knife. If you're not very careful, you may cut into the roots.

After the plant is out of its old pot, tap the root mass lightly so that any old, loose soil will fall away and delicately enough so that none of the roots go with it. The plant should then be moved up to the next size pot, a plant that's been in a six-inch pot should be moved up to a seven-inch one and so forth.

When the plant has been firmly seated in with fresh soil mix, water it with vitamin B-1 solution to minimize the shock of transplanting and set it back where it was. For the next month or so, give it less water than it's been accustomed to getting. The root system will need a month or so to adjust to its new surroundings, an adjustment that too much water will make unnecessarily difficult.

At this point in a plant's life, most of its energies will be directed toward extending and developing its root system, so don't expect sudden miracles for your repotting efforts from those parts of the plant that are visible to you. If anything, the newly repotted plant will appear to be less active than it was before you repotted it, and it may even produce some decidedly inferior growth for a time. With some slow-growing plants, you may have to wait as long as six months to reap the visible rewards of your repotting efforts. Be patient and don't panic. Panic leads to too much water, too much fertilizer and some very real damage.

Pots

Far and away the best pot for all house plants is that old standard, the common garden variety, red clay, unglazed pot. Clay pots breathe, absorb moisture, expel moisture, draw salts out of the soil, and provide a working buffer between the roots of the plant and the air outside. Plastic and ceramic pots merely contain the soil and, if they've got holes in their bottoms, drain.

If you're fond of decorator pots, don't plant directly in them. Instead, put the plant in an unglazed clay pot and put that pot inside your decorator container. Wooden containers are excellent substitutes for unglazed pots, but they tend to rot out, and they're not terribly reliable when it comes to holding and directing water. If adequately water-proofed, they lose their porosity and behave exactly like their ceramic, plastic, and metal counterparts.

At all costs, avoid putting a plant in a container which doesn't drain. A plant so potted has two additional and powerful strikes against it from the start. For one, if it's given just the slightest bit too much water, that water will sit at the bottom of the pot and start to rot out the roots. For another, excess fertilizer and mineral salts, which can't drain away, will accumulate until they're so concentrated that no plant, however hardy, will be able to withstand them.

If, in spite of my sage advice, you're still determined to grow something in a container that doesn't drain, fill the bottom of the container with a layer of broken crockery so that excess water, salts, and fertilizer residue will be trapped there below and away from the roots. Add a layer of charcoal over the crockery to keep the water and soil from stagnating, and make sure you always water with the restraint and judgement of a diamond cutter. Better yet, drill a drainage hole in the bottom of the container and set it in a saucer.

For myself, I've never seen a decorator container that can touch a clay pot for simplicity and elegance of design or a glaze that can match the patina that builds up on a clay pot which has been in use for awhile. More often than not, it seems to me that decorator containers often detract from the beauty of the plants they contain, just as a plant can detract from a container that's truly beautiful in and of itself. Perhaps now that plants almost invariably come in plastic pots, the simple beauty of the clay pot will become apparent to more people.

Pests & Diseases

The one great advantage that house plants have over their outdoor neighbors is that they are far less apt to be exposed to pests and diseases. Occasionally, however, disaster of some kind will strike. When it does, remove the infected individual or individuals and isolate them completely, in a separate room if possible, before they can infect other, healthy plants.

If you're introducing a new plant to your collection, especially one which hasn't come from a reputable plant source, it's not a bad idea to quarantine it for a month or so in order to make sure that it's clean. I once volunteered to babysit a friend's plants and failed to notice in time that some of her plants were suffering from mealy bug. Before I realized it, a few of my own plants had become infested, and it took me more than five years to completely clean one of those up.

Mealy bugs resemble tiny pieces of very white cotton, and they're usually found on plants in the crotches between trunk and stem, stem and leaf, and on the undersides of leaves. Since they live in the soil as well as on the plant itself, they're almost impossible to get rid of. I've even heard one very reputable house plant expert recommend destroying an infected specimen rather than risk keeping it in the house where it might infect other plants.

Stubbornly and perhaps foolishly ignoring this sage advice, I kept my infected plants, isolated them, and finally cured them. I did so by going over the plants again and again with a cotton swab dipped in acetone (nail polish remover) and touching the mealy bugs lightly with it. To handle the bugs in the soil, I misted the top of the soil very lightly with rubbing alcohol from time to time, being very careful to see that none of the alcohol reached the roots, since it would have pickled them if it had, and that's very definitely something to be avoided.

Scale is another fairly common and highly communicable house plant problem. Scale appears as tiny brown or black buttons about an eighth of an inch in diameter usually, but not always, on the woodier parts of plants. I've cured a plant of scale simply by going over it again and again and picking off the scales with my fingernails. For really serious scale problems, there are petroleum sprays available from the nursery. These sprays don't work chemically. They simply and very physically smother the scale in oil.

Occasionally, a flying insect will find its way into the house and deposit its eggs on a house plant. This year I was surprised to see that an ivy of mine was apparently being eaten by something. A close examination of the plant revealed a number of tiny inch worms. I prowled through the leaves and removed as many of the offenders as I could find by hand. Then I took the plant outside and applied a strong, fine mist to it and got rid of some more. For a few days after that, I continued to prowl through the plant until I was satisfied that I'd got every last one. The ivy then went into the hospital where I forgot about it for awhile. Unfortunately, one inch worm managed to allude me, and it reached maturity unnoticed and at the expense of the ivy which, despite all these hardships, is now making a splendid recovery.

By and large, however, if something appears to be ailing a house plant and if you can't locate a culprit, the chances are a hundred to one that the plant is suffering from something other than pests or disease. What's wrong with it almost certainly lies with its environment, with the amount of water, heat, light, and moisture it's getting or isn't getting. If you approach your diagnosis from that standpoint, instead of imagining mysterious diseases and invisible bugs, you're much more apt to set the plant straight before it's too late.

New Plants

If you're uneasy about your abilities where house plants are concerned, don't be tempted to buy large, handsome and expensive specimens. Such plants have almost surely attained their grandeur under ideal growing conditions, probably in greenhouses where temperature, humidity, soil, water, and fertilizers are scientifically controlled by experts to produce maximum display in a minimum amount of time.

A plant grown for long under ideal conditions will become rigidly demanding. Throwing it suddenly into the relatively hostile atmosphere of your house may give it a greater shock than it will be able to survive, and you'll be out the plant, its price, and some confidence and peace of mind.

Younger, smaller plants are always considerably cheaper and, like young dogs, can learn new tricks faster and better, tricks like how to survive in your house. If they don't learn that trick, they can be inexpensively replaced by specimens which might.

The temptation is to repot a new plant as soon as you get it home, and that's a temptation to be avoided. A new plant will already have suffered the shock of removal from its original environment, the trials and tribulations of shipping and handling, and the strangeness of a new life at the nursery or plant store.

The only thing the plant will have to call its own when you get it is its hopefully undisturbed root system. Disturbing the root system at this point by repotting the plant may disorient the plant completely. Instead, give it a shot of vitamin B-1 and let it stand around for a month or so until it's had a chance to get acquainted with its new environment. Then repot it if it's necessary.

Failure

Everybody fails with some house plants at some time and often for reasons they're not quite sure about, no matter how much experience they've had. If you manage to keep half of what you bring into your house for longer than a year, I'd say that you were edging toward success.

When something fails, throw it away and try to forget about it. If you fail repeatedly with a particular kind of plant, go on to something else. That's exactly what I've had to do with ferns. I love ferns, and I'd love to have a house full of them, but I just can't seem to make them grow. I've learned to make some deteriorate more slowly than others, but that's hardly a measure of success. Still, I plan to try again—someday.

20 SOURCES OF PLANTS

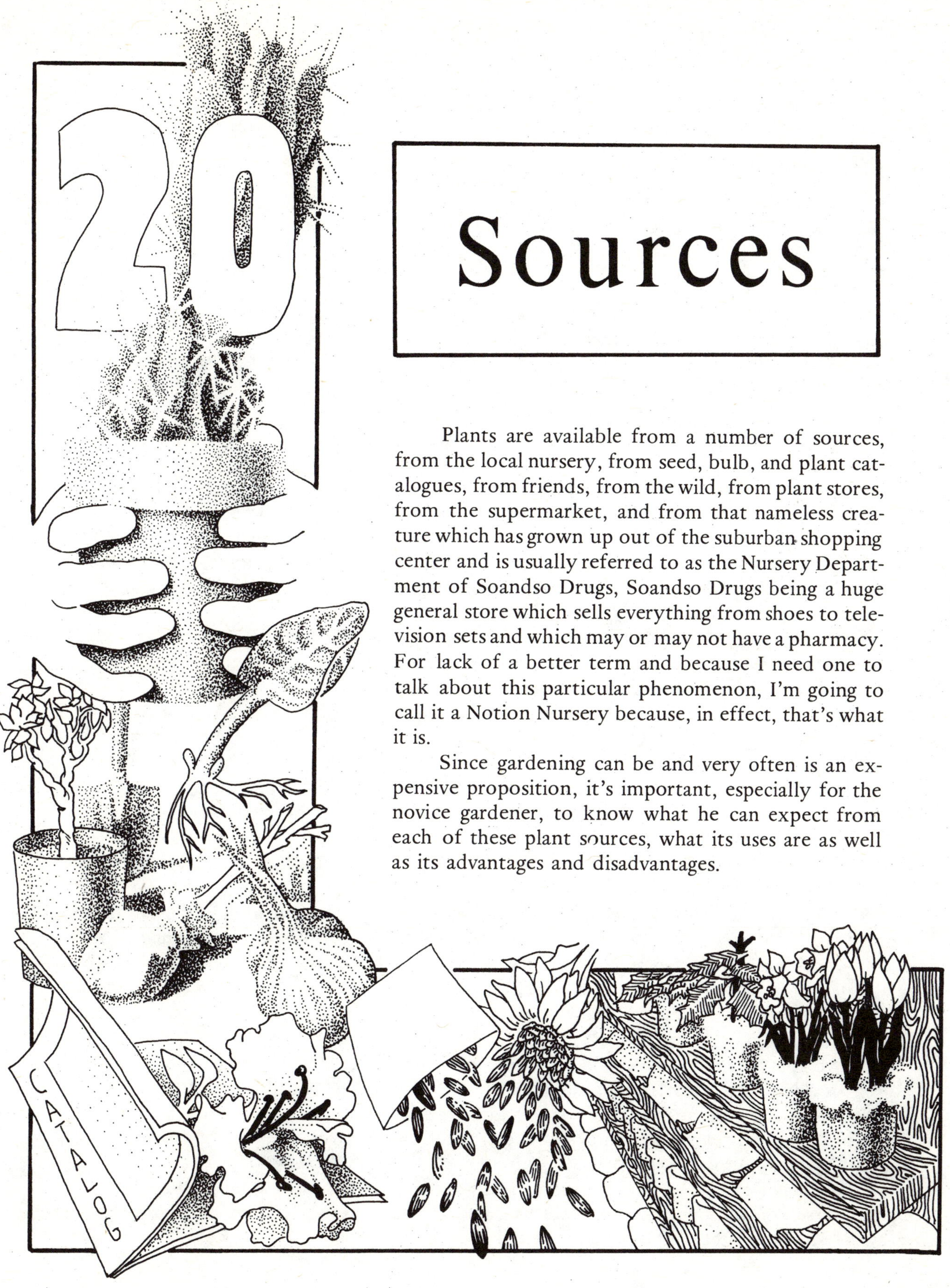

Sources

Plants are available from a number of sources, from the local nursery, from seed, bulb, and plant catalogues, from friends, from the wild, from plant stores, from the supermarket, and from that nameless creature which has grown up out of the suburban shopping center and is usually referred to as the Nursery Department of Soandso Drugs, Soandso Drugs being a huge general store which sells everything from shoes to television sets and which may or may not have a pharmacy. For lack of a better term and because I need one to talk about this particular phenomenon, I'm going to call it a Notion Nursery because, in effect, that's what it is.

Since gardening can be and very often is an expensive proposition, it's important, especially for the novice gardener, to know what he can expect from each of these plant sources, what its uses are as well as its advantages and disadvantages.

The Local Nursery

The local nursery is almost invariably the best source of plants. It has—or should have—the widest selection of plants, and it very definitely should have the best quality. The survival of the people who run a nursery is dependent wholly on plants and plant-related items *and* on your return patronage, just as your patronage should be dependent on your receiving sound plants along with sound gardening advice.

If you're after a particular plant, you go to the nursery for it. The nursery, if it's a good one, should have the plant or, if they don't, they should be willing and able to order it for you or to tell you where you can get it yourself.

You also go to a nursery with a particular gardening problem, with a piece of a plant you want identified, with a pest problem you want help in solving and, in general, with all your gardening questions. A good nurseryman should be as pleased to answer your questions as he is to make a sale. If he's not willing to talk to you or pushes you into buying something you really don't want, it's time to shop around for another nursery.

The willingness of a nurseryman to spend some time with you is one way of identifying a good nursery. Another way is to keep an eye on the stock. A good nursery won't devote a lot of space to pushing notion items. In the spring, you won't, for example, be confronted at the entrance with hundreds of foil wrapped pots of tulips and daffodils in full and glorious bloom. Instead, the nursery will carry a wide selection of these and other bulbs in the fall.

For a time, I dealt with what I knew was an inferior nursery simply because it was the nursery closest to home. One day I dropped in and asked for a Chinese elm, a common Bay Area street tree and hardly an item to excite wonder in anyone. My request was first met with incredulity and then with the patronizing assurance that what I really wanted was a Japanese maple. I, of course, blushed at the man's ignorance and walked out never to return again.

This gentleman, who claimed to have worked for the nursery for five years, had failed an acid test. If you're interested in acid testing yourself, it's not difficult to set one up. You simply become an instant expert on some small facet of gardening—irises, for example—by reading a book on the subject and concocting four or five general questions which you ask innocently during your next visit to the nursery. Allowing some leeway for reasonable differences of opinion and for the fact that no one can know everything, you should, from the answers you get, be able to determine just how knowledgeable your nurseryman is.

If you have several nurseries available to you, pay a visit or two to each of them before you settle on any particular one. If you can locate a nursery where the people take a real interest in plants and the people who grow them, you'll find that you'll often be coming away with more than your purchases.

You will, of course, be paying for the quality, variety, and professionalism you get from a good nursery. Good nurseries are expensive, and for that reason it's sometimes better to go elsewhere for some items, as we'll see.

Notion Nurseries

From a distance, notion nurseries look vaguely like the real thing, but they're not. For one thing, the people who staff them are more likely than not merchandisers and clerks instead of real plant people, and they shouldn't be trusted for advice no matter how readily it may come and feasible it may sound.

Notion nurseries also cannot be counted on to have a particular plant. Their line of stock isn't well-rounded and isn't intended to be. Instead, it's determined by what's currently available to them from the suppliers in the largest quantities and at the cheapest prices. It doesn't hurt, of course, to see if a notion nursery might happen to have a plant you want, but if they don't, don't let yourself be talked into accepting a substitute that you may be sorry about later.

Notion nurseries tend to specialize in what I'll call glitter items, like azaleas in full bloom at twice the price you'd pay for them out of season at a real nursery. You may also find when you get one of these azaleas home that it's been forced in a greenhouse to sell as a gift through a florist outlet and that, because of being forced, it's seriously out of whack with the natural cycle of the species. Getting it back into whack may prove a greater strain than the azalea can survive, and if it doesn't survive, you'll be out the price of the plant and the plant as well.

My main objection to notion nurseries, at least to the local ones, is their ever-increasing tendency toward marketing everything in four-inch pots at, currently, thirty-nine cents a pot. It's criminal, I think, to sell a single annual at this price when the same plants are available at the nursery at a dollar a dozen or thirty cents per plant cheaper, and it's madness to pay four-hundred-and-fifty percent more per plant when all you get for your money is a three week head start on growth, some extra dirt, and a plastic pot for your trash can.

On the other hand, thirty-nine cents for an asparagus fern, any number of other perennials, and for house plants in the same four-inch pots is a real bargain. At a real nursery, you probably couldn't make equivalent purchases for less than seventy-five cents or a dollar.

Garden hoses, garden hardware of all kinds, flower pots, fertilizers, peat moss, leaf mold, steer manure, ground bark, and soil mixes are often much cheaper at the notion nursery, sometimes by as much as half the regular nursery price, and it's for items such as these that I use the notion nursery most.

Seeds turn out to be the same price and quality at both kinds of nurseries because, it seems, the seed business is a concession and seed racks are stocked and handled in both places by the companies which produce and package the seed. Seed packets are dated so that they can be pulled before the seeds become sterile. To be on the safe side, look for the date to make sure you're not getting last year's seeds.

I've had very bad luck with bulbs from notion nurseries, and I suspect it's because they've been overlooked for a couple of years in some warehouse and discovered again long after they've lost their vitality. For bulbs, the local nursery or a bulb house is the safest bet.

A Eureka lemon bought from the local notion nursery produced no lemons at all but did put out quite a few oranges, so I would recommend a real nursery for citrus fruit, since it's very difficult to tell what kind of citrus a citrus is until the fruit has matured.

Catalogues

Besides being a lot of fun, catalogues offer you a much wider variety of seeds and bulbs than are available even from the best stocked nurseries, and sometimes they offer items you simply can't get anywhere else.

Catalogues have their pitfalls, too. For one, they show you a picture of a prime specimen raised under ideal conditions and photographed at the peak of its glory, and they indicate that, for a very reasonable price, you can get a packet of seeds that will produce for you the very same wonder in your own back yard. They don't tell you that it may be difficult if not impossible for anyone but a professional to supply the conditions necessary to make the seeds germinate. They may tell you, however, that certain plants are easy to grow from seed and, if they do, you can believe them.

Generally speaking, most annual seeds are fairly easy. You are only apt to run into real trouble with perennials, and then not always. I use seed catalogues mostly for ordering marigolds, especially mule marigolds, which I've never found at a nursery and which, like all marigolds, are very easy to grow from seed. (Mule marigolds are hybrids which, because they're sterile, bloom continually in their mad, vain quest to reproduce themselves.)

I also use a seed catalogue for ordering vegetable seeds because of the great variety of different kinds of peas, beans, tomatoes, corn, and so forth that they offer, a much larger variety, in fact, than you'll ever find on any seed rack in any nursery.

If you're into growing tulips, daffodils, and any of the myriad of other bulbs, a bulb catalogue is like a wonderland, and spending too much time with one can, if you're not careful, ruin you financially. Everything looks too good, especially after you've done some experimenting and discovered, as I have, that most of the picture promises made by a bulb catalogue will come true.

Try to resist ordering garden hardware and supplies through seed, bulb, and plant catalogues. Such items are almost always available to you much more cheaply from the nearest garden supply outlet, which also won't ask you to pay additional shipping and handling charges.

I don't recommend ordering living plants from catalogues unless they're specialty items which aren't available to you in any other way. You'll pay more for a mail order plant than you would for the same plant at a nursery, and the specimen you get will be weakened by packing, shipping, and handling procedures. Plants, no matter how well packed, don't do well out of the ground and in the mails.

Gardening magazines and journals often contain ads for specialty catalogues—iris, orchid, rare plant, cactus catalogues, what have you. Such catalogues are interesting and educational to look through whether or not you have a particular interest in their subject. They're usually free or very cheap, and they're well worth sending for if you don't mind running the risk of exposing your name and address to yet another mailing list.

From the mailing lists gardening has got my name on, I'm forced to conclude that gardeners are considered to be an especially sappy and soft-hearted lot. The other day I threw into the trash an unsolicited box of Christmas cards sent to me by the "friend" of a woman who had supposedly illustrated them with a pencil she'd strapped to her nose. Certain parts of my anatomy were touched by this plea for funds but, as it happened, none of them was my heart.

The Plant Store

About three years ago, to put it sappily, the florist and the nursery got married and produced the plant store, which is, as far as I can tell, something entirely new under the sun. The plant store is designed to serve only the needs of the indoor gardener, the house plant enthusiast or freak, if you prefer.

From what I've seen of these stores, they vary a great deal in what they offer the customer, and some, offering very little, haven't, I've noticed, lasted as long as the plants they offered for sale.

As you might expect, plant stores are on the expensive side, but expense aside, a good store usually offers a wide variety of plants, some of them relatively rare, along with sound advice about how to care for what you've purchased.

"The Indoor Gardener," a plant store with which I am in no way affiliated, on College Avenue in Berkeley is, of all the plant stores I've seen, the nicest. It's ingeniously and beautifully laid out and a joy to visit if you're in the neighborhood. My slender wallet and total lack of self-discipline when it comes to buying plants keeps me from visiting it as often as I'd like to.

If you're interested in house plants, in starting or adding to a collection and if you're dubious about your abilities where house plants are concerned, it would be well worth your while to find a store like "The Indoor Gardener," which could provide you with plants, advice, diagnoses, and courage when your house plants and spirits are flagging.

The Florist

The florist is the place where someone who doesn't know anything about plants pays a lot of money for a plant in order to give it to someone else as an expensive gift. If the person who receives the gift doesn't know any more about plants than the giver, the gift may be well received, but if the recipient is a gardener, he may greet the gift in much the same way as an accomplished philatelist would greet a book of trading stamps. Not very well.

Florists may be fine for cut flowers and corsages, but unless they've got a lot of the plant store about them, they leave much to be desired when it comes to plants. Their total plant stock is usually divided between forced flowers in foil wrapped pots and cutesy arrangements of small house plants in ceramic dishes topped with a ceramic statue or a bit of driftwood.

The forced chrysanthemums, azaleas, and poinsettias are invariably so out of whack with nature and themselves that it's better to throw them away when they've finished blooming than it is to bother trying to convert them back into something that will grow in the garden. The little house plants in the cutesy arrangements can probably be saved if you repot them separately as soon as you get them, which will probably hurt the feelings of the person who gave you the arrangement, but in my book that beats watching the little buggers die.

Friends

Getting plants from the gardens of your friends has the great advantage of not costing anything, unless of course you have very strange friends. It also has one serious disadvantage which should be considered before accepting or soliciting a donation.

Along with the plant, you may be getting something you haven't bargained for, a new kind of pest, a new weed, and worst of all, a new soil disease, which will be very hard to detect and possibly impossible to cure.

Strict precautions are supposedly taken with commercially sold plants so that this kind of thing doesn't happen, but I can't help but entertain doubts about the thoroughness and universality of these precautions. I also can't imagine myself turning down the gift of a plant on the grounds that it might not meet my standards of garden health. When a gift is offered, I accept it in the spirit that it's given, and if any new problems turn up, which none have as yet, I'll rack them up to kismet and learn to make do.

Cuttings, seeds, and bulbs from which all soil has been washed are much less of a threat than plants which come with soil attached.

The Wilds

Bringing plants in from the wilds has the same advantages and disadvantages as getting them from friends as well as a unique disadvantage of its own. You may find that by so doing you're breaking a law. More and more wild plants are being protected by law because, like so many of our birds, their very existence is being threatened by us humans, who, along with cockroaches and seagulls, occupy the very bottom of the Endangered Species list.

Before you load your shovel into the car and set off into the country after a plant, you should give some thought to what chances your intended acquisition has of surviving in your garden. If you're not going to be able to provide nearly the same kind of environment for it as the one you're taking it from, you'll be wasting your own time as well as making a small but unnecessary rent in the already badly torn fabric of nature.

Seedlings & Seeds

When you're buying seedlings from flats or in pony packs at the nursery, don't follow your instincts and buy the biggest plants. Large seedlings will almost surely be root-bound. If the roots are too badly bound, they won't be able to expand beyond the root ball once the seedlings are in the ground, and the plants will slowly strangle themselves to death. Small plants are always a better bet and have a much better chance of reaching maturity and of reaching it faster.

If you're interested in starting your own plants from seeds, it's very much worth the effort, especially in terms of the money you'll save if you're successful. The seed packet will usually tell you if it's best to sow the seed directly in the ground or if it should be started elsewhere first.

For starting seedlings out of the ground, I use the plastic pony packs I've saved from previous visits to the nursery. Nothing you might construct at home could possibly be better, cheaper, or more convenient than these small plastic containers, which, if they're handled with care, can be used over and over again.

Before planting the seed, the containers should be filled with any good potting mix (see page 225) and thoroughly wetted down. The seed should then be planted at the depth recommended on the packet. If you have more seed than you want plants, two seeds can be placed in each section of the pony pack container. This will help to insure that something will germinate in each section. If both seeds germinate, which is a distinct possibility, the weaker of the two plants can be removed later.

After planting, the containers should be placed somewhere where they will get filtered sun or morning sun only. Since snails and slugs are a particular threat to young seedlings, the containers should also be placed up off the ground on a table or bench.

The containers should be watered frequently with a spray fine enough so that it doesn't in any way disturb the soil. If the soil is allowed to dry out, the young seedlings will of course perish. Just how frequently they'll require water will depend on the weather, but it's a good idea to check them on a daily basis, particularly just after the seeds have sprouted and the roots are very near the surface of the soil.

After the seedlings have reached a height of three to five inches, depending on the species, they're ready to be placed in the ground, preferably in a bed prepared for planting in the same way that you'd prepare a vegetable garden (see pages 190 to 191) or, lacking that, in holes into which organic matter has been dug to a depth and width of nine inches.

Transplanting should be done when the weather is on the cool side and/or in the late afternoon or early evening to help minimize shock to the young plants. Shock can be further minimized by watering the new transplants with a solution of horticultural vitamin B-1. You'll find the directions for the solution on the bottle and the bottle at your local garden supply outlet.

Bulbs

There is an almost endless variety of plants which grow from bulbs and other thickened root structures such as tubers, rhizomes, corms, and tuberous roots. It would be impossible to discuss everything pertinent to the growing of each of these in anything smaller than a tome. Such information is readily available, however, along with the bulbs you purchase by catalogue or, if asked for, along with the bulbs you buy at the nursery. Still, there are a number of generalities about bulbs which fit into the scope of this book and may be of some use to you.

Generally speaking, bulbs can be divided into two main categories, those which naturalize and those which do not. Naturalizing simply means that a bulb can be placed in the ground and left there permanently to grow and multiply without being further disturbed by the hand of man except when division becomes necessary or desirable. A bulb which doesn't naturalize is one which must be dug up and stored after it's died back every year, a bulb which, if left in the ground, would succumb either to rot or some disease or insect pest.

Whether or not a bulb will naturalize depends on where it's grown and what conditions it's grown under, but by and large, the spring bulbs we tend to think of as Dutch—tulips, hyacinths, daffodils, and jonquils—don't naturalize unless the winters are cold and the summers dry. These bulbs are expensive, and if you're not willing to put in the effort of pulling them, preparing them for storage, storing them, and replanting them every year, they're a poor investment. If your time in the garden isn't unlimited, what time you do have might be better spent in growing something which doesn't require so much tedious labor for a comparatively fleeting amount of delight.

If you're determined to grow spring bulbs of this kind, grow them in pots. After they're finished blooming, potted bulbs can be set away out of sight to die back, something that all bulbs must be allowed to do before they're pulled, and something they must be allowed to do completely and at their leisure if they're to rejuvenate themselves fully.

Dying back is a process that can take up to three months to complete. It's an ugly process to watch, and with spring bulbs, it begins to happen just as spring starts to get into full swing, when you want your garden to look its best. All this makes bulbs, unless they're judiciously placed, poor long-term landscape assets.

Spring bulbs which naturalize easily, like scilla, also go through the ugly and inconvenient dying back process, and they can present other problems as well. I have scilla—commonly called bluebells—popping up all over my garden. Every time I move some soil, I seem to move some scilla with it, and I can forsee the day when, if I'm not careful, I may have scilla everywhere crowding out less vigorous and more desirable early spring growth.

Translated, this means that any bulb which naturalizes too well can become a real problem for the gardener, a problem that isn't easy to solve because much of it is hidden under the ground for a good part of the year. If you're trying to remove problem bulbs, you may even find that they've become intertwined with the root mass of a valuable plant and that they can't be extracted from it without doing the plant serious injury or even killing it, something the bulbs themselves may eventually accomplish simply by continuing to grow and multiply at the nutrient expense of the plant they've infested.

For all these reasons, I recommend bulbs to the novice gardener with strong reservations. Before adding any new bulb to your garden, make sure that you know what you're getting into and that you're not going to get in over your head. This advice, strong as it is, shouldn't stop you from considering bulbs altogether, of course. I wouldn't part with a single one of my peonies without putting up a fight. They're simply too beautiful and cause me too little trouble, and they die back in the fall, rather than the spring, after having contributed an outstanding display of summer foliage to the garden.

Shrubs & Trees

Most shrubs and small trees are sold in either one or five gallon cans, and at a well-stocked nursery, you should be able to get the variety you want in either. The question is which. I strongly recommend the one gallon purchase. It will cost you less than a third of the price of a five gallon specimen, and its chances for survival in your garden are greater because the plant is younger and will more easily adjust to the double shock of transplanting and a new environment.

With the five gallon can, you may get a year or two head start on growth, but what you'll really be paying for is the cost to the nursery of transplanting a one gallon plant into a five gallon can.

Bare Root Stock

If you're interested in roses, fruit trees, or any other deciduous trees or shrubs, the most economical time to acquire them is in the winter when they're available at the nursery in bare root stock.

Most any plant which loses its leaves and undergoes a period of winter dormancy can be lifted bodily from the ground and, bereft of its soil, shipped inexpensively to the nursery, which then passes the savings on to the customers.

If you wait until late winter or early spring, the selection of bare root stock available to you will be smaller, but the prices may be even lower because the nursery will then be faced with the trouble and expense of planting what's left themselves or of losing it.

Before planting, bare root purchases should be soaked overnight in a solution of one tablespoon horticultural vitamin B-1 to one gallon of water, and the more of the plant you soak the better, although the roots should naturally get first consideration.

Cuttings

Another way of acquiring new specimens is from cuttings. Cuttings may be started in a number of places, in pots, in flats, in plastic bags, and directly in the ground. Pure vermiculite, pure river sand, or one part of either to an equal part of organic matter makes an ideal rooting medium.

If you wish to start cuttings directly in the ground, find a place in your garden that gets a lot of light but very little or no direct sunlight. Prepare the soil in the area by adding into it to a depth of nine or ten inches enough organic matter and river sand to make the soil light, loamy, moisture retentive, and fast draining.

In general terms, a cutting should be a twig approximately eight inches long. Before planting the twig, the larger leaves and all the flowers and buds should be removed from it. After you've done that, dip the lower end of the slip into hormone solution or powder and stick it into the soil up to its middle. (Rooting hormones are usually available anywhere plants and garden supplies are sold.) To increase your chances for success, plant four or five times as many cuttings as you want plants.

What plants are suited to this kind of propagation is a reasonably complex matter, but by and large, any plant that has a fairly woody structure is a possible candidate. Experimenting will cost you very little in terms of time and money and can be a lot of fun. Common sense should dictate that such things as annuals and bulbs can't be slipped, and it won't be worth your while to bother with any grafted plants such as roses and fruit trees. Cuttings from these plants have a good chance of sprouting, but they'll never amount to anything because they're not capable of developing strong root stock, which is why they were grafted in the first place.

Cuttings, like seedlings, have to be babied, watered gently and never allowed to dry out. Once it's clear that a new plant has established itself—and this means much more than the emergence of a few little leaves, it can be moved out into the garden. With cuttings started in sand or vermiculite, an intermediate stage in a loamier soil may be necessary in order to acclimate the plant to the rigors of life in the open ground.

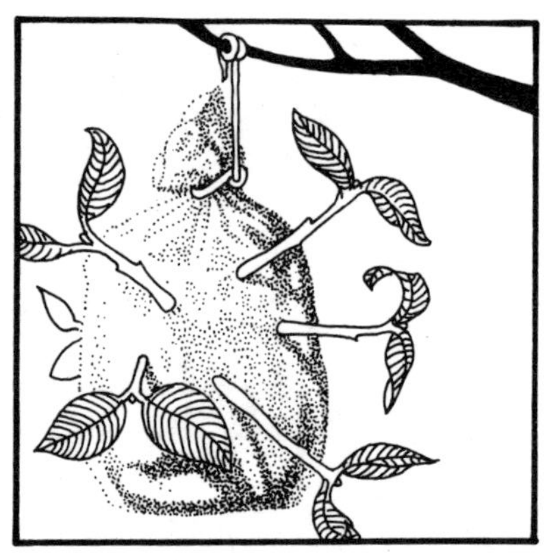

Fuchsia Bag

Someone, I can't remember whom, recently came up with a new way of starting fuchsias using a plastic produce bag. The bag is filled with pre-moistened peat moss and tightly tied at the top. Small holes are poked through the plastic with a pencil and into each hole a cutting, dipped in hormone first, is placed. The bag is then tied to the lower branch of a tree and left there unattended until the fuchsias have sprouted. At that time, the bag is carefully dismantled, the roots of the fuchsias carefully separated, and the fuchsias permanently placed in the garden.

I don't see any reason why any number of other kinds of cuttings couldn't be started in just this way. This system of propagation is ideal, too, especially for the forgetful gardener, because there is no way that moisture can escape from the bag and allow the peat to dry out before the cuttings have rooted and are ready to be transplanted.

That unfortunately is not the whole story on acquiring new plants through propagation. I've overlooked air-layering and leaf cutting to name but two more methods, but like too many other things, the whole story is again beyond the scope of this book. I have, however, laid down the ground rules and hopefully, with what you now know and with a little common sense, you can start experimenting on your own with no small chance for success.

Propagation, like all other facets of gardening, is something best learned by doing, and no book can help beyond a certain point. If you fail occasionally, it's of little consequence. I fail sometimes, and sometimes too often. All gardeners do. It makes the successes, and there are bound to be some, ever so much more spectacular.

21 GARDEN LANGUAGE

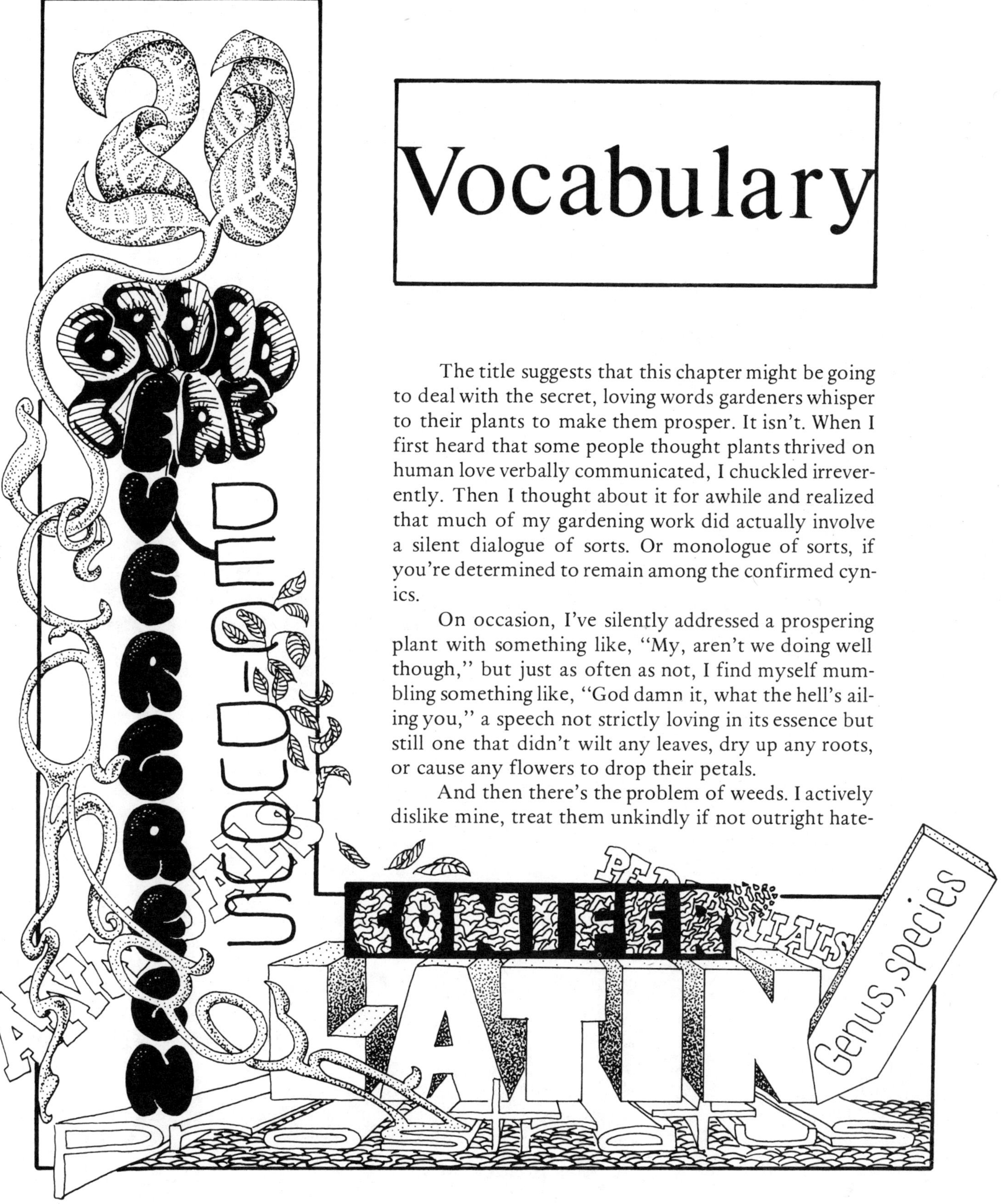

Vocabulary

The title suggests that this chapter might be going to deal with the secret, loving words gardeners whisper to their plants to make them prosper. It isn't. When I first heard that some people thought plants thrived on human love verbally communicated, I chuckled irreverently. Then I thought about it for awhile and realized that much of my gardening work did actually involve a silent dialogue of sorts. Or monologue of sorts, if you're determined to remain among the confirmed cynics.

On occasion, I've silently addressed a prospering plant with something like, "My, aren't we doing well though," but just as often as not, I find myself mumbling something like, "God damn it, what the hell's ailing you," a speech not strictly loving in its essence but still one that didn't wilt any leaves, dry up any roots, or cause any flowers to drop their petals.

And then there's the problem of weeds. I actively dislike mine, treat them unkindly if not outright hatefully, and yet they persist in popping up and flourishing if they're not promptly checked. If my flowers thrive because I love them, who is it, I ask, that's whispering sweet somethings to my thriving weeds? Is some malicious neighbor lurking weed-lovingly just on the other side of one of my fences? Is there a secret cult of weed-lovers piously at work in some nearby basement? Or do weeds get all the love they need from the Evil One? And do weeds even know they're weeds and, if so, how? Perhaps they see themselves as mysteriously unpopular flowers, which, like persistently unpopular people, are always forcing their attentions on you, blowing their latest mouth wash in your face or letting you know that their armpits are dry at last.

It is, indeed, a boggling subject, this mysterious communication between man and marigold, perhaps even a silly one, and it's certainly one that's best handled here in the dropping of it. What I really want to talk about in this chapter is plant names, particularly their Latin ones. I also have a few parting words on tree terminology.

Plant Names

Plants generally have two names, a common one and a Latin one. It would be nice for the gardener if he never had to deal with the Latin names at all. Latin is a foreign language to everyone, and Nursery Latin is even more foreign than the other varieties, Church and Classical, to name two.

I don't think I've ever heard two nurserymen mispronounce the same plant's Latin name in the same way, and I've been corrected myself after offering a reasonably Classical rendering of the spelling of a plant's name with a pronunciation that was totally unreasonable from any standpoint. Latin in the nursery is awkward at best, and the use of it there usually leads to a great deal of mumbling, much pointing and gesticulating, and finally, the humble reading of a tag.

Unfortunately, Nursery Latin is sometimes necessary. Common plant names often fail to communicate any real information. For example, people who don't know plants may think they know what a daisy is, but people who know plants know they don't. A nursery may have as many as ten or fifteen totally unrelated plants all of which are commonly referred to as daisies. If you ask for a daisy at the nursery, you'll be asked in turn what kind. You may then say you want an English daisy, an Alpine daisy, a painted daisy, an African daisy, a Shasta daisy, and so forth.

Even this much information may not be adequate. Common names get mixed up, and in some cases they may change completely from region to region, so if you want a Shasta daisy, or what I call a Shasta daisy, and you want to be sure you get one, it's best to ask for a *Chrysanthemum maximum*, which may surprise you because you may have thought that you had all the chrysanthemums you could ever want.

"Daisy," as it turns out, refers only to the general configuration of certain flowers, in home-grown dictionariese, a flower the petals of which radiate usually but not always singly from a central hub, the colors of which petals and hub usually but not always occupy the white to yellow color range. That and nothing more specific than that is a daisy.

The tags you find on plants at the nursery will usually bear two Latin words, such as *Acer palmatum*, the first word designating the plant's genus, a division of its family, and the second its species, a division of its genus. Family designations, such as *Liliaceae* (the lily family), never appear on tags, are rarely mentioned by anyone but botanists, and are usually only of academic interest to gardeners as, for example, did you know that both onions and orchids belong to the lily family and that roses and raspberries are both members of the family *Rosaceae*?

There's nothing mysterious about the terminology of *Acer palmatum*, the scientific name for the Japanese maple. *Acer* is the Latin word for "maple." *Palmatum* means "palm-leafed." Why botanists chose to call the Japanese maple the palm-leafed maple is anybody's guess. We'll have to assume that their reasons were sound, but they could just as well have called it *Acer japanicum* or even *Acer niponensis.*

If you find a tag at the nursery which reads *Acer palmatum atropurpureum,* it indicates a separate variety of Japanese maple, one that developed in nature and differs slightly from the others, in this case in leaf color. You won't, however, find such a tag because nature produced no such tree. Instead, you'll find a tag which reads *Acer palmatum 'Atropurpureum,'* which, through its single quotation marks and capital letter, indicates a separate variety but a horticultural one, one that was developed not by nature but by man.

Atropurpureum is the Latin word for "black-purple" and, for reasons that I can't even begin to imagine, refers in the case of *Acer palmatum 'Atropurpureum'* to the *red*-leafed Japanese maple, a tree that I would have called *Acer japonicum 'Rubrum'* for obvious reasons. Science, in its unceasing quest to delimit and clarify, sometimes seems only to add to the general confusion unless, of course and by the same token, we must come to think of Old Glory as the black-purple, white, and blue, the Fourth of July as a black-purple letter day on which we celebrate our independence and our ability to wipe out the Chinese Black-purples should they try anything funny. Come to think of it, though, the red-leafed Japanese maple does have a black-purplish cast to it.

A Latin dictionary will help to clear up a lot of the mystery surrounding plant names for anyone who's interested in pursuing the subject further. In some cases, however, a dictionary might not prove entirely satisfactory. You could search through a Latin dictionary forever for the *schmidtiana* of *Artemisia schmidtiana* (Angel's hair) and never find it. This particular species of artemisia was obviously named after someone called Schmidt, either to honor him or because he was the first to discover it.

Some Species Names

If you don't want to bother with a Latin dictionary and only wish to pursue this subject just a little further, I've selected a short list of fairly common species names, which will give you an idea of the areas which they cover. The species name, remember, is the *palmatum* part of *Acer palmatum.*

albus, alba, album. These words mean "white." The endings differ according to whether the generic name is masculine, feminine, or neuter. *Acer* is a neuter noun in Latin so a white maple, if one existed, would be an *Acer album.*

artemisoides means "shaped like the artemisia plant." The suffix *-oides* means "in the shape of." Recently, the local news media conducted a campaign warning people not to eat mushrooms of their own picking because of a sudden proliferation of that highly poisonous creature, the *Amanita phalloides.* I was much amused to hear the species name so freely and blatantly brandished over the air-waves since, if *phalloides* were translated into English, it would become a media no-no of the very first water.

canadensis refers to any species which is a native of Canada, just as *mexicana* or *californica* refers to species native to those general areas.

communis designates the most common, ordinary, and usual species of a genus. The terms *vulgaris* and *officinalis* are two more ways of saying the same thing. None of these terms is pejorative, of course.

concinna means that the species referred to is particularly valued because of its shape. *Sophia concinna* is not a plant. She's an Italian movie actress.

crassifolia means "densely foliaged." The suffix *-folia* always refers to the leaves of a plant. *Cuppressifolia* means that a species has foliage suggestive of a cypress tree. *Ficifolia* means that the leaves of the species are shaped like those of a fig tree. Victorian botanists used to use ficifoliates to cover up those damnably embarrassing *Amanita phalloides.*

chinensis means "Chinese." So does *sinensis.*

glaucus, -a, -um designates a blue or bluish species of a genus.

grandiflora means "large-flowered," the suffix *-flora* always referring to the flowers of the species. Hence, *terniflora* means that a particular species flowers in groups of three.

maculata means spotted. In his "Sweeney Among the Nightingales," T. S. Eliot refers to a "maculate giraffe." Mr. Eliot was being redundant. Giraffes, on the other hand, have very little to do with gardening, although, if properly trained, they come in very handy when it comes time to prune tall trees.

occidentalis means "Western." *Orientalis* means "Eastern," and these terms can refer either to hemispheres or to sections of the same continent.

prostratus means "low-growing, prostrate" and is generally used to indicate that a particular species is a ground cover.

puchella means "very pretty," as in *Correa puchella,* the Australian fuchsia, and *Sophia puchella,* the Italian actress. Forgive me.

ruber, rubra, rubrum means "red."

rhodanthus, -a, -um means that the flowers of the species so named are shaped like roses.

scandens means "climbing" and is used to indicate a vining species.

semperflorens means "ever-blooming," as in *Sophia biflora semperflorens,* or *Sophia semperbiflorens.*

sempervirens means "ever-living" or "evergreen."

tormentosus means "twisting, interlacing."

Although that barely scratches the surface of specific botanical names, it should go a long way in obviating any fear or awe they might inspire in those who, in one way or another, haven't marched with Caesar into Gaul. The botanist who named the Australian fuchsia (*Correa puchella*) the very pretty correa couldn't have been overly impressed with the weight and solemnity of the task he'd undertaken. Even Latin has its jokes and, as evidenced by Pompei, its bathroom graffiti.

The Great Tree Confusion

In this book, I've bandied the words "evergreen," "deciduous," "conifer," and "broadleaf" about without explaining the distinctions between them, distinctions which aren't clear in everyone's mind and which are helpful to know if you ever get involved in a conversation about trees.

The terms "deciduous" and "evergreen" are exact opposites and are mutually exclusive. A deciduous tree is one which drops all of its leaves at about the same time, without exception—or one that I can think of—in the fall of the year. An evergreen tree is one which keeps its leaves throughout the winter and for the rest of the year as well. A tree which drops some but not all of its leaves in the fall is called semi-deciduous.

Pines, firs, junipers—trees with needles or needle-like foliage—are commonly called evergreens, which they are, but they're more properly referred to as conifers, "cone-bearers." The dawn redwood (*Metasequoia glyptostroboides*) is a conifer but, unlike most conifers, it loses all of its foliage in the fall and is, therefore, a deciduous conifer and not a deciduous evergreen, which would be a contradiction in terms, an oxymoron, if you find it pays to increase your vocabulary.

Trees which don't have needles or needle-like foliage but which have leaf-like leaves are called broadleaf trees. Maples, elms, birches, oaks, loquats, and sycamores all belong to this group. Among broadleaf trees, some are evergreen and some are deciduous. Most oaks, for example, are deciduous, but the California live oak is not. It keeps its leaves the year round, as does the loquat. These latter two trees are referred to as broadleaf evergreens.

Every tree in the world can be classified as one of the following:

1. Evergreen conifer
2. Deciduous conifer
3. Evergreen broadleaf
4. Deciduous broadleaf

Just as there is no such thing as a deciduous evergreen, there is no such thing, to the best of my knowledge, as a broadleaf conifer, although strictly speaking, this is not a contradiction in terms, since it's theoretically possible that a tree which has broad leaves could also produce cones. Apparently, however, none do. I suspect that it's here in the unapparent mutual exclusiveness of "conifer" and "broadleaf" that we can find the source of most of the confusion surrounding tree designations.

22

APOLOGIA PRO LIBRO MEO

Apology

It seems I've written a book very different from the one I started out to write. I had intended to concentrate on practical things and have found myself, perhaps too often, waxing philosophical and even, on occasion, stooping to levity which, I know, some people find unforgivable. I can hear voices in the distance muttering, "Well, that's all very interesting, I guess, but I still don't know what to do about these gladiolas or whatever you call them."

Those voices humble me—in so far as it's possible to do that. The only response I have to them, and a weak one it is at best, is that writing this book has taught me a great deal about gardening and, for that reason, I'm convinced it has some value—if only for me. For those who have found something of value for themselves, let me suggest that they, like any good editor, take a blue pencil to those parts that they found worthless or annoying and strike them out now and forever.

I approached gardening slowly and step by step from the age of seven. Always the amateur, I worked hard at keeping my amateur status. I avoided gardening books, the lure of scientific approaches, large generalities, and anything that smacked of formal education, and I did so partly out of laziness and partly in reaction to years of formal education, to discipline imposed from above rather than discovered from below. I am, unfortunately, one of those hapless creatures who learns almost everything by doing and almost nothing from listening. If I don't hear a specific answer to a specific, handwrought question, I'm soon asleep.

You may have fallen asleep long ago yourself in spite of what I must now confess has been my intention all along, to involve you in gardening, to addict you to it if possible. Without any interest in gardening beyond the compelled maintenance of a piece of property, you are, I'm afraid, almost doomed to failure from the start. For you, gardening can only and always be a series of hateful, endless, unrewarding, unrelated, tedious and tiresome chores, and there are a thousand more profitable ways to spend your time than by imposing such torture on yourself.

If you are one of those people who is stuck with a garden and is congenitally incapable of getting at all interested in it, a landscape architect may be the best answer. That may sound like too expensive a solution to your problems, but in the long run I don't think it will be.

A landscape architect can concoct for you a virtually maintenance-free garden, one that you'll enjoy looking at, one that you can avoid without guilt, and one that will, as the modern saying has it, improve your property value. In five year's time, you can easily retrieve the cost of the architect in what you've saved in spring spending bursts at the notion nursery and by paying out good money to unskilled, temporary help, who often, bless them, end up doing more damage than good. You'll also have avoided countless family arguments and enjoyed any number of weekends that would otherwise have been lost to you.

If this book has convinced you that you really are a confirmed non-gardener and sends you off to a landscape architect, you've learned something from reading it. If, armed with a grasp of its contents, you can steer the architect away from executing his own dreams and into executing your needs, the book will have been worth the price you paid for it or the time you spent getting it out of the library.

On the other hand, it may be that you really do enjoy working with plants and don't have very much trouble making them thrive and prosper for you, but there's still something wrong with your garden. It could be that your garden really isn't one. A real garden, in my book, is much more than the sum of its plants. A landscape architect might be able to help you a little with design and make you think a little bit more like an artist and a little bit less like a farmer.

For myself, I've learned from writing this book, from the sometimes insurmountable problems I had in organizing and thinking about it, that gardening is something much larger for me than I knew. I now have to face the cornball fact that gardening is my religion, a rather practical religion to be sure, but a very real one nonetheless.

Gardening teaches anyone who's willing to listen some of the basic processes of nature as well as the unrelenting and omnipotent force of those processes, and it does this in an age when man is all too often attuned only to the artificial structures of his own device, when his pride is highest and most false. But I won't press this religious business any farther. Back yard philosophy is one thing, metaphysics and theology quite another.

If you enjoyed the book, if you found it helpful, or if you have any criticisms or suggestions about how it might be improved, I'd appreciate hearing from you. If other editions should follow, there's no reason that, with the help of others, they couldn't be improved. I'd like to think that this book, as it now stands, might only be the acorn from which something a little more oaklike might eventually grow.

INDEX

A

B

C

D

E

I

J

N

O

P

Q

R

S

T

U

V

W

Z

Name________________________________

Address ______________________________

State ___________________ Zip_________

Send to:
John Muir Publications
P.O. Box 613
Santa Fe, New Mexico
87501

Enclosed is $6.00 plus .39 for postage and handling
(New Mexico residents please add 4% State Sales Tax)

Booksellers, please contact Bookpeople, 2940 7th Street, Berkeley, California 94710.